I Thought It Would Be Different
WITH A NEW PURSE

**Shed Stress, Drop Guilt, and Care for
Yourself While Caring for Others**

Praise for *I Thought It Would Be Different With a New Purse*

"You have done the seemingly impossible: you have entwined clinical research with the most charming storybook tales to create a jewel of a *self-help* book that takes us into the heart of who we are. I want to share this with everyone I know! I love you both for that enormous insight."
—Carolyn Woodard, MSc

"Lynda and Leslie's stories are humorous, down-to-earth, and engaging. Let them be your guide to a happier way of caring for yourself as you care for others at the same time. Every woman who reads this book will see herself and the challenges we all face daily. Their three-part solution gives you a clear roadmap to carrying less stress and less guilt while navigating life's challenges."
—Ann Ladd, PhD, LCSW, The Connecting Place

"I LOVE your book. If you have ever felt a tug-of-war between caring for others and yourself, this book is for you. With a lighthearted and warm style, Lynda and Leslie have written a book that feels like a conversation between friends. They make neuroscience understandable and relatable, while sharing the challenges and joys of relationship. I was encouraged by it and a bit sad when it was done. The invitation to pick it up again in the last line was lovely! This book is a gift to revisit regularly for yourself and to share with others."
—Melri Wright, Co-Executive Director, Ledge Leadership

"Any woman who struggles with the balance of caring for others, while still attempting to care for her self, will feel heard, understood, and supported in reading *I Thought It Would Be Different With a New Purse*. Lynda and Leslie skillfully weave solid neuroscience research into a witty, anecdotal, and conversational format, making the science more palatable and understandable to all. And finally, Lynda and Leslie invite you, the reader, to be part of the conversation, continuing the support, potentially, beyond the final pages of their book."
—Sheila Hammond, MSc, AAMFT Clinical Fellow (retired)

"Lynda and Leslie, with their combined lifelong expertise in the world of human dynamics, have creatively used the metaphor of a woman's purse to aid the reader in understanding the neuroscience behind stress and how to manage it effectively. In *I Thought It Would Be Different With A New Purse*, we learn how we store our *purse-onal* stress in our collective purses and how, as dutiful caregivers, we try to juggle the often exhausting demands of workplace and home-life balance—and the negative impact this has on our nervous systems.

With an illuminating, intelligent, humorous, and always compassionate style, the authors take Dr. Stephen Porges' scientifically based polyvagal theory and creatively teach how our sense of safety, danger, and threat can impact our behaviour. They show us a way to get our Sparkle back by following their unique formula that leads to nervous system regulation, allowing us to feel, think, and connect better in our busy, and at times overwhelming, lives.

Being a lifelong caregiver in both my personal and professional life, I certainly could have used Lynda and Leslie's lovely guidance years ago to gently inform my overworked nervous system how to compassionately care for others without losing my own *Sparkle*. The metaphor of the oxygen mask comes to mind when flight attendants say that in the unlikely event of a cabin pressure emergency, put the mask on yourself first before attending to others, as you cannot really be helpful to those you care for if you are unconscious."

—Gaye Gould, MSW, RSW
Psychotherapist, private practice
Author of *The Compassion Junkie:*
From Diapers to Depends, It Never Ends (releasing soon)

I Thought It Would Be Different

WITH A NEW PURSE

Shed Stress, Drop Guilt, and Care for Yourself While Caring for Others

LESLIE GILLESPIE
LYNDA REES

Capucia LLC
211 Pauline Drive #513
York, PA 17402
www.capuciapublishing.com
Send questions to: support@capuciapublishing.com

Paperback ISBN: 978-1-954920-91-0
eBook ISBN: 978-1-954920-92-7
Library of Congress Control Number: 2024904439

Cover Design: Ranilo Cabo
Layout: Ranilo Cabo
Editor and Proofreader: Karen Burton
Book Midwife: Karen Everitt

Printed in the United States of America

Capucia LLC is proud to be a part of the Tree Neutral° program. Tree Neutral offsets the number of trees consumed in the production and printing of this book by taking proactive steps such as planting trees in direct proportion to the number of trees used to print books. To learn more about Tree Neutral, please visit treeneutral.com.

Our Intention and Disclaimer

This book is based on our own experiences, learnings, and perspectives as white heterosexual cisgender women. There is very little in the world of psychology and relationship systems research that is absolute. This book represents how we have interpreted and integrated what we have studied and experienced. We want to hear about your experiences, learnings, and perspectives, so that together we can deepen our understanding of what it means to be truly human. Your voice matters. The tales in this book are fables, except where we tell you something about one of us. The ideas in this book do not replace consultation or treatment with a health care professional.

We dedicate this book to our mothers, Lela Lucille and Mary Catherine,
who cared for and carried so much for those they held dear.

Ode to Our Mothers

Some lies have been told
And you are a little afraid

Have you forgotten the truth of who you really are?
Softly now, you will recall
How a beautiful baby cried her spirit into the world
And sang "I have arrived."

Gentle now
Do not fret
Everydayness can cloud
The memory of your
True
Vibrant
Self

Your sparkly toes—that dance the sugar into your soul
Your sparkly soul—that loves and is loved
Your sparkly love-shine—that leaps from your heart
Your sparkly heart—that shines like a star

You were born a star
You just forgot

As you busily tend to all
Your Sparkle feels dim or not at all
Like stars under the clouds
The light still shines

Your Sparkle core
patient
gracious
vivacious
tenacious
        —awaits.

You own your Sparkle Power. You just misplaced the ownership.
Delicious, sparkly you,
Delight in your Sparkle again and delight in the love you shine.

Contents

Foreword

I am honoured to have the opportunity to introduce readers to this book. I believe that writing it has been a labour of love. Aimed predominantly at women, but not exclusively so, Lynda and Leslie have used the metaphor of one's purse to explore the complex and often exhausting balance involved with caring for others while at the same time caring for self emotionally. What is unique about the book is that its compassionate message is based upon scientific research, but its imaginative delivery style makes serious subject matter accessible, informative, and easier to understand. The authors have managed to integrate several modalities of therapeutic research into a practical compassionate message of self-care. They seem to know that women exhausted from the struggle may be looking for nurturance, support, and understanding more than being expected to absorb the data presented by research studies.

Authors Leslie and Lynda bring to readers a wealth of experience. They each augmented professional careers (one in law, the other in nursing) with entry into the fascinating field of relationship dynamics to initiate a friendship and collaboration that has spanned over thirty years. Reading this book is like being allowed to sit in on a conversation between two seasoned practitioners who use anecdotes to dissect the complex nature of individual reactions as these individuals interact with other people. These anecdotes describe different scenarios, allowing a glimpse at the inner dialogue most people may recognize as part of their own inner processing. What we learn is that there seems to be a universal innate need to be connected, so our instinct to help/care for others has a biological component. It is really an innate human quality. While this is reassuring, adding oneself to the equation is revealed as the task at hand. Managing this inevitable struggle thus becomes a valid lifelong task.

Two questions arise: Does this have to be either/or? Is it not both/and? Then *how*? How do we do both? Is it selfish to suggest caring for ourselves when there are so many needs presented to us by others on a daily basis designed to take our attention elsewhere?

Let us listen in on the conversation—perhaps its creative use of language will stimulate reflection on your own situation and provide a catalyst for some needed self-compassion and ideas for practical change. The whimsical nature of their approach suggests it does not need to be an onerous task. There is some foundational wisdom at its core. Let us add some joy to our perspective!

During these turbulent times, I personally welcome a discussion about balance. A retired professional myself with multiple people in my life to love and worry about and multiple interests to pursue, I am a fellow purse-carrying traveller. I believe that we are going to need each other to face the many challenges ahead. Tools for including oneself in the equation in a healthy way are welcome. Lynda and Leslie remind us that it is possible to have more than one emotional experience at the same time, e.g., curiosity and dread or curiosity and awe. And sometimes a pause can seem as beneficial as a longer rest. Messages conveyed with humour, joy, wisdom, and hope and a recognition of the need for sharing go a long way. Thank you.

Jean Brown, RN, MSc, RMFT
October 2023

To Our Readers

Why did we write this book?

A lawyer and a nurse, we met in grad school and immediately recognized a fellow giver, passionate about becoming relationship therapists. We wanted to love and care for others, yet we didn't want to be people who cared for others at the expense of our own health and sanity. Unlike our moms, we realized we didn't have to carry our stress alone. What began as the two of us meeting weekly to support each other turned into our powerful approach for caring women. We use our Reignite Sparkle Solution daily, and we are thrilled to share it with you.

INTRODUCTION

The Story of the Purse

Rushing to a meeting, we scamper to the car, juggling purses and briefcases. Our minds race, retrieving the information from the meeting we just left, worrying about the meeting we are rushing to, checking our hair and makeup in the car mirrors before we exit. Engaged in busy conversation about all of this and throwing our baggage into the back seat, we begin to pull out of the parking space. Leslie remembers we need the parking ticket to exit the garage. Lynda begins to fish around for it in her purse.

No ticket.
Hand dives in again.
No ticket.

Where is this all-important ticket to parking garage freedom? Time ticks away. The next meeting is approaching, and we can't get out of the garage.

To ease the stress, Leslie comments to Lynda how lovely this new purse is, "Well, it seems so spacious and there are so many pockets. It looks so organized." Lynda continues dive-bombing around for the magic ticket.

And then Lynda utters, "I thought it would be different with a new purse!"

Isn't that it? We women are always on the lookout for the best, newest way to help us take care of ourselves and organize our lives and the lives of others. We recently took stock of our purse collections in current circulation and came up with the following tally: Lynda 18, Leslie 22.

Because one purse is a better size or colour for this or that occasion, whether we are at work or not, whether we are travelling or not—we always need the right purse!

With each purse comes new hope. This purse will organize us better, this purse will make us look professional, this purse will make us look sassy, this purse will make us look _____. You fill in the blank, but the bottom line stays the same:

> *This purse will be the best answer to the current situation.*

Of course, the funny part is you can change your purse all you want, but you still need fundamental items inside the purse. What's inside counts.

Part of You Hesitates

Hi. C'mon over and have a seat. Put your feet up and take a moment if you feel like you can. Perhaps the problem is that in even taking a moment to stop, to read, to reflect, you feel guilty. If that's true, then picking up this book is a luxury, and it was probably written for you.

Are you a woman who cares about others so much you know about others' minds, agendas, and feelings more easily than your own?

Being their number one fan makes you happy. You have made a practice of this. You want to take care, really good care, of the people in your circle: spouses, children, friends, colleagues, extended family, and even the extended family of the extended family—all those lucky enough to be loved by you. But perhaps, what once worked very well for you may not be working anymore, and you find yourself feeling surprised, mad, and guilty. Your energetic adventures and positive spin on life have led to misadventures—some of your own making, a lot out of your control.

All the self-help articles and emails about how you can improve your health, have great relationships, eat less sugar, exercise more, meditate, be mindful, be happy, feel less guilty, and floss your teeth while on Twitter (X) have simply tweeted you out. They magnify your guilt because now the mantra is: *Self-care is the pinnacle, and if you do not do a good job of self-care, you will die* (or at least live a sorry, miserable life).

If this speaks to you, then all this information about self-care can make you feel:

Rebellious

- *I can't take time for me. I need to go to the nursing home or pick up the kids or get the groceries or do the org chart for work or floss the cat's teeth.*
- *Well, no way. I have gained this fat by being good to everyone else, and now I feel punished by having to take more time to lose it.*

Or Ashamed

- *I have a mirror that I avoid.*
- *I should know better.*

And the Ultimate

- *I'm too stressed to think about me.*
- *I'm not sure I care. There is too much going on.*
- *What the heck is self-care anyway? I read all the self-help books and underline them by hand and highlight them in my tablet, and I still goof it up.*

We don't only know about this because we have listened to women who say this. We know about this personally.

Your Own Story

Every woman who cares for others has her own story.

When you are told to take care of yourself, part of you hesitates. When books and shows and webinars evoke the merits of self-care and drawing boundaries, a part of you hesitates about the possibility. Logically, it makes sense to take good care of yourself. The facts are more than compelling. The stats abound.

Yet, part of you hesitates to care for yourself.

We love the awesome care and marketing regarding our health. For too long, women's health was not even on the back burner. It was not even on the stove! In December 1952, the *I Love Lucy* show described Lucy's delicate condition in French, *enceinte*. She could be pregnant in Paris, but not in New York City? After all, she and Ricky did sleep in twin beds.

Our sex lives, our entire health issues, are historically hidden—not up for discussion.

Many women's illnesses are difficult to diagnose. Perhaps, it is symbolic that our symptoms are just as hidden as we women who do not wish to draw attention to ourselves when others are in need. Women have scrapped the quiet imposed by culture and embraced advertising resplendent in colours of pinks, reds, and teals—celebrating our brave bodies and quests for healing with walks, runs, fundraisers, galas, and high heels.

Yet part of you may still hesitate about your precious health.

You may have seen a friend or family member suffer. You may have helped them through it, and for a while, you vowed to put yourself in the equation of life too: *There will be room for me in my purse.* But after a little while, you go back to old habits and put everyone else first because part of you hesitates.

Perhaps you watched someone die. Your friend or sister or mother was not purposely unkind to herself, but you find yourself—in your grief—mad about the stress she was undertaking while caring for others.

And still, part of you hesitates to care for yourself.

You may have had a health scare yourself—mental, physical, emotional, relational, or all four, the jackpot.

And still, part of you hesitates.

Sometimes you clean out your purse and repack just your things. Yet gradually your *purseonal* square footage dwindles down to a cracked mint dispenser and a used tissue among others' keys, sippy cups, and golf balls.

It is really, really, okay. Have a tissue. No, not the balled up, wrinkled one. Here's a fresh one. There is no shame at all in caring so incredibly through your whole being.

Aunt Dora

With caring intention, we open our purses just like this.

You go to Great Aunt Dora's retirement home and are feeling quite full of verve and love. You bring that pack of cards you shared with her growing up. You waltz in with your fun plan for a nice visit and an old-fashioned card game.

Fran, a tidily dressed support worker—with an authoritative badge on her chest that spells out, FRAN—looks directly at your large carryall and sees you pull out your deck of cards. "Mmm. Can't use those here." She shakes her head authoritatively.

You put on your friendliest smile, extend your hand, and say, "I'm sorry. I'm not sure what you mean. Oh, and I'm Betty by the way. Nice to meet you."

The support worker draws a line under her badge with her capable finger, nodding a stiff greeting.

"Fran," you complete.

Fran says, "No, NO! Can't use that deck. The print's too small for Nora here, and they haven't been sanitized."

"Oh, but Fran! These are my Aunt *Dora's* personal deck from home, and they are quite clean."

"Nettie, those are the rules, and if I had to break them for Cora here, well, you know, that's a slippery slope."

Fran continues to inform, saying that one can only use the retirement home's large print playing cards and strongly suggests that you go down to the card room, so you don't disturb Aunt Flora's roomie.

"Okay," you say.

Then Fran says, "What day would you like to play cards?"

And you reply, "I was thinking now, of course, because I drove two hours and took the day off work."

She says, "Well, that won't do because the room is closed for cleaning."

And you start to get a little edgy as Aunt Dora states, "That's all right, dear. It's the thought that counts."

Then Fran says, "Well, we must clean the room, and that only happens on Wednesdays. After all, we pride ourselves on cleanliness, and you wouldn't want your aunt to get C. difficile, or MRSA, or COVID 19, would you?"

And then you feel like a total insensitive nimrod because Uncle Elmo died of an infection in the hospital. *Oh gosh, I did play cards with him, too, come to think of it.*

And your sparkly sense of love and caring dwindles steadily and slowly like an old birthday balloon.

Nila

Or how about?

You say you'll help your granddaughter Nila with her homework. You loved school after all. Nothing like the feel of finely sharpened pencils and the smell of new notebooks to have you recall the energy of school, your friends, and your favourite teacher.

Nila pulls out her laptop and downloads the assignment from the cloud. How poetic it sounds.

You look over her shoulder and say, "Wait a minute, honey. I just need to grab my readers." *As if they will help.*

Nila begins to review the posted assignment. "Oh, Shakespeare," she groans.

Excitedly you squeal and say, "Oh honey, yes, Shakespeare. I am good at this. Just call me Portia, spelled with an *i-a*, not a *s-h-a*. You know I always got at least a 95 in Spelling!"

Nila turns her head towards you, raises one darling eyebrow, and asks, "What's Spelling?

You quickly recover, remembering the laptop has spellcheck. *How old fashioned of me.* You lick your lips that feel kind of parched. You say to yourself, either "Let it Go," Disney-style or "Shake It Off," Ms. Swift-with-a-capital-S style and remind yourself not to worry. The task at hand, your beloved bard, awaits.

And then Nila says, "Got the download open," and you both peer at the one-line task:

Translate the Merchant of Venice into seventy-eight tweets.

Benny

And finally, an example of failure from the animal kingdom.

Benny, the family's beagle hound, is listless, dragging his perfect little bum lower to the ground. His eyes are sad, and he is hiding under the end table in the living room.

Your heart weakens at the edges. You crawl on your tummy to peer under the table. Benny is miserable. You make soft soothing beagle-loving murmurs, "Benny baby, what's up?"

You try to reach in to grab his collar to see if you can gently drag him closer to you, and he growls and bares his teeth.

Yikes. You are scared of him, mad at him, worried about him, and love him all at the same time.

This horrific gut-wrenching sound rumbles from within Benny. You continue to reach for your beloved, distressed dog. One more rumble roars from the little guy's insides, and Benny barfs all over your hand.

Luckily, the offending rawhide bone—that Benny swallowed whole—is among the contents. Benny, feeling much better, runs out from under the table, strewing his now spilt stomach junk everywhere.

Benny got Bruce-the-St. Bernard's big bone all the way down his gullet. Somehow, when you unpacked the groceries, picked up the phone to answer the charity drive, and mopped the floor with your foot, you left out the wrong size treat.

Gulp.
Literally.

You say to yourself, *What a lousy parent I am. I almost killed the dog.*

Each of these stories illustrates the tenderness of your soul; your yearning to have all your loved ones safe and happy jumps to the forefront, forcing you to the back.

We feel so intensely the pain, fear, and sensitivities of those we love. It is not that we see them. We feel them. We are constantly making decisions that include information about others. Very quickly, we weigh and assess their needs, all the time.

We've heard so many women, including us, say things like:

- *I can't help it. It's just me.*
- *My mom always had our backs first, so that's what I do.*
- *My mom never had my back, and I never want to be like my mom.*
- *I know I give others a break, but well, not me. I gotta motor through.*
- *My Dad told me to never neglect my family as he had.*
- *So much on my plate. There's no time for me. Maybe next year.*
- *They're all stressing me out.*

Whose stress is it? It's hard to know. When we spend time with the people (team meetings, working on a project together, doing homework with them, going to appointments with them, or nursing their broken hearts—all of which we choose and want to do), we will have stress.

What Results from All that Caring?

After continuous and exhausting infusions of your caring, one or more of the following happens:

- You are exhausted when usually you're not.

- You are overloaded and feel there is too much stress in your life.

- You make it through a stressful period, expecting to bounce back, and are as flat as a week-old club soda.

- You have serious health issues.

- You have annoying, but not life-threatening health issues, such as tummy upset, shoulder pain, joint pain, back pain, rashes, breathing problems, frequent colds, infections, or ulcers you never had before.

- You are plagued by worrying and dark thoughts: *Where the heck is the sunny side of the street?*

The Pièce de Résistance

Then? The very people you care about and cherish in this world are less lovable, more annoying, and not adorable. You don't like the people you care about. You feel guilty about feeling this way. You certainly don't tell anyone. You are too ashamed that you can't continue to juggle all you used to. You feel mean-spirited.

You don't feel like yourself.

We call it *Care-y Stress*. You carry stress, so you have Care-y Stress—a secret tug in your heart, mind, and gut created from the act of caring for people intently. People's life stress and your life stress mix together. You cannot figure out whose stress is whose. You try to take care of relieving their stress and then forget about yourself. Not taking care of yourself upsets you. You act out on the people you love. Then you feel guilty and upset.

We hear your plea: *Please just quietly give me a book, so I can fix my darn self by myself.*

Since there is a book about it, the feelings you have must be shared by other women. Just maybe you are not a terrible, awful person for having these feelings.

There is a way to get through this zany cycle. We will challenge the opinion, *everybody first, fuggit about me, I'm fine*—uttered as we hobble about, propping up the arm of an elderly relative or combing the hair of a squirming toddler while on the phone to a desperate friend as we send a complicated email to work. We will not judge you or ourselves for taking care of others and perhaps forgetting ourselves.

We are going to celebrate the intuitive, caring, incredibly smart knowledge that taking care of others is, at its core, survival of the finest. We truly celebrate why you hesitate. It's totally understandable. Our caring instincts are first biological, then nursed along with the messages we have ingested from family, school, ethnic heritage, society, and culture. All of this plays a huge part in propelling us forward into caring for all and sundry. So, you are not perfect at taking care of yourself and everybody else at the same time. We hope you are curious to know how

You can have a purse of your own and still love and encourage those you love.

Yar-hoo you.

CHAPTER 1

What Do You Carry in Your Purse?

Lynda's fervent battle cry for the hope of a new and different purse ran deeper than we thought. The search for the hidden parking ticket in the folds of Lynda's new purse was fuelled by our stress.

We were dashing to deliver our stress workshop. We loved giving stress the old heave-ho with the able assistance of boas, tiaras, sunglasses, and great shoes. We nixed the therapeutic workshop title and offered these events as *Fun Forums*.

We used a nifty exercise we learned from Kathy Norman, called "Open Your Purse," to see how we all share so many aspects of a shared problem.

Our goal was to teach people how we carry both stress and *Happy* on us every day.

We invited women to "find two items you carry in your purse that make you feel stressed."

They boldly opened their purses and easily declared items that represented stress to them.

Then, we asked them to "find two items you carry in your purse that make you feel happy." The same items that could make some people stressed could bring other people joy. This demonstration allowed us a simple way to have people experience the bodily feelings of both stress and joy as they related the feelings and stories associated with the objects.

But the demo came alive to us in another way. Not only did women carry both symbols of stress and happy in their purses, they also wore these symbols on their faces and relayed them in their voices. As women described the various objects in their purses, we who listened jumped on a virtual roller coaster ride.

When a brave woman waved her debt-ridden credit card or the appointment card for her mother's many medical appointments, our hearts stood still or slowed to honour the depth of stress she endured.

We cried over:

- The big print notebook for an aging mom's failing eyesight
- A broken animal cracker from the doctor's visit for a child they worried so very much about
- A loved ones' failed exam crumpled into a ziplock bag
- The speeding ticket

Emotions clogged our throats. Sadness, grief, anger, fear, and guilt entered the room.

Rummaging through their purses, women joyfully pulled out their child's picture or their dog's hair ribbon.

We laughed as these objects spilled out:

- A grandchild's tyrannosaurus rex
- A faded flower, the fragrant memory of a special night out
- A tennis ball on the ready for a son's road hockey practice
- Car keys, instant jingle bells for a new baby

We could feel our hearts swell, smiling inside our chests. Emotions skipped lighter—joy, love, and happiness entered the room.

The shifts were real and palpable. Respect, tears, and laughter danced a strange waltz in the room. We felt the physical sensation of energy as it moved and shifted, minute by minute, heartache by belly laugh. Our hearts grew like the Grinch's when he saw Cindy Lou's despair and hope. Our eyes welled at the poignancy of unexpected changes in a woman's life.

Energy

Energy is as real as the rent and as invisible as the Tooth Fairy.

Energy is hard to see, and we might wonder if it is even present. Yet, we believe many things exist without visual proof because we see the effects of their presence. We do not question the validity of gravity, humidity, air, WIFI at the coffee shop, or cell phone signals.

Energy, as invisible as it may be, somehow seems acceptable for physics, space research, or medicine in terms of diagnostic tests, but still, you can't really see it.

Energetic moments scare us when we feel blue,
sense a storm in the offing,
shiver with hairs eerily alive on the back our necks,
are shocked by walking on a static carpet,
or feel the tension when we walk into the room.

Energetic moments delight us when we bubble with excitement,
drink in the warmth of sun on our faces,
anticipate seeing someone we love,
are surprised by a wonderful gift,
or are in the presence of people who are joyful.

Still, when we talked about energy to participants, clients, and especially our families, we were often met with: *So, you really believe this energy stuff, eh?*

Invisible and Mysterious

Energy is not only invisible, but also mysterious.

Energy might seem more acceptable in the healing professions. Energy healers often use physical interventions without words. Some just use their own movements near the body and do not even touch the person. It can seem like hocus-pocus. When we do not know or understand something, and that something seems mysterious, we can feel protective, confused, and defensive.

Energy's invisible and mysterious nature has puzzled us too. Raised as good little girls who ventured into practical professions in medicine and law, proof and verification were our gold standards. None of that touchy-feely, chanting *hoo, hoo, woo, woo*! Thank you very much.

So, we did what any logical brained nurse or lawyer would do. We studied. But as so often happens, it was a calm and collected person who captured the reality of energy for us intellectual naysayers.

What the heck is that noise?

And why won't it stop?

We noticed our office landline telephone was making strange Morse code-like noises, intermittent and distracting. We weren't even using the darn phone. This was quite agitating. The sound was unpredictable and interrupted our conversations with people. Assuming the old phone had done its job and deserved retirement, we unplugged it and sprang for a new phone.

Happy with our new purchase and delighted with its sleek, new features, we knew we had fixed the problem. We plugged the new phone in and—*static, static, static*—freaky uncomfortable sounds returned! Why didn't we spring for the more expensive phone?

That week someone else noticed the noise. "Oh, don't worry about it. You just need to move your cell phone. I think the cell is sitting too close to the landline, and the different frequencies and sound waves create static. Same thing happened at our office. If it bothers you, just move the cell phone a bit."

Doh! Thank you, Homer Simpson. Similarly, the women participants illustrated how energy flowed or kinked in and around us.

The Garden Hose

Imagine you have a lithe, curvy garden hose. Water flows through it, and you reward the universe by sharing happy H_2O with all living things. You brighten the flowers, and you perk up the blades of grass.

Then the water drops to a dribble.
Or stops all together.
You have a kink.

The water is still coming from the tap, but it is not completing the route to your spout. The water is still there, but it is not flowing. The *energy* flow culprit is a kink in the hose. The kink can be caused by many possibilities. The hose got wrapped around a chair leg. The hose was tangled. Something fell on the hose. Doesn't matter. Same result, no flow.

Listen folks, the hose wasn't looking to get a kink in it. Garden life just happens.

There is patio furniture out where you water.
There is wear and tear on the hose.
There is a tree or bush in the way.
There could have been a huge storm.

Yes women, we are just like the garden hose. Our energy flow can be a no-go or a paltry dribble. Sometimes we rejig the hose, and for a moment the water bursts out and we have an energy super soak. When the route to our spout is blocked, we usually try to figure out where the kink is in the hose so we can get the water moving again.

It's the same with our energy. We are energy, and energy moves. Energy is both in and around us, and it moves all the time. When we have an **Energy Kink**, we need to rejig something to get the flow going again.

But what really brought home our red-eyed study of books and the kazillion bucks of cash and time we spent on excellent conferences trying to *get* energy were *women's hearts.*

Collecting Our Energy: The Heart

As little people, when we wanted something so very much, vibrating with possibility or quivering with fear—we would say these magic words, *I wish with all my heart.* Our small worlds seemed big and sometimes out of control, and oh so very important. We both remember telling our mothers our chaotic tales of friends who did not like us, or the doggies who growled at us, or the fact that our toy had just fallen apart—blubbering away in search of answers and, more importantly, support.

Both our mothers would say to us, "Now, now. Let's start from the beginning."

The heart does rule the head. In their groundbreaking book *Heartmath Solution*, Childre and Martin explain how our heart emerged as the first organ to develop, before our brain and nervous system. The heart has her very own brain, separate and apart from our big ole head to track what she felt, knew, and did before the brain and other organs came along.

What does that mean? Our hearts have their own memories, and these memories are deeper and different than brain memories. The heart has more history and different experiences because it is older. Our hearts kept us going until our brain and nervous system were more developed. Your heart deserves quiet and focus to decipher all this life-affirming info as it performs nonstop. Every minute, she pumps your entire blood volume, five quarts or so, through the sixty-thousand-mile length of your circulatory vessels. Beating approximately100,000 times a day, she deserves any break you can give her (Leal 2021,128).

This heart knowledge is central to our well-being.

According to Rollin McCraty in *Science of the Heart, Volume 2*, our heart's intuitive voice calls out to us about the state of our nation— your unique and precious nervous system stage. Heart information dances through our insides in unseen, yet real ways. Hormones and neurotransmitters chemically and energetically share the heart's latest news. Heartwaves pulsate like little space stations within us. All this info swirling within us can be documented and verified by our heartwaves. Electrical impulses paint patterns within our hearts. Electrocardiograms showcase these picturesque highs and lows.

When we are happy, flowing, and feeling well, our visible energy is SmilesVille. In Bermuda, one can watch the ocean waves at play, flowing from vigorous to gentle, anticipating the next wave in a seamless ebb and flow. Like a Bermuda beach within us, our heartwaves roar or gently ebb, and the time between each wave is different. The more readily and easily we go from one heartwave to another, the more vibrant, healthy, and happy we are.

Our energy is coordinated. Our heart is in the loop. Everyone knows that coordination is *de rigeur*. Thank you, Grace Kelly and Audrey Hepburn. But when stress grips us, we look askance or tight-faced. We bellow robust rants or detail our upsets with deflated discourse. Our heart energy waves inside of us are too crazy high or too dull low with not much time difference between the waves (McCraty 2015, 3–28). Out of the loop, de flipping loop.

Energy waves and mappings inside a person are a physical matter that explains how doctors test for health stuff. But energy swirling around outside a body, transmitting the happiness or stress inside a person to the outside world? C'mon now. We would need a signed affidavit or an important medical document to secure our belief about that.

Then of course, there was the landline phone and the cell phone phenomenon. We experienced that together. It seemed a little wooey-hooey. But it shouldn't have.

The most rip-roaring, powerful energy in the human body is the heart. The largest source of electromagnetic energy within us is our heart. We glow as our heart power shines outside of us. With an electrical field sixty times greater than what our brains send out, that heart energy is more than one hundred times greater in strength than the brain's and can be detected up to nearly one meter (three feet) away from the body in all directions (McCraty 2015, 36).

One way to imagine this heart energy emanating outside of us is to compare it to a weather report. In the Atlantic, hurricanes are followed closely. We think nothing of the nice blue maps on the Weather Channel. When danger lurks, we eagerly look for the storm's eye, as swirling tendrils on TV and computer screens paint high tides and big waves. We rely on these visuals to decide whether not to batten down the hatches.

Heart hurricanes or the breezes of cardiac calm map out our inner storms and inner zens. Energy zings out from hearts, swirling around all the time. Just imagine the colourful patterns our hearts would make on the Weather Channel. If we did, we would see our energy touching others' hearts, making people smile or frown, laugh or cry as we radiate our heart energy.

Each heroic heart in our workshops pulsed with energy. Each heart emitted energy. Each heart received energy.

And all these energetic comings and goings were vibrantly talking to each woman's core: her automatic nervous system. Clear as a bell in each woman's soft-featured face and in the engaging lilt of her voice, emotional energy was visible. The sadness or frustration in a woman's taut face and higher pitched, faster-paced voice magically made emotional energy visible too.

We then knew that what we had studied about energy was the real deal. Others' energy somehow was bumping up with ours. Each radiating heart shared its power. We felt stirrings within us, remembering our stories of connection or loss in our own lives. We absorbed energy. Emotions relayed energies throughout each of us. We felt them and we relayed them. Our nervous systems lit up or hunkered down. Energy was now familiar. The mystery had lifted.

Another person's stress became our stress. Their stress was felt within us. Their fast-beating hearts became our fast-beating hearts. Our very own bodies felt uncomfortable, as we privately recalled those times we felt *stress* too. Their happiness became our happiness, and *their happiness* was felt within us. Their calm-beating hearts became our calm-beating hearts. Our very own bodies felt energetically relaxed as we privately recalled those times we had been happy too (Childre and Martin 1999, 160).

We hoped the "Open Your Purse" exercise could teach women how quickly our body's automatic nervous system goes amok when stress ensues. The *sympathetic branch* of the nervous system revs people into actions to protect themselves. Items in their purses could demonstrate how soon women felt this physiological pull as they gasped at an unpaid bill. At the same time, women carried items that could invoke a more relaxed response, engaging the *parasympathetic branch* of their nervous systems. That is what we knew about the science of stress back then.

We realized this exercise revealed women's powerful heart engines in a way no book could ever have taught us. When a heart was pulsating in a feel-good way, that heart attracted more hearts to join in. Absolutely compelling and magnetic.

Experiencing how women sent out loving heart energy, drawing people more easily into their purses, we thought this magnetic pull that drew others near to them explained how women care for those in their circle so consistently. This unspoken heart language allowed us to feel calm, energetically attentive, and happy. Their loving hearts were teaching our nervous systems how to be safe in the presence of others.

Women's Stress and Women's *Happy*

Women bore both stress and happiness—which we will fondly call *Happy*—in their purses and wore both on their faces and their nervous systems. This emotional energy was an alchemy of them and theirs.

An alchemy of them and theirs?

Wait a minute. Wait a gosh darn minute.

Staring us right in the face was the other glaring truth that women showed us. This amazing heart energy, with its ability to connect and collect other people, revealed another surprising result. Sure, this purse-sharing frivolity unveiled the massive energetic power of our loving hearts, but we were left with questions.

What made women stuff their purse with other people's stuff in the first place? And what made them keep the stuff in their purse?

A Purse Phenomenon: Other People's Stuff

This result occurred repeatedly. Every time, in every event, in every town, women showed us the exact same thing. Women carry a lot of other people's stuff smooshed in their purses. We mean *a lot*. And not just the expected stuff, like their younger children's toys and snacks. Oh, no—teenager's stuff, bigger people's stuff, friends and relatives' stuff.

So much stuff that their own stuff was buried underneath.
Or they forgot to put their own stuff into their purses.
Or their own stuff had fallen in the foot well of the car as they
  jostled around in their purses en route to someone else's
  appointment or need.

The two of us never noticed the same phenomenon in our own purses because we did exactly the same thing. We get stressed by the very people we love. Without knowing it, our stress hormones kick into gear. It affects every part of our body.

One of the stress hormones, *cortisol,* overflows inside us, urging our nervous system to speed up or slow down. But too much cortisol can wreak havoc in our bodies, keeping us on alert for similar experiences, making it hard to think clearly or learn new things, inflaming our insides (Graham 2013, 206–207) and even encouraging weight gain to pad us up for any future assault (Chutkan, 2013, 174)

We try to carry others' stuff and their lives. Our energies and their energies are all mixed up together. Others' lives can become more important than our own.

With each opening of their purse, women were holding onto their loved ones' stuff for safekeeping, and they felt relief and safety within their beings too. Somehow this safety thing was super comforting for one and all.

We thought it was just women's hearts, but there was more.

The strength of their hearts enabled them to do this brave feat, but why on earth would they—and we—carry this stuff so automatically? It was as if our purses just popped open to anyone who needed something, or we thought needed something. We all did it as if our lives depended on it.

While we watched this open purse action in our neck of the woods, a researcher in another town was discovering why women open their life purses for safekeeping and how their caring beings were able to do it. We knew it took heart and a lot of nerve to love so openheartedly all the time. Little did we know how right we were.

Women are nervy—in a very good way.

CHAPTER 2

Viva Las Vagus! (Not Vegas)

When women valiantly care for and hold places for people in their purses, they turn a groundbreaking theory advanced by scientist Dr. Stephen Porges into a vivacious feature film. These purses paint the research for us in technicolour. Clever women participants, heavy purses in tow, revealed what nervous system science was working at behind the scenes.

Before doing anything to save our sorry souls, we need to seek connection. In this seeking, we end up carrying people.

It was not only an unexpected finding but a stressful one. What was this carrying behaviour all our participants did? Did this action have anything to do with what we had taught about the stress reaction? Or was it explained by these strong hearts that loved so dearly?

Both were true.

Our Nervous System at Safe

The best way to set our nervous systems at *safe* is in the presence of someone who feels safe.

When people are comfy safe—not stressed—they not only survive, they blossom vibrantly. Our nervous systems crave human connection to feel safe (Porges 2017, 7–8). We need to feel safe to *purr* at calmly energetic. Purring means fluid movement with no odd knocks or clunks, no unwanted noise or emissions, no stopping or freezing, and no clogs. When you are set at safe, you are in purr-fect running order (sorry we couldn't resist). Scientists call it homeostasis.

Dr. Porges researched the vagus nerve within the parasympathetic branch of our nervous system that cozies up to the heart. This research showed that the parasympathetic nervous system is not just about the relaxation response. He discovered people always reach out to find safety with others first when they sense trouble brewing. If we sense we are *unsafe*, we resort to our nervous system's ancestral and solitary defences, but it is not the first thing we do. This truth shakes up everything we thought we knew about stress.

The Safety Protocol We All Know

A person learns to set their nervous system at *safe* with the help of somebody else's safekeeping actions. This action of carrying others is a wonderful example of nature's attempt for us to come together in times of good and in times of stress. But what we choose to hold in our purses also revealed more of what Dr. Porges knew to be true.

Purses are sacrosanct. You never go in someone else's purse, and they don't go in yours! Why do we have that rule?

Safety.
Purses keep things safe.

We keep our loved ones' stuff safe, stowed within the bottomless pits of our purses.

Our actions of carrying our loved ones' stuff shows how deeply we try to keep them safe.

Items we choose to keep in the folds of our purses, such as pictures, a package of sugar, a baseball ticket, a dog treat, or song lyrics, reveal the essence of safety we wish for the people we adore.

You might feel safety when:

- Seeing a sunset as you relax with someone special
- Sipping a warm cup of cocoa as you huddle together after building a snowman
- Cuddling a puppy or kitten that sighs on your chest
- Hearing the ump's cry of *Safe!* after the mad dash toward home plate
- Smelling a favourite aroma wafting from the oven
- Hearing a song you love

We want our loved ones to sparkle with emotions we all know about and cannot articulate. The generous folds of our open purses yearn to provide a safe place where remnants of these emotions can colour our loved ones' insides. Yup. Our purse-carrying behaviour is all about keeping those we love safe. Teaching those we love how to be safe does not get any bigger than that.

Take a bow you purse-totin', purse-poppin', fearless woman. Loving so courageously takes a lot of nerve. Literally.

Visiting Vagus

Like many people who spend endless hours in Vegas honing a winning strategy, Dr. Stephen Porges dedicated many hours studying the vagus nerve locale. While the rest us were getting cheap flights to the only Vegas we knew, he visited Vagus daily in his office lab.

Vegas, a town of wild exhilaration and devastating blows, a city of possibility and fear, gathers disparate people together. Both jubilant celebrants and lonely souls connect in this neon neighbourhood. Like Vegas, the long meandering vagus nerve also courts social celebratory connection and is on the lookout for when we are in lonesome sole-soul territory. Las Vegas is a cavalcade of lights, smoke, and mirrors portraying promises of dreams coming true with a little luck. Yet as anyone who has visited that happening town can tell you, the true nature of a human can be found amidst the showy glamour and oxygen-infused casino rooms. The setting might be false, but Vegas reveals the real lowdown on the humans who visit her.

The vulnerability of fortunes-in-the-making shows a lot:

- The safe or risky soul
- The happy or sad player
- The hopeful or the hopeless

The vagus nerve reveals our essence.

Housed originally in the brain, the *vagus nerve* is cranial. Vagus, meaning *wandering* in Latin, is aptly named. A traveller to her core, vagus is the only one of the cranial nerves to leave the shelter of the skull and hit the road to explore the entire body. Lengthy vagus begins her journey throughout us, venturing forth from our brain stem behind our ears. A bundle of nerve fibres like a roadway inside of us, vagus connects to many vital body parts. We are talking the big guys: heart, brain, lungs, gut, liver, kidneys, spleen, ears, eyes, throats, and vocal cords. This nerve is vital for health as its massive size enables it to shimmy lots of information throughout us (Rosenberg 2017, 7–8).

Vagus gets around. A good traveller, vagus texts her homebodies a lot (or sends postcards if she's old school). Similarly, vagus loves to continually report info to the body, mind, and emotions about her adventure without us knowing anything about it.

You might think the brain connection would be the big contributor to the vagus knowledge base, but only 15 percent of what vagus tell us about ourselves is brain stuff. On the other hand, 80 percent of what she tells us comes from our gut and organs. That's a lot of inner knowingness. In addition, vagus gets about 4 percent gossip from our throat and vocal muscles and 1 percent from skin around our ears (Habib 2020, 2).

In his early days, Dr. Porges explored the worlds of obstetrics and neonatology. You know, baby stuff (Dana 2018, x). The two of us pored over many books, attempting to understand Dr. Porges' theory and how it applies to caring women. We jotted down notes and chatted together over steaming mugs of coffee. We began where he began—baby stuff.

Leslie exclaimed excitedly, "Human babies. Oh, they look so perfect, and they are so handy at asking for what they need without saying a word. What a feat, given they need so much help, especially at the start of life."

It seemed Dr. Porges might be solving a huge puzzle for us about how our biology and human need for connection is intertwined. He showed the progression from reptiles to who we are now (Porges 2018, 51).

Reptile Reflections

The two of us pondered. We had never really considered snakes, crocs, frogs, and toads in any detail before. Reptiles don't need a connection gig. Never did and still don't. Snakes, alligators, lizards, and frogs expel their eggs to the outside world, then slither or hop away.

Eek! How cold blooded! Lynda still shivers at the memories of the cobra snake that reared its head and hissed at her when she was a mere little girl in India.

Solitary sojourners, reptiles function perfectly without need for instruction, reflection, wisdom, or encouragement from other reptiles. Ever look a snake in the eye? Didn't think so. They don't gotta open a purse to those they love. To answer Tina Turner in her song, "What's Love Got to Do with It?" a snake's reply is: *nothing.*

Reptiles must be careful all right. But the only one they ever count on, ever, ever, is themselves. With all its gut knowingness, the reptile does quite nicely, thank you, detecting changes in sensation, temperature, and in general what-is-around-me stuff. Reptiles don't need others to help them at all. They don't know how to cuddle, sigh, or purr with delight. Satisfaction to a reptile is simply: *I'm here, aren't I?*

We chatted about how a baby snake comes to be, commiserating over a reptile's lack of romance. Lynda madly wrote down our thoughts:

- *No soft candlelight or sexy music required. No lovemaking schtick.*

- *Fertilize and drop that egg. Plop. A little later, crack, crack, egg opens.*

- *Little reptile senses the texture of the ground around it, and slithers, hops for sustenance.*

- *Reptile doesn't hope for a campfire singalong to know where to find the gang.*

- *Reptile never started with a gang, so it has no idea what "Hail, hail the gang's all here!" means.*

Connect and carry? Fuggit about it. The singular reptile does not know the sense of another beating heart or the sweet action of being fed by a nurturing, generous other. Reptile does not know the cuddle-up warmth of sucking its thumb, drifting off into slumber, or the melodic rocking of a parent's movements. Reptile cannot miss being with another reptile once out of the egg because reptile never had something to miss. Reptile saves itself all on its ownsome. No connection. No relationship.

Reptile Slogans

I figure it out. I'm a solo act.
Hide. Freeze. Slither. Hop. Flop.
Just another game of solitaire.
I save myself.

Then reptiles stay alone forever. Leslie, with a little catch in her throat, uttered, "This is just so sad," and felt for this reptile that can't feel back. With emotion tingling Leslie's soul, she started humming the melody to "People," a Streisand tune that never fails her and cheers her onward. She continued to hum a few more bars.

Lynda exclaimed, "We humans need each other!"

We knew, just as Virginia Satir—the mother of family therapy—intuitively knew, we are "people makers" (Satir 1972, 196). Dr. Porges had something to say about this transition from reptile to human. We were hooked before we even knew his whole theory. Unlike reptiles, the human embryo has no sense at all of being singular. The sperm and egg do their *Glad to meet ya, hi dee ho* and voilà! Little zygote finds a safe, comfy place to hang out. A short-term lease in the womb room is perfect.

The Inside Purse

We start as a Little Doodle in someone else's purse. We land in the womb room. We are carried.

Right from the get-go, people sense, know, and grow because *We* are more than *I*. We can only grow as we. Little Doodle's energy is all mixed up with mom's energy. Always in relationship, our biology only knows connection to other warm-blooded sorts. We downright percolate with connection. Warm-blooded, fired up, and wired up for closeness, we need to be nestled. We need to be snuggled.

If nothing untoward happens, Little Doodle can languish in the comfort of safety. Floating and growing in her own little bubble, Little Doodle delightfully enjoys the room service feature *momma body* offers. Inside purse-holder momma obliges, providing food, water, and shelter. This landlord-tenant setup is gut-to-gut, heart-to-heart, visceral for both mom and this new kid on the block. Two energetic chatterboxes, Little Doodle embryo and momma wordlessly share nonstop between their two changing bodies. Blood, air, lymph, heartbeats, skin to skin, their entire nervous systems entangle deliciously together.

When all is well, Little Doodle gets about forty weeks of togetherness rent free. No thinking, no asking—every need can be met, snug in this warm-blooded purse of another human being.

At that, we needed a break. We turned up the tunes. Music always soothes our nervous systems when we are a little revved up. Sister Sledge's "We are Family" rocked in the background. Soon, we began humming and moving our bodies. This helped us to get back to what we were reading and thinking about.

Little Doodle's first sense of family envelops her. Intricately tied to another body, her own little body energy experiences the ups and downs and the just-right settings of her developing nervous system. Little Doodle does not think about or see clues for safety. Her ability to know what's safe is quicker than that. She connects and carries clues from her insides and outsides using *neuroception*: underground, automatic, wordless (Porges 2017, 19).

Momma body consistently and continually monitors the world, the people in it, and her own inner workings to make sure momma is safe from threat or danger. Little Doodle's nervous system responds to the changes in mom's nervous system. These changes are uncomfortable and not desirable but usually manageable (Mulkey and du Plessis 2019).

The basic nervous system safety plan momma still has from when she was a little unborn doodle herself has not changed. To stay alive, her nervous system is always available to her and can go full throttle if needed. When momma feels safe, her nervous system is calm, and she can continue to grow and enjoy life in the company of safe others. There is no perfection, of course. If momma's nervous system is more highly amped or less energetic, Little Doodle will ride that setting with her.

Dr. Porges highlighted the vagus nerve that has everything to do with safety. Focusing on one thing, the health of this nerve can make us all connect with kindness as we carry less. As Dr. Porges knew, when our nervous systems sense safety, we focus on learning and growing without diverting our resources to fending off foes. When safety weaves through us, our foundation is solid (Tucci, Weller, and Mitchell 2018, 92).

The Safety Signal

Safety gives us the all-clear to sparkle.

When momma body registers safety, she hums and purrs at *just right*. Little Doodle hums and purrs too (Porges 2017, 9). Within the womb, she stretches and moves as needed without fear. Within the womb, Little Doodle rests and stays still as needed without fear. Her heart rate and blood pressure pulse in an even pace. Her muscles relax. She breathes deeply at just the right pace. She enjoys the pleasure of skin sensation as she receives nurture. She eats, digests, and sleeps well. She smiles and sometimes sucks her thumb. She never senses being alone when momma's nervous system purrs just right. Warm comfort wordlessly bespeaks safety.

Little Doodle's Slogans

"With a Little Help from my Friends" by Lennon and McCartney (1967)
I need a nervous system that is safe.
Relate is great when it is safe.
I need you to be safe for me to flourish.

"Gosh," Leslie said: "We come into this world inside of another person, and we develop and grow only in the world of other people—forever. It never stops. Ever."

Little Doodle was never detached from this physical momma body; she was always attached to another human being. She was never physically alone. We anticipated what was next for Little Doodle, tucked into momma's purse—birth. Sudden. Abrupt. No plan of action. Whether natural birth or by intervention, all Little Doodle's basic connections to food, water, and shelter are cut off. She is embarking on this trip naked, no suitcase, no map, no smartphone with a GPS.

Little Doodle's nervous system—entirely on its ownsome—freaks out. Little Doodle has been at this stress rodeo before, but not in such a dramatic way. She is now auto-primed on a continual whole-body scope of what is safe, what could threaten, or what could be without-a-doubt dangerous. Her nervous system is always on the lookout. Her organs, skin, blood vessels, lymph, fat, and muscles are on the ever-ready. She has no clue of her *neuroception* that always looks out on her behalf. A resourceful little thing, Little Doodle even starts recording stressful moments to avoid, and these notations stick like glue inside of her (Graham 2013, 41). We started calling these gooey recollections **Sticky Notes**.

Never, ever, in her lovin' Little Doodleness has she experienced this terror. Alone. Totally disconnected. Ouchie! This really hurts.

This alone feeling is a zone she rails against with all her might (gosh, if she could speak):

What on earth? she cries.

Earth? What's that? she wails.

Geez Louise, I was a womb tenant? Did I not read the fine print?

What's my Little Doodleness to do?

Incapable of words, yet full of sensation, she senses, *I'm unhappy.* At this tender age, even without a fully developed thinking brain, she senses different parts of her within her wondrous growing mind energy. If she could stand up and stomp her little foot, she would. Trying to help her, different parts of Little Doodle try to cover all the angles of this sudden disaster. Some parts of her are darn scared. Others are just flippin' angry. Some parts pretend she didn't sense all this unsafe ickiness.

Lynda sighed deeply and spoke with caring fervour, "Oh, this is so alarming. She must start breathing on her own. She must get her heart beating all on her ownsome. She must find food. She must stay warm. She has no words. She can't stand up. She wants another heartbeat to calm her, for that cuddle-up sensation she just left a few hours ago. Gosh, poor thing, this alone stuff is for the birds. The safety she knew was the connecting stuff. Little Doodle needs another human being to keep her safe."

The fear we first felt for her transformed into tremendous awe as we thought about her blind fortitude and valiant energy. She only knew how to be carried inside mom, mixed with mom's energy. They spent a long time exchanging their cells with each other (Cómitre-Mariano et al. 2021).

We knew Little Doodle would need a lot of heart and nerve to leave the womb room. We then remembered there is even more that Little Doodle needs. Little Doodle comes to life's party with her **Body, Mind, Emotion, and Connection Energies.** (To satisfy the scientific part of you, see a longer explanation in the Appendix.) She needs to learn how to use her four energies.

These energies are the essence of her humanness. She depends on the warmth and kindness of safe people not only to give a helping hand when in trouble, but to also assist her energies to grow and flourish. She needs another safe person to see, know, and experience all her separate parts and her sparkly self. It is not an alone job. She is right to feel terror.

If you feel that you were not always the most relaxed purse provider, please do not fret. Nervous system maintenance is the lifework of all us doodles. Taking time now to learn about it is a testament to your goodness and caring. Opportunities abound for growth and repairs no matter what we may have tried before (Graham 2013, 183).

Next: Little Doodle needs help from safe and sparkly human beings to party on her own life stage.

CHAPTER 3

Theory with Heart: Polyvagal

Little Doodle changed her address and desperately wants a return to sender. Leaving the womb room for parts unknown takes a hero heart and a lot of nerve. How can Little Doodle survive, let alone grow?

Little Doodle has her own nervous system stage in which she stars in the party of life. She has a nervous system comprised of the brain, brain stem, spinal cord, and multiple nerves to help her (Rosenberg 2017, 7). The automatic nervous system can be thought of as the interplay of various nerve messages working all the time to help us survive.

We are usually not aware of their constant work on our behalf. In the same way we do not think consciously of each heartbeat that drums or breath we inhale and exhale, the nervous system just works away, doing its thing. There are two branches of nerve pathways in the automatic nervous system: the *parasympathetic* and the *sympathetic*. As we studied the polyvagal theory put forward by Dr. Stephen Porges, we began to call this automatic nervous system the three **Purse Sisters,** named **VeeVee, SpeeDee and DeeDee.** You will learn about their Purse Sisters act in Chapter 8.

How Little Doodle's Purse Sisters whir internally in any given moment defines her individual stage and determines how Little Doodle will think, feel, say, and act. The Purse Sisters have *one* goal: keep Little Doodle safe and alive. When her Purse Sisters use their neuroception to sense safety, she feels okey-dokey. Her Body, Emotion, Mind, and Connection energies flow. Little Doodle's insides, fully charged with energy, feel swell.

Then, Little Doodle can **Sparkle.** Sparkle is Little Doodle's core essence of wise compassion that is with her throughout her life. On the other hand, if any of Little Doodle's energies become kinked, her Purse Sisters neuroception senses she is unsafe and will try to protect her. She won't feel so good and will no longer be focused on normal growth, maintenance, and clear thinking. Her Sparkle is dimmed and hard to notice.

We all have our own nervous system stages in which we star in the party of life. Sometimes we are drama queens, sometimes we are heroines, sometimes we are icky fallen stars. How our nervous system Purse Sisters are whirring away internally defines our individual stages in any given moment and determines what we think, feel, say, and act. Their fascinating relationship—moment to moment—affects the four energies of our whole being each and every nanosecond.

As we continued to read and reflect upon Dr. Porges' polyvagal theory, it became crystal clear: people need people beyond helping each other out of a pickle. (Although it is important to get out of a pickle too.) People need safe people to teach each other how to live and excel in their own precious nervous systems. Without safe people, we might eke through life. But to shine at our loveliest, healthiest best, safe people cinch the deal.

Little Doodle's system is at rest when she is around safe people. She can learn, grow, play, and take care of her own energy without mixing with energy around her. Little Doodle's nervous system can quickly protect her from unsafe sorts. In a mere blink, with the help of SpeeDee, her heart can race high, or with the help of DeeDee, sink way down low—constantly charging like a Belmont racehorse or droopily dragging like Eeyore the donkey.

Baby Doc Talk

Early in his career, Dr. Porges was super curious about the parasympathetic nervous system's vagus nerve, the heart, and babies. Having met pre-birth, the heart and this important vagus nerve have a permanent and eternal bond. As close pals, vagus nerve activity can be measured and researched by checking in with the heart. This measurement is a huge deal. According to McCraty, *heart rate variability*, the range between each heartbeat, shows us how our nervous system is functioning at any given time (McCraty, 2015).

Dr. Porges' research revealed that the vagal nerve could regulate a newborn baby's heart rate in a healthy way. His findings and report were published in a journal read by neonatologists and pediatricians. He hoped this info would be helpful and even encourage clinicians to check for a baby's vagal activity.

One baby doctor, a neonatologist, wrote Dr. Porges. This doctor faced a perplexing puzzle. How could the vagus nerve be helpful to babies? From his training, this baby doctor knew the vagus nerve was related to a serious danger for newborns called *bradycardia*. In this condition, the vagal nerve could slow down a baby's heart rate to the point of death. In short: *Dr. Porges, kindly explain.*

Rather than be daunted by this challenge, Dr. Porges made it his mission to solve this apparent dichotomy. For months, Dr. Porges carried the colleague's letter in his briefcase, a constant question tugging at his scientist heart. How can the vagus nerve protect some babies and be life threatening for others? One vagus nerve? Two opposite effects? Dr. Porges termed it a "vagal paradox" (Porges 2017, 59–61). The tension built.

The Paradox

How would this paradox be solved?

The two of us read and re-read Dr. Porges' ideas that emerged in his search to answer this dilemma. He dug deeper into understanding the vagus nerve right down to its evolutionary roots. An intense read indeed. Like mystery novel addicts, we hungered for the answer.

We needed chocolate.

Sadly, only breath mints were available in our purses. We both savoured the sweet tingle on our tongues, so grateful this same mint could freshen our breath as we still had many writing hours ahead.

Leslie jumped out of her chair, "Golly, poly, two! Two! Two nerves in one. Hey, this is what Dr. Porges is talking about."

Dr. Porges revealed the solution to the vagal paradox. He saw that the vagus nerve had two parts (*polyvagal*, not to be confused with the ointment you are carrying in your purse right now in case someone you love gets a boo boo). The heart buddies up with the vagus nerve in two directions. This discovery of the two parts of one vagus nerve in the parasympathetic branch of the nervous system changed everything.

Two Vagus Parts Diverge: North and South

Each part of the vagus nerve takes a different road. Each road provides important but different benefits. These two roads in the parasympathetic nervous system exit the brain stem and stroll through our body. Both vagal parts directly connect to our ever-loving hearts and our life-breathing lungs. Then they part company.

DeeDee

The first part of the parasympathetic branch of the of the vagus nerve is called *dorsal*. We call her DeeDee. The oldest Purse Sister, DeeDee starts out in the brainstem but is of an age when fashion was frivolous and does not wear a *myelinated sheath*, so she slowly goes south to the heart and lungs and connects to organs below your diaphragm or the middle of your back (Porges and Dana 2018, 53). DeeDee ventures deep into our lower insides, creating, receiving, and relaying gut-knowingness. DeeDee provides an ancient protection feature that reptiles still rely on. DeeDee can slow a body down to super slow, feigning death in front of a foe or freezing the pain, if *ick*, the foe digs in. Human doodles have this dorsal defence available to them too (Levine 1997, 96–97).

VeeVee

As people came along, the parasympathetic branch of our nervous system developed a second part of the vagus nerve: *ventral*. Ventral vagal may sound like some weird piece of housing material requiring duct cleaning, but it is our hidden gem, central to our vibrant health and warm human connection. We spent so much time thinking and talking about ventral vagal she felt like a pal. We started calling her VeeVee. She ventures in the totally opposite direction from dorsal. In comparison to DeeDee, VeeVee goes north, moving upward from the heart and lungs, connecting to our face, throat, eyes, and ears. Fashionable and technically advanced, sassy VeeVee wears a *sheath*, a myelin cover around her collection of nerve fibres. This chic covering enables her to scoot information more quickly and efficiently throughout our bodies.

Dr. Porges saw that premature babies (born before thirty weeks) are not born with enough of a functioning VeeVee. Of course, a preemie baby's heart rates, digestion, and connections with people could be at risk. The older DeeDee path could slow down the heart rate so super low that it could harm Little Doodle. VeeVee aids a baby by moderating her heart rate, which if left to its own devices, would beat much faster or way too slow.

With two parts of one vagus nerve, Dr. Porges solved the vagal paradox. Porges found that VeeVee manages the brake for the nervous system. Lynda found herself twirling in her chair with wild abandon, clapping her hands together, when she finally realized, "VeeVee uses a brake and frees up Little Doodle's energy to party."

Like a well-intentioned umpire, VeeVee calls *safe*. The nervous system rests and lets the Body, Emotion, Mind, and Connection energies do their growing, healing thing. Little Doodle's system will be at rest when she is around safe people. She can learn, grow, play, and take care of her own energy, staying connected without mixing her energy with those around her.

When VeeVee senses things are safe for Little Doodle, she uses her brake to help her buddy heart beat just right—not too fast or too slow. VeeVee stops Little Doodle's protections long enough for her to venture near others and hang out with safe people. Little Doodle receives the precious gifts of time and fellowship.

Yowser. Safe connection is a "biological imperative" (Porges 2017, 7).

We smiled.
We laughed.
We jumped.
We danced.

Then serious contemplation trickled into our jubilant celebration as we realized Little Doodle's automatic nervous system may be at safe, but does she know what a safe person even looks like? In addition to having to be fed, changed, picked up, held, attended to, and never left alone, Little Doodle needs to find safe connection to both keep her safe and to help her own energies work smoothly. To do this, Little

Doodle must identify who is safe and who is not. She must let others know that she is a safe bet too. How hard can it be?

Gulp.

We shook our heads. Feeling parched, Leslie reached for a glass of water and wondered out loud, "How can she recognize a safe human being? She has only experienced another person from the inside out. While she sucked her thumb, all cuddled up in her prior womb room, Little Doodle had her eyes closed. Even if she had opened her eyes, all she could see was a glorious mass of muscle, fibre, and organs."

While in the womb, Little Doodle sensed mom and the environment's impact on her. Her skin touched mom and felt bumps and movements, both comforting and disquieting. She had stirrings of what sounds were comforting and what sounds were scary.

But what happened when she left the womb? Could she recognize a person's face? Nope. Not on her ever-loving life. Literally.

Dr. Porges figured out that where VeeVee travelled must be the key. He saw that VeeVee winds north and upward from the heart and lungs to the face, trailing round the throat, almost dancing underneath cheeks, eyes, ears, and throat. He could now see the path that this explorer nerve followed. Like a Peary discovering the Arctic Pole, a Cabot sailing first to the Northwest passage, VeeVee's northward navigation from heart to face bespoke her heroism. He calls this the "face-heart path" (Porges, 2018, 57).

A person coos, speaks softly and with a light rhythm, looks kindly into Little Doodle's eyes. Little Doodle's own VeeVee begins to stir. She coos softly and with a light rhythm, looks kindly into bigger doodle's eyes. Little Doodle's VeeVee comes alive by the love-filled adult's VeeVee. The face-heart path in one person wordlessly talks to the face-heart-path in Little Doodle. Little Doodle's VeeVee feels good and talks wordlessly back. She likes it! She wants to do this connecting thing more. She begins at a tender age to open her purse. Little Doodle's own VeeVee pathway is coming to life's party.

Little Doodle has this face-heart path within her own skin and has not yet been able to fully experience its power. This path beneath her face comes alive as she meets people in the world outside of her original safe home. This could be just what a Little Doodle needs. Her VeeVee could receive info from others' seeing, hearing, and voices. Her VeeVee could give out info from seeing, hearing, and using her voice.

No Thinking Involved: Social Lessons for a Little Doodle

In the womb, Little Doodle can't think much about clues with her newbie brain. Doodles are gifted with neuroception: non-thinking knowingness throughout all her tissues.

Sense-o-matic baby.

What if VeeVee targets unique aspects of people, like types of eye gazes, hearing voices, and other sounds, head tilts, and body poses? Although she would have heard voices or music while leasing the womb room, she wouldn't know about the rest. Little Doodle can use her neuroception to zero in on human stuff. And what if, at the exact same time, VeeVee acts like a dedicated umpire, vetting which of these human clues might be safe or unsafe for Little Doodle? Warm open eyes, melodic murmurs, and open-faced attentiveness could quell her sweet heart into calm repose.

Safe! cries VeeVee, enticing Little Doodle to sit tight, all is right. While angry sounding growls, high pitched noises, stark stares, or turned away heads make VeeVee shout, *Unsafe!* spurring Little Doodle's nervous system to be **On Guard**.

VeeVee will be shaped by others forever.

This tutoring and learning start when Little Doodle is a wee bit of a thing, and this continues throughout her life. Her VeeVee is never stagnant. People need safe people to teach each other how to live and excel in their own precious nervous systems. Without safe people, we might eke through life. But to shine at our loveliest, healthiest best, safe people cinch the deal. VeeVee does her best to vet safety. It's not perfect. Like any well-intentioned ump, VeeVee can **NeuroGoof**. Sometimes she senses something is safe when it is not, or something is unsafe when it actually is safe (Lindaman and Makela 2018, 231).

Safe people in our lives make us. Unsafe people can break us. VeeVee helps us sort out who is safe and who is not.

Overall, VeeVee can teach a little human how to safely hang out with her newfound pals. The doctor knew we would always need versions of what Little Doodle needed. Our nervous systems are continually shaped in relationship. That is how we roll.

VeeVee helps us sort out who is safe and who is not.

Even though this might be your first official introduction to your VeeVee, she has loved you from at least the moment you were conceived. She adores you. She works away constantly. This intimacy you already have means you can call her by her pet name, VeeVee.

If we were to blog about VeeVee, we imagine extolling her virtues like so:

 Are you a caring person who is looking to find calm in your heart, lungs, and gut?

 Do you want to share a trip with like-minded and like-hearted fellow travellers, who have your back?

 Do you want your days and nights to be filled with heart dreams, not drama queens?

 Do you want conversations where you can look at others in the eyes, listen and feel listened to?

 Do the sounds of calm, pleasant, caring voices invite you to stick around and enjoy hanging out for a while?

Then come to VeeVee, baby

Next: See VeeVee's face-heart path come alive in a familiar tale about a woman and her dog.

CHAPTER 4

That Purse 1960s Style:
A Goner for the Big Galoot

A tale about Margie from the 1960s, when women dressed up to do their daily errands.

Margie was almost ready to go out shopping. Her hat on her head, having already applied her lipstick, she stood at the door, putting on her gloves. Margie was looking forward to leaving the house and the chores for a while to do some shopping for herself, a rare treat. Margie had a deep generous heart, yet she was nobody's fool. She had a basso profundo voice and had no trouble telling others her opinion. A woman ahead of her time, she seemed firm and fixed on the exterior, but her devotion to family and those she loved spoke of her marshmallow interior.

As she righted her hat, a sigh.
Margie felt eyes on her.
Another, bigger sigh.

The big boxer dog looked longingly at her, cocking his head. She could have sworn a tear formed in his eye as his goober-y lips trembled. Ever the practical one, Margie put her gloves on with more fervour. She said, "There, there, you big old baby. I will be right back," knowing full well she would be out for several hours. A tinge of guilt and hesitation gripped Margie.

Margie was not hallucinating. Her body craved connection. When Margie was a Little Doodle, connection to another safe human being was a matter of life and death. Years later, Margie's body percolates with this incredible yearning. In less than a nanosecond, Margie was a goner for the big galoot.

Faces and Hearts Meet

Using their VeeVees' face-heart paths, each felt safe and caring toward each other. Betraying her brusque bravada, Margie's insides melted—so many marshmallows on an open flame. Judge whined in dulcet tones. He did not yip or bark or wail. It was a gentle, persistent soft bark, a sound reflective of his anticipatory grief. That gentle sound zeroed in and landed on tiny muscles in Margie's ears. The pupils in Judge's eyes enlarged. Their luminous growth both drank in and roped in Margie. As if seeing her for the last time, his eyes tried desperately to imprint the vision of Margie completely into his being, in case she never came back.

That same imploring look also drew Margie in and touched her deep in her unawares. The forlorn gaze pulled on Margie's heart strings. To knock it out of the park, Judge added an adorable head cock. His big brown head leaned to the side, and subtle though it was, leaned in a bit towards Margie.

Sound.
Eyes.
Body language.

Under Margie's hat, gloves, and going-out-shopping clothes, her body responded without thought or analysis. Margie had no awareness of her body's automatic dance with her boxer. Her neuroception infused the dog's neediness within her being.

The warm blood of Judge met the warm-bloodedness of Margie. Margie's organs and nerves attended to the clarion call of a loved one in need. In that snippet of doorway time, her hand on the front doorknob, little muscles in Margie's ears heard Judge's soft, persistent pleas. Margie's eyes embraced his large begging eyes and cocked head. She felt his leaning-in body in her own body.

Margie's body answered him back. She murmured, "There, there, old fella," in soft, kind tones. Her ear muscles stretched open to suss out the true nature of the dog's possible distress. Margie's eyes widened and drank Judge in too. Margie leaned in toward Judge. Margie attuned to her beloved dog's woe. Immediately her face and body became a beacon of love radiating to Judge.

This love between Margie and her beloved dog took a lot of nerve.

The VeeVee Connection

Right beneath Margie's and your beautiful faces, vibrant VeeVee navigates life's waters, seeking safe passage and calm energy. VeeVee's face-heart path is people-oriented, delicately intertwining itself with your throat, ears, and tiny muscles in your face. VeeVee senses others around her while simultaneously teaching you to speak, look, and send information out that you, too, are safe to be around. VeeVee speaks quickly and directly to the oxygen that fuels you as she winds into your heart and lungs, the portal organs that sustain you with blood and breath.

VeeVee is all about kindness, safety, and connection, but not because she is gooey and romantic. She relays to people that you are safe to be with, that your lovingness and caring will ensure that your loved ones have you as an ally in times of danger and times of joy. The beauty of polyvagal theory is that it shows we are designed to connect. The intent of reaching out to others is our nervous system's first attempt to survive. Surely together, people with whom we feel safe and not alone will help us each live longer.

VeeVee is the poster girl for team. Safety first. VeeVee's connection to your eyes, throat, ears, and heart show people that you are a safe bet. Using these same links to your body parts, VeeVee helps you decipher which people in life are safe connections for you. This bio-design detail ensures the longevity of humanity, the entire species.

Pretty important stuff indeed.

No wonder you connect with your peeps. You want to show them you are safe to be with, there for them through thick or thin. At the same time, you benefit yourself and your chance for survival by having safe people close to you. VeeVee's superb survival design is the nervous system's multitalented seeker of calm and safety.

Quality Not Just Quantity

VeeVee searches for those who will be good and kind to you, who will help you in times of danger and share with you in times of calm. It's not just the number of people but the type of people you are with. As any good shopper knows, quantity is great but only if it's the right quality. If the ship is going down, you need all hands on deck. You don't want a group of unsafe people feeling alone, crying out, "Everyone for themselves!"

VeeVee knows:

- Only safe people help each other when danger abounds. *I am with you. You are not alone.*

- Only safe people help you when you are not safe but must excel in this game of life. *I will teach you how to be safe.*

54

It's not always easy. Sometimes the people you thought were safe were not, and those you thought were unsafe were safe. VeeVee tries to sort out what's safe from the energy inside you and around you. She can NeuroGoof, but her intent is pure.

A bassett hound of curiosity, brave VeeVee searches for:

- Sounds that denote safety. A low growl or high pitch won't do. Pleasant lilting sounds flowing in an even frequent pattern delight.

- Sights that mean safe. Those willing to look you directly in the eye kindly—not glaring or staring—meet VeeVee's approval. VeeVee even vets the wrinkle lines around others' eyes and mouths, detecting upward motion of the skin as people smile.

- Information from your insides as they sense safety or foreboding. She consults your heart's beats, lungs' breaths, gut's tingles, or easy digests. She even detects if the tiny hairs on your neck are rising softly, or bristly On Guard.

Margie and Her VeeVee

When Margie was with Judge, she was not simply hearing Judge. If she was, her brain may simply label his whines *annoying* and leave him be. Margie was not just sensing Judge either. Margie was doing all the above and more. Margie's Body, Mind, Emotion, and Connection Energies—through her agile, curious VeeVee—were resonating with the information outside and inside of her. And then, her very same VeeVee conveyed all this juicy information to her as a felt experience. Margie did not use her logical thinking brain. She did not think or perceive. She did not think about what was best for her and the dog. She used her neuroception.

Margie was social.

She connected with Judge.

She experienced the love for a good dog, a buddy for whom she would do anything. And in return, his faithfulness to her filled her insides with glorious love. Both experienced *safety*. Margie and Judge absorbed each other within the fibres of their beings. Their eyes, ears, faces, and hearts engaged in a constant dance with each other. They felt it as a marvellous experience they both wanted to do over and over again. Dr. Porges reveals the human guidance and support system all people need: the "social engagement system, nature's gift creating connection" (Porges, 2018, 51).

Margie tuned in to her beloved dog's woeful plea. Immediately her face and body became a beacon of love radiating to Judge, *You are safe with me*. In the blink of an eye, chemistry within Margie worked with her VeeVee. Margie received a blast of *dopamine*, a feel-good neurotransmitter. We will see later that this quest for dopamine might get a tad messed up if relationships aren't always happy (Banks 2015, 58).

Whether Margie had carried a baby or not, she was built with an inside purse designed to focus on carrying someone else. As a female, she experienced higher levels of chemical and hormonal juice to seek safety for another human being, including the hormone *oxytocin*. Margie could feel cuddly and soft toward Judge. Oxytocin is a super cool connection promoter. When Margie used oxytocin, she made more of it (Taylor 2002, 21–28).

As well, compared to males, Margie's emotional brain is larger. This contributed to her intense ability to caretake, nest and bond, read emotional cues, and be more sensitive to physical touch (Amen 2007, 79).

Margie didn't feel *for* Judge.

She felt *with* him.

Margie could mirror the action of another and feel their feelings too. *Mirror neurons* created her ability to empathize, to feel another person's feelings as if they were her own. This mirroring information passes through a part of the brain called the *insula*. One of insula's gifts is to connect information to Margie's own emotions. She feels what Judge feels. This allowed Margie to encode the sense of another person, even a dog, inside of her. Judge really got inside her brain and body (Banks with Hirschman, 2015, 4–8, 208–210).

You Connect with People and Yourself

Like Margie, you let people know that you welcome them through your eyes, your kind voice, and your patient listening. You show them you are safe. When your body registers safety, your VeeVee glows with welcome and acceptance. The four energies in your body flow.

Connection brings you full-face listening. You are curious. You are available to yourself and to another in the moment. This rewarding feeling keeps you on the lookout for safe-and-loving kind of folks and shows them you are good folk too. When you reach out, you have the best chance to protect all of us from danger. Smart, huh?

VeeVee not only seeks safe others, she also calms your insides down so you can be present and make good decisions. She helps set your nervous system to a calmly energetic pace. Your body gets the memo *all is okay,* and you feel lovely. As VeeVee uses her neuroception and senses safety, she helps you feel calm and good in the presence of safe and trustworthy others. You connect.

Always in School

All VeeVees are constant teachers and students in life.

With each moment your VeeVee meets another's VeeVee, you train each other how to use your own VeeVees. When you connect in safe relationships with yourself and others, you can create and maintain a safe VeeVee state within you. When others connect in safe relationships with you, they can create and maintain a safe VeeVee state within themselves.

The result? When safe people are together, we all feel our best. Safe people help each other's insides grow, develop, and feel good. We constantly want to be in safe connection with others. It's not because we want or even like to help everybody; it's because we need to.

Say that once again. *We need to.*

Your VeeVee inspires you to always check on everybody. It's a felt experience trilling in your tissues. This ability to connect so wholly to another human being and have the responsibility of breathing and beating their hearts for them is as big as it gets. It is in our tissues.

Seriously girlfriend, think about it. It does not matter one iota if you have a child or not. You are built for this.

You feel another person as if you were that person.
At one time, we were all part of another person.
Their joy is ours.
Their pain is ours.

Your innards have all these intense possibilities for experiencing others. You were never making this intense feeling up. And when you reach out, oxytocin and dopamine in your body amp up, and you get the added bonus of feeling swell (Buczynski and Vigil–Otero 2019, 15).

When VeeVee calls *safe*, you are inspired to lean into the heart-tugging cues from those you love. Margie's and your mirror neurons reflect the actions of others within your very beings. Oxytocin flows. Dopamine production can pop like a champagne cork. Margie and you can be playful, restful, intimate, fun, frisky.

And the huge bonus? You and Margie can freely focus on caring for yourselves as you easily enjoy the people in your life. It's wonderful and breezy to connect when you are with another being who is also calmly energetic and in the moment with you.

But what if someone else is stressed, distracted, or worried? It's hard to stay calmly energetic and focused. Your VeeVee, using her neuroception, senses their upset. Your energies kink. You might even want to ease their dilemma. (After all, their behaviour is bugging you.) You can quickly put your needs to one side. You can open up your purse and let people inside. Just like that, without thinking, you can make the easy error we all do.

You go from *connect* to *carry*.

Next: That's what Margie did.

CHAPTER 5

Margie's Intentions Get All Mixed Up

Margie's whole being vibrated with the needs of an ever-lovin' dog in that doorway moment. It was fine until it wasn't. The playful lovingness took a turn. Judge had anticipatory grief. It wasn't real. Margie was not abandoning him. It was simply enough that he sensed he might be alone very soon. He didn't feel so good. His hangdog behaviour filled the doorway.

As Judge saw Margie's gloved hand remain on the front doorknob, his neuroception trilled, *This is awful. I am going to be alone!* His pleas grew horrific and repetitive.

The Cry

A whimpering whine of destitute loneliness wheezed from Judge's pores. Judge lowered his boxy carriage and laid his big head on his long front legs. Woeful brown eyes pleaded his desperate case. His cries increased in frequency. A big boxer heart, on the verge of an absolute breakdown, beat a mournful tune on Margie's broadloom. It gnawed at her insides when the woeful dog sighed and practically pulled out a violin to play his lonesome blues.

Willy-nillies invaded Margie as Judge turned his upset into an epic movie. It all happened so fast. Without thought or plan, Margie's insides shifted. As her energies kinked, her stomach knotted, her heart raced, and little sweat beads blossomed on Margie's forehead. Judge's dramatic agony ignited Margie's caring intentions. Margie's insides lit up in caring neon. All Margie knew was *I gotta stop this.*

Their two energies smooshed together. The soft barks sailed through her ear muscles, drizzling within her, drenching her heart, lungs, and hormones. The pleading eyes met her own open pupils. The image of Judge's liquid brown neediness swirled into and around Margie's open optic nerve, placing the dog squarely in her mind. As Judge's ears perked up and stood at begging attention, his face became more open and available for Margie to capture. Tiny muscles in Margie's cheeks mirrored his exposed canine cheeks. The tenderness of this irrational, illogical moment infused Margie.

Margie's connection combo—her VeeVee, her dopamine, her oxytocin, her mirror neurons—was designed to work in tandem with the thinking power of her Mind Energy. Margie had her brain to help her discern who and what were safe.

But Margie also had habits and messages within her that developed long ago, before her brain fully developed. Before she was about seven years old, much of her learning was downloaded by rote. During her younger days, Margie did not have the capacity to make reasoned and clear decisions. But, at those tender ages, she did have the neuroception and chemistry for connection whirring away in her body energies. She could respond quickly on behalf of her survival needs with the aid of this neuroception and connection chemistry—without the assistance of her yet-to-be more organized and thoughtful brain.

A lot of living happens before seven years of age. Numerous habits and messages were established during these formative years. Lots of times, Margie had put her needs aside when another seemed in need.

She was a *good girl* and could not discern how to juggle all interests, including her own, until she was older.

Only as her brain and Mind Energy developed could Margie consider different aspects of situations she encountered. With her prefrontal cortex in tow, she could then think about what had happened before in similar times, what was happening now, and what could happen if certain actions were taken. In a short pause, she could choose to engage these thoughts.

Even in a doorway moment, this choice is possible. Without practice, though, choice may not be probable. Without pausing and choosing in this doorway moment, Margie confused connecting with carrying.

The Doorway Moment

The pure simplicity of connection with Judge seemed a distant memory. His bellyaching weighed on her. The peaceful ease morphed into a task to be handled.

Gloves off, finger by finger.
Hat pin removed.
Coat off and placed in closet.

Judge successfully jumped into Margie's purse, replacing her shopping list. Margie sighed as she walked back to the kitchen and put on an apron. Judge's bum wiggled madly, ears up, prancing behind her. Even though it meant a change in her own plans, Margie saved Judge from his loneliness and popped him into her purse. Part of her was glad to care for him, and it made her happy. Part of her felt so responsible to care for him that she forgot about her own needs.

Margie donned her apron for one simple reason—she wanted to be happy. Margie wanted the happiness that radiates from caring. Margie wanted Judge to be happy.

Margie loved Judge.
Judge and his slobber.
Judge and his shedding hair.
Judge and the way her two children adored him.
Judge and the way her husband scratched him behind the ears.
Judge and the way she talked to the big, blubbering baby.

In that moment, Margie hoped putting her needs aside to attend to Judge's woe would be wonderful and would make her happy right then. Her own needs were put aside, of course. This dog needed her. Feeling safe with Judge was nice and all, but carrying Judge differed from connecting with Judge. Her focus of responsibility shifted to just helping Judge as she dropped her very being.

Margie forgot where Judge ended and she began.

Other parts of Margie had plans that depended on her going out. Even Judge would benefit if she left for a while. Dog food was on her shopping list! Without stopping to think about how both she and Judge could continue to feel safe, her nervous system was askew. She ended up feeling and acting off-kilter. Despite her caring intentions, Judge carried on, satisfied his mission was accomplished. Margie started to feel sorrowfully alone. She had to fend for herself now.

A Few Possibilities

Scenario One

Margie returns to the kitchen, a little miffed at the dog and her decision to stay to avoid his unending stare. She thinks about the kids who don't exercise the dog enough. If they did, Judge would be asleep under the dining room table, exhausted from his exercise. In a bossy tone, she barks at the dog, "You always get your way you big, old brute," and thinks of how tonight the kids are going to get a good lesson on dog walking.

She toys with the idea of an ad in the local paper: *Boxer. For sale. Now.*

So stirred up she can't decide what to do next since her day's plan had been hijacked, Margie storms out of the kitchen to clean the living room she had already cleaned two hours ago. Both Margie and Judge want to keep their distance from one another, alone and fuming.

Result: Not feeling happy.

Scenario Two

As Margie ties her apron, her nerve endings are raw, and her insides jump. Her mind races. "Judge, I am so sorry."

Margie nuzzles his neck and gives him some of the hamburger she had put out for dinner. Other thoughts creep in. She had needed to go out to pick up a couple of other things for dinner and the dry cleaning too.

A pang of guilt jolts her gut. Margie is alone with her racing, apologetic mind. She feels guilty and so, so sorry for the dog, the kids, her husband. She begins to thread together the *I'm sorry* for when everyone comes home because she is serving the smaller meatballs without the famous tomato pepper sauce.

If she pleases them enough, maybe they will see her good intentions and overlook the mini meatballs that look so lonely on the great big plates.

Result: No hint of happy.

Scenario Three

Margie's insides feel all a jingle. She cannot concentrate and she cannot sit down. She scarfs down a few cookies in the cookie jar and then grabs a butter tart. Smearing peanut butter on the butter tart, she plops down in front of the TV and mindlessly switches channels, not an easy feat because there is no remote control. It is the 1960s.

She calls Judy and gabs about nothing. Judge is licking his lips because his water bowl is empty, but Margie is so busy on her phone call. Suddenly she says, "Oh my. Judy, gotta go" because she hears water running in the sink that she left on and sees she had meant to fill up Judge's water bowl an hour ago.

Now Margie finds that magazine with the new recipe and flips through it, distracting her from the bills she had hoped to get to that day. Judge makes a big harrumph and collapses under the dining room table. He is exhausted from following Margie from room to room and for what? On the run, flitting from one thing to another, Margie did not even pet him, say hello to him, or water him.

Forget about food. Maybe he could find a butter tart crumb. Poor Judge. A lot of good all that woeful pleading at the beginning of the day did. To top it all off, Margie is running all over. He can't get her attention to let him outside. Judge does his business under the dining room table. It's up to Margie alone to pick up the sh—shared gift deposit by Judge. Egad.

Result: That discovery does not a happy Margie make.

Scenario Four

"Well Judge, if we are staying home together, let's make the most of it."

Suddenly, the boxer finds himself on the back deck getting hosed down, rubbed, and scrubbed. As he shakes off the soapy residue, Margie then starts a banana loaf. When she searches for the eggs, she realizes that the fridge is in a terrible mess and begins to clean the shelves.

After this, she sorts out the children's sock drawer —a task they never seem to do. She is satisfied that this very helpful organizational assistance will make it faster for them to get a move on in the morning. Her plan is this extra time will allow the children to walk Judge in the morning, (There are two children at home; they can alternate mornings.) and this will alleviate her afternoon problem of leaving a lonely dog. Once this helpful plan is in place—as set out by Mother yet again—all will certainly be well, and she will no longer have the guilts when she sets out to shop.

Luckily, she has a large Bristol board left over from her science project last week—er, Bobby's science project—and she sets to making out a colour-coded chart for the children's dog-walking responsibilities. She wipes her brow, tightens up her apron strings, and returns to the kitchen to finish the banana loaf.

She reviews the list of ingredients in her own mother's neat script and realizes, *Heck, I did not even need that many eggs.* She smiles to herself and proceeds to the fruit basket to peel the bananas. No bananas. Yep. That was on her shopping list, neatly prepared for her now truncated jaunt. The smile begins to flatline. She hears a funny noise, a sort of long hmm and a repetitive thunk.

Judge is trying to dry his ears off by sliding on the silk carpet. Oblivious to Margie, he slides up one side then the other side of the exquisite silk, sighing his satisfaction as he rubs his floppy, doggy ears. All alone, Margie wishes she had one more arm. Margie juggles herself silly as she reaches for the dog, the dog leash, and the carpet cleaner.

Result: Happy is down for the count.

Scenario Five

Margie is at odds and sods. Quite stymied with her change of plans, she is not sure what to do next. The happy energy she felt when she decided to stay home is a distant memory. She is revved up and frozen at the same time. Part of her knew she needed to do something. Going out had been a way of escaping the worry she felt when alone. Tied to home and her apron through Judge's imploring eyes, the worry regarding her friend Gina and her husband Bill's job and her kids' future poked unexpectedly at her.

She pulled out a crossword to focus on something clear in black and white and to shut out the afternoon. She didn't bother to top up Judge's food and water bowl. She let the housework go.

At the end of the day, the kids danced in, puzzled at the lack of singing and nice smells coming from the kitchen. "Mom! We're home!"

Margie taps her pen on her crossword and with a flat frosty tone says, "Well, I can see that. I'm not blind. Fill up the dog bowl. Play outside so you don't make a mess." Caught in her own puzzle, Margie stayed off on her own, even though that had been her last intention.

The kids shrug their shoulders at each other. Bobby kind of sighs as he drags the big bag of dog food close to the silver bowl with the big J on it. He guesses it wasn't the right time to show Mom the gold ribbon he got for the longest jump in track that day.

Result: Definitely not happy.

Scenario Six

Margie wrings her hands. She feels heartsick and overwhelmed. She couldn't leave the dog. Yet her plan for the day was ruined, and she didn't have a backup. The kids would be home in two and a half hours, and she won't be able to make that spaghetti dinner she promised them. She is all out of the canned tomatoes that topped off the dish.

And yet, if she attempted to leave again, she would have to face those big brown eyes. She could call her friend Brenda who always knew what to do, but if she does, she is admitting failure at *Life 101*. As nice as Brenda would be about supporting her, she knew Brenda must be inwardly exhausted with Margie's helpless pleas.

Margie felt spent as if the air was leaving her. Her inevitable migraine made its triumphant return. All Margie can do is take a nap. Judge, sensing that Margie's migraine dulled any hope for a companionship snooze fest, lopes away, tail down, a Boxer's equivalent to a frown.

Result: Shush already, I have a headache. Happy is too loud.

Scenario Seven

Margie just stops. She can't think—or move—or function. Unlike scenario four in which she can muster up a little sarcasm and zing it out, or in number five in which she can sigh out how miserable she feels, she just *stops.*

Totally numb and checked out, no one will be able to warm her up. Not Judge, the kids, or the husband.

She is gonesville.

Result: No happy. No unhappy. No Margie.

Yup. And this is about a dog. Not a friend, child, spouse, romantic partner. These seven scenarios do not a happy Margie make. Nor a happy Judge, nor happy kids, husband, or friends. Despite Margie's vigorous caring efforts to make Judge and, later, her family happy, the dog, the kids, and the husband all seemed aloof, distant, and edgy towards her.

Didn't Judge realize she had given up her day for him? Him, who spent the day begging for more attention or snoring under the dining room table. And later, when everyone came home, they all snipped at her or avoided Margie and her requests. *What the heck?* Did everyone, including the shedding dog, not see how hard she worked to make the whole show work?

Gosh, she suddenly felt none of them *got* her. Boy, even with all this loving family, she felt misunderstood, unseen, alone. This hurt.

Rejection pained Margie.

A brain part, the *dorsal anterior cingulate* (dACC), registered her pain of being rejected and ignored as real as if Margie had slammed a drawer on her fingers. Ack, her dACC! (Banks 2015, 40–48) In stark contrast to the dopamine reward Margie got when she stayed at home with Judge, rejection gave her a genuine ouchie.

"Okay then," she says to no one in particular, "I opened my purse for this? All I was trying to do is to show you I love you and want you to be happy."

Where was that happy she first felt when she stayed at home with Judge? The connection she wanted seemed far away. Hat and gloves on, she marched off to the corner store unbeknownst to her family to pick up a magazine.

Times may have changed in many ways.
Sweet, you have the identical caring intentions.

CHAPTER 6

Back to the Future:
I Opened My Purse for This?

Travelling back in time to 1967, we left Margie marching off to the store. A white, middle-class woman, she was aware a women's revolution was afoot. As a young girl, she heard about suffragists fighting for equal rights for women: the right to vote, the right to equal education, the rights to healthcare, and the right to fair employment. She had been through WWII. Men went to war. Women stepped up to do the things men traditionally did and still took care of the family. She learned it was possible to take on male responsibilities. She also saw what happened when men returned home, and she ended up doing what she did before the war. So now, when she read about *women's lib* in the news, she thought this was a good thing.

Margie heard rumblings about a woman named Betty Friedan. Friedan challenged patriarchy, writing about women who were dissatisfied and unfulfilled in their lives. Women thought this situation was caused by their marriage or that something was inherently wrong with them. Betty called it "the problem that had no name" (Friedan 2013, 57–78).

On top of that, women had less access to resources or power because of race, religion, income level, ability, age, gender identity, or sexuality. Since 1967, women have in many ways attempted to stand up to patriarchy and address these inequities (Gilligan and Snider 2018, 6). Our global worldview has expanded since then. Still, the favourable bias today seems more toward we who have more privilege as white, middle class or elite, cisgender, heterosexual women (Beck 2020, 9–12). Regardless of our access to resources or power, women share one thing in common: feeling responsible for all things *relationship*.

In 1990, Bepko and Krestan wrote about how we as women take on the messages of culture and society to be emotionally responsible for all in our relationship circle, look good, try to be nice, and not be selfish. We should do it all cheerfully, of course, but also feel guilty and ashamed for not being perfect.

Men were also affected by these messages of culture and society to go out there and win, be the leader, protect those they love, make great money, be the best lover, and while doing all those things, try not to be a sexist jerk.

As women and men, we were both caught in a cycle of reinforcing each other with these cultural and societal messages even if we wanted equality. As women, our focus was on the thoughts, desires, and needs of others, forgetting about our own needs, thoughts, or desires (Bepko and Krestan 1990, 5, 29–57, 166–167).

In addition to this cultural reality, we found that many religious or spiritual systems, teachings, and practices deepen these messages.

Since the 1990s are long gone, you might suppose these cultural, societal, and religious messages no longer apply. On the surface, it seems as if our experience as women has changed. Yet we are hearing similar stories of women being responsible for everyone at home and at work, including others' thoughts, feelings, and actions, and ignoring our own needs. It is a constant push-pull trying to juggle everyone's needs at home and at work and putting our own needs on the back burner. Statistics confirm women continued to do most of the caretaking and took on the bulk of responsibilities during the pandemic of 2020/2021 (Watt, May 24, 2020; Dessanti, 2020).

We assume all our time and attention must be given to others and even a moment of time for ourselves is selfish (Nagoski and Nagoski, 2019, 87). We might as well have a little Sticky Note attached to our insides that says, *Be responsible for everyone. Forget about yourself.*

Life is different today than it was for Margie. So much has changed, and yet these cultural, societal, and religious messages continue to influence us. In fact, when women try to break free from these messages, they feel judged, unsafe, and alone. It's as if these messages are time-stamped from a time before, and we end up feeling, thinking, or acting as if they are ours today. In essence, these messages are handed down over and over again through the generations. These inherited messages are part of what schools VeeVee on how to use her neuroception to sense what is safe or unsafe for us to think, feel, know, believe, and do.

Your caring intentions carry on. You keep trying to connect with those in your circle. You want to be a connected friend, parent, lover, partner, co-worker. When these connections go smoothly, they can make you smile. But you might notice that these people in your life—those you love and to whom you are dedicated—can exhibit the same extreme actions that Margie did.

Like Margie, you can quickly put your needs to one side in these situations. You are designed to watch out for those you love. You ripple with caring intentions all the time.

Day-to-Day Encounters

It still can go something like this:

You go to the nursing home after you mailed your Dad's letters, picked up his prescription, bought pajamas size medium-not-large because he is smaller than he was and he can't keep anything down other than a protein shake, which he wants you to pick up at the wholesale place not the ritzy drugstore, but for goodness sake why bother because he says, "I won't drink the darned stuff anyways," and you make arrangements to take him to the eye doctor for next Tuesday only to find out he won't go next Tuesday because that is Bingo day at the home—

And all of a sudden, you feel alone and assaulted by Dad's selfish, ungrateful, and bossy energy.

So rude! I opened my purse for—this?

Or

You have lunch with Marcy. It has not been easy to arrange because of both your schedules, and you have two cases of protein shakes in the trunk, grateful they don't need to be refrigerated while you pause for once, for lunch, in a nice restaurant, with your buddy. You are worried about Marcy. She is going through a rough time with her relationship and her job. You think this lunch will be great as you have both been running on empty. You can finally take an hour to reboot the old engine. Bliss.

You arrive first, and she soon joins you. She apologizes everywhere for her five minutes of lateness. *Responsible Marcy, just trying to please everyone, making herself less than—how very nice.* You settle in. You feel yourself breathe for the first time in a week. Marcy takes the lead in the catching up and describes her current work situation. As she continues her update, you feel aghast on your friend's behalf. Your buddy's new job expectations sound outrageous, and Marcy appears truly exhausted.

You say, "You have a lot going on, how exhausting!" (You kind of feel like apologizing, too, but you don't know why.)

And she replies, "It's okay. It's my fault anyway. I'm sorry to go on this way."

Your eyes bug out, "Your fault?"

"Well, I am old guard after all. Twenty-two years of perfect service and excellent work reviews—but, gosh, maybe they are right. I don't know the new computer program that the twenty-two-year-old installed, and I'm sorry and everything." Marcy sighs, reaching for her water. She continues, "Oh and, how are you? I'm so sorry I didn't even let you talk. Good gravy, I'm even failing friendship."

You begin to say that you don't think she has a correct perspective on her job, and she says, "I'm sorry. You are right. I should not have brought it up."

And you say, "No, that's crazy. It's your life. It's important. Of course, you tell me about that."

Marcy replies, "Oh darn, I am so sorry. You are so right. My bad! I just keep goofing up. I am SOOO sorry."

"No, no," you say, "you are not wrong."

Marcy protests, "Well of course I am. (sigh) That's why Dan left me. Oh, I'm so sorry. There I go again back to me. Now, how are you?"

You exclaim, "Wait a minute! Dan left you? Dan, who has been my friend for twenty years?"

Marcy sputters, "Oh I am so sorry, my double bad. What a shock for you. I'm sorry."

You spill your wine glass that has not been touched. Yes, you know what's next, and you wait for it.

Marcy says, "I'm sorry."

Despite all your best efforts, it seems Marcy is so caught up in pleasing you that you might as well be invisible. What a lonely lunch.

So rude! I opened my purse for—this?

Or

On the way to your board meeting, you drop off your teenager Abbey for the umpteenth time to get her braces adjusted. She is in tears because she feels so ugly, and Ryan only has eyes for her best friend Reena. You love her so much that you don't mind reassuring her that she is the most beautiful girl on the entire planet. You tell her you will look at the possibility of new shoes to detract from her mouth.

You pause, looking for a special bonding moment. You turn to her as you park the car and say, "Abbey honey, I just wanna tell you it will all be okay, and you are the most beautiful. . ."

And—she is texting away, oblivious to the sincere plea in your eyes for connection. And there it is: your angel is a far cry from her heavenly halo as she totally ignores you, attending to everyone and everything else as you try so hard to focus on her. She's just not there. You feel ignored, unseen, and alone.

So rude! I opened my purse—for this?

Or

Your sister Janice calls you. She tells you not to worry. *How nice!* you say to yourself. *Someone is looking out for me.* Although you are puzzled because you didn't even know that you were worried. Good ol' sis. Somehow, she sensed your simmering angst about your work deadline.

She repeats, "Don't worry. I handled it all. I put Dad's stuff in colour-coded file covers. I have emailed you the meanings of each colour in a file called the meaning of each colour, and I bought enough underwear to last Dad a year. I didn't buy any more than that because we must be efficient. I talked to the doctor at noon today. I didn't tell you about the phone call because you are always so distracted with your work. I didn't want to bother you. The doctor says Dad should make it to next year, but well, one never knows about these things. The doctor asked if I could speak for both of us so, of course, I said yes, but I did sign you up for the nursing home bake sale. It looks better that way you know. Don't worry, I have brownies already frozen. That will be perfect for your contribution."

You want to ask your super-gal sister about what she meant by Dad maybe not making it for a year and how she feels about that and then how you wish she would have told you about the meeting as you had questions for the doctor and golly, you are really feeling sad about Dad—

And she says, "Not to worry. I made a chart of all your anticipated questions and made the appropriate check marks as the doctor answered them. The doctor said I was a very devoted daughter, and it was just a shame she hadn't met you yet, but hopefully before the year runs out and when there are major decisions to be made, she might get a glimpse of you."

You are gobsmacked. You want to appreciate your sister and all her hard work, but you are so steaming mad at the audacity of it all. At the same time, you feel guilty for not attending the meeting—the meeting you didn't even know had been set. You want to say, *Hello Janice, I'm right here. I do have an opinion, several in fact. . .* CLICK. Did she actually just hang up?

And there you are, staring at the phone, feeling so alone.

DING. A new text:

> Hi Sis (smiley face emoticon). Check your snail mail! I sent for that handheld vacuum cleaner on TV. I noticed your house could use a little tidying up. No need to thank me. Happy to do it (smiley emoticon with jazz hands).

You are just about to blow a gasket. *Will the new handheld vacuum pick that up?* Honestly, there is such a thing as being too helpful.

So rude! I opened my purse for—this?

Or

You want to tell all these wild happenings to your work buddy Wilma. You two often meet at her place about once a month. You share wine and war stories and help each other in your respective roles at the company. She's a good egg, and you two certainly have been through some rough patches in your respective lives. Her kids are in high school, and she is wanting them to do well at school like she did, but they unfortunately are struggling academically.

You plop down on her couch, anxious to tell her all about a project you are working on that is your baby.

"Careful," she says, "I just had the sofa cleaned."

You squirm to attention and blurt, "Geez Wilma, you are not going to believe the week I have been through. You're just not going to believe it!"

Wilma puts one finger to her perfectly painted lips. *Say what?* Is Wilma actually, shushing you? You now notice the smartphone with earpiece placed perfectly in her diamond jewelled ear. You realize she's talking to someone as her manicured nails tap furiously away on her tablet.

Wilma snips, "The placement counsellor at Alex's school misplaced his transcripts, and I am sorting and cataloguing the archives." She also has a glass of white wine, yet neglects to offer you one. Wilma's eyes are focused, staring out, as she taps her perfect nails on the tablet, clear on task, oblivious to you. Icy, calculating, cool as a cuke. You smooth out your skirt, stand up, and peruse the sofa, making sure you have not left a mark on said, newly cleaned couch.

You have never felt more unclean, unwanted, and alone. The frosty chill is palpable.

So rude! I opened my purse for—this?

So

The next day, you think that maybe your honey Ed will help you fill in the rough edges etched into your being from this calamitous week. He knows all the players, and he knows and loves you. His eyes look a little glassed over too. At first you think, *like Wilma's*. But, no, somehow his eyes are more pleading and scared. Your gut churns. *No. Just when I need a safe place to land after Wilma's unforgiving couch.*

"Hi honey," you say. "Everything all right?"

"It's work," he says. *Oh boy, work, that unforgiving mistress.* He continues, "I'm beside myself. It's too much."

You genuinely feel sorry for him. You try to put your arm around him. He slumps. You ask, "Guess this is not a good time to talk to you about Janice and what she did with Dad's doctor?" You had so wanted to slump first.

"What's that, dear? Janice is so responsible. I wish I had her mojo. Maybe they would appreciate me more at the office if I did. Gosh. I just feel so helpless."

And that is exactly how he looks, defeated with the pleading eyes of a hound dog. You feel that strange pull in your gut when someone you love is so needy. There's no one else but you here, or so it seems.

Alone again with no support from your helpless honey.

So rude! I opened my purse for—this?

Or

You now leave your husband's droopy demeanour. You make some dumb excuse to escape to the TV room downstairs. Maybe there, you will slip into soap opera solace. Those characters you recorded know exactly what you need. They got you, girl. Their goofy agony and serial love affairs make your life look rosy.

And then, Georgie. Your sweet twenty-eight-year-old child Georgie is sitting on your coveted couch. You think, *This child has been there four months, or was it eight? When did this child finish school?* For a moment you forgot. Georgie has staked claim in the den. Chip bags, pizza boxes, two beer cans, and a—you don't even want to know what that is!

You instantly flick these offending items away as you approach them. Georgie is immersed in the video game; the pings, the pongs, and explosive sounds abound. Your once loving, fun, engaging little child sits listless, immune to your presence in the room. As if frozen, Georgie doesn't move except to the habitual responses to the absorbing video game.

You feel for Georgie who can't find a job. You are tempted to say, *Come on already, Georgie. Do I have to light a fire under your butt? Mama loves you and Mama needs the remote.* You flail in front of them, but they only have eyes for the TV screen. *Honestly.*

Georgie is so totally frozen, it makes you want to scream: *You don't see me, hear me, or know me!*

So rude! I opened my purse for—this?

There You Are

I love them all, but I'm not happy. I'm fed up! I wanna tune out and ignore my never-ending to-do list or curl up in a ball and hide with the dust bunnies under the bed. But maybe what I really want to do is—

Here are tempting ideas I would never do, or I'm just about to do:

- Tell Dad I'll get Janice to buy his pajamas from now on. She'll buy a six-month supply and put each one in a hermetically sealed bag. Good luck with that, Pops!

- Put my fingers in my ears and call out "La-la-la. I can't hear you," when Marcy says *I'm sorry* one more time.

- Tell Abbey I have no idea where her phone is after I set it on silent and hid it in the garage.

- Over-the-top apologize to sister Janice. Admit with dripping sarcasm my hopeless incompetence. "Thank you, thank you, thank you, Janice. I never would have thought of talking to the doctor while I was picking up Dad's protein shake, returning his pajamas for the third time, and listening to Dad call you a buttinsky and say, *Don't tell your sister.* Yes Janice, you are the queen of care. Who am I but a meagre minion with a university degree and a ginormous size heart?" *I'd like to finally put a cork in her ongoing litany of personal successes.*

- Spill red wine all over Wilma's couch.

- Give honey, Ed, a wedgie as I tell him to *man it up!*

- Look at my child Georgie and say, "Child this hurts me more than it hurts you" as I accidentally drop my purse, so heavy with everybody's junk, onto the open computer. Is that a crack you see?
  I hear, "Mom, you have finally lost it!"
  I say, "Well, what do ya know? The child can speak."

Just like Margie, you can feel totally flabbergasted. This really hurts you. You and Margie have spent your whole time thinking of others and trying to be a good responsible woman in your work and your relationships. You haven't minded offering so much of yourself as the reward is great. You and Margie have continued to share yourselves, forgetting yourself in the process.

You both meant well. Margie wanted to connect with Judge that Tuesday afternoon, even though she had different plans. You wanted to get a little boost from your family and friends. But look what happened. In all scenarios, the results were consistent. All the players felt eventually less happy (ignored, snapped at, pushed out, confused). Productivity dwindled to zip. All the relationships needed a repair.

Caring for everybody at your expense? You hope if you care for everybody, you will achieve your impossible dream: *they are happy; I am happy.* Despite best intentions, everybody that you both loved was out of sorts and frankly, miserable. Neither of you got any of your personal needs met that day including the need for everyone to be happy.

Instead, you and Margie end the day in the noxious nightmare—*ain't nobody happy*. Ridiculous!

No one notices what a kind, caring person you are. You feel more alone, unseen, and unappreciated than ever.

Alone, and cortisol-infused, Margie and you need a margarita, a nunnery, or both.

CHAPTER 7

Hasty Happy Purse Dump

Contemplating which flavour margarita or nunnery to choose, you and Margie very well might be feeling unhappy, unappreciated, and alone after such vigorous attempts at cheerleading others.

Guess what you and Margie might do or say? *Enough already! We are going the extra mile, and they all have the nerve to treat us this way? What kind of hijinks are these people getting into?*

Surrounded by these characters to whom you once devoted your heart and soul, you now crave happiness. You thought that making them happy would keep them happy, but more than half the time, they are still unhappy. You deserve redemption and justification for all your hard work. You want to grab happiness. You need a happy fix.

Just give me a hint of happy. Puhleeze.

We call it **Hasty Happy**: the quick fix for momentary gain. A well-intentioned attempt at carrying less so you can be more caring to yourself. The reactive salve for a relationship wound, the wretched recapture of yourself amidst the chaotic frenzy of stressed loved ones. Hasty Happy lights up your dopamine delight, and changing it up makes you feel better, all right, for a moment. It's a hasty hint of happiness, but you adapt to the change you made. Then, it just doesn't feel so fantastic anymore. The happy high you once felt peters out (Lembke, 2021, 47–68).

Hasty Happy

A Hasty Happy is like:

- The momentary bandage-fix to address the crying doggie, whose imploring face made all the other details in the scene fade to black

- An emotional doughnut, after two weeks of salads

- The extra glass of wine after that two-hour call with your auntie, negative Nora

- A *Well, you too!* as you flip your fingers under your chin in their direction

- The *Wasn't I right all along?* when you watch a loved one flailing as they ignore your helpful advice

We bet you know the Hasty Happy very well. As do we. What's a purse-totin', lovin'-hearted woman to do?

Reclaim her purse. That's what.

It may be hasty, but it sure is happy—at least in that grand moment when you treat yourself to *the purse dump*. You eventually haul out your purse, lift it over your head, and dump it on the floor.

You dump that sucker upside down and shake its very innards. You might accompany this dramatic flourish with *Aha!* or *Take that!* or *Argh!* or *My poor sorry purse!* or *S★★t!* You dump your purse with such ferocious flourish. In that moment, you don't care about others. You may even feel some satisfaction that you are free of their Hasty Happy.

Just like our purses, we fill up our lives with our loved ones until their caterwauling, sorry-isms, freaky frostiness, or know-it-all energy gets our ire up, and we dump them out of our life momentarily. In your Hasty Happy hullabaloo, loved ones lay ceremoniously and symbolically on the floor, joining the ranks of old mints, broken lipsticks, and balled up tissue.

Get outta my purse!

The blood flows deliciously fast through your veins. You lick your lips like a lioness after the kill. For one brief, shining second you are Queen of your world again. You look at the mountain of mayhem spread on the floor.

You breathe.
Then, laugh.
Maybe even cry.

Here is all the stuff you could not find. Magical, the hidden gems you discover. There are always hair ties, hand sanitizer, and your favourite lipstick that you mindfully put in, never to be found again until you dumped your purse. Purse dumps can be subtle, quick, and turn on a dime. You feel fine—until you don't.

The Key Story

You are lost in conversation at lunch with your bestie, unaware of time, lingering over the latte, cherishing this sacred corner of friend time in your busy life.

The cheery server asks nicely if he can settle the bill with you two as he is changing shifts. Relaxed, you both realize the hour, laughing, waving your arms animatedly. You apologize, but *not really*, for staying too long at the table and make motions to pay.

The server says, "Think nothing of it. Your laughter has made my day. It's infectious."

You are emanating those lovely, coordinated in the loop, heart energy waves. Strangers pick it up. If we could examine both you and your buddy inside, we would see the *just-right* energy flow sparkling inside of you. Your VeeVee is soothed, as you feel loved and supported.

You reach into your bag for your credit card and toss it on the bill. You two agree to split it. All is well. Phones with calendars, you two plan your next get-together. You hug each other as you depart before you warmly say eye-to-eye, "Bye for now." The sun is shining. You slowly turn your mind to your next event of the day, buoyed and joyed by your long lunch with your pal who adores you.

As you approach your car, you reach for your keys. *Ugh.* This purse is so pretty but has so many pockets. You start fishing. The keys are not there. *Well, that's ridiculous,* you say to yourself. *I drove here, didn't I?* Logic reigns. *Okay, so where the heck are they?*

You fish longer and deeper. Your breathing is becoming faster and shallower. Your hands are clammy. *Well, I know they are in here.* And now you might be adding other gems, such as: *I can't believe this. How can I be so stupid?* or *If that server hadn't been so cute, I might not have dropped my bag and jostled all its insides. His good looks caused this chaos!*

As you talk to yourself, you feel annoyed, tense, less happy, and more anxious. You fiercely dig in each and every pocket. You look in this nook and that cranny. No, no, no keys. The review of the day begins. You retrace your steps. Could you have dropped your keys on the way to the restaurant? Did you take out the keys to show your pal the pic of your dog that graces your keychain? If you did, now you are mad at your pal for asking about the dog. Then you get mad at yourself for being mad at your friend. Then you feel sorry for her that her cat is sick. Now shaking your head, you utter, "Get a grip, nimrod!" and take a deep breath. *Who can I call? Do I go back into the restaurant?*

You go back into the restaurant.

You look a little different because your lipstick is chewed off from biting your lip as you worriedly combed through your purse. Your once coiffed hair is amiss from running your frazzled fingers through it. You look like Tippi Hedren in the Hitchcock movie, *The Birds,* after she was attacked by the winged mutants in the creepy bedroom. The smiling eager hostess who greeted you earlier in the day now seems too gratingly cute.

"I'm sorry to bother you, but I think I may have left my keys here. I was over there," you point, "at that table by the window." You breathe a little easier as the hostess looks you in the eye and nods. Confidence returns as you know this action step will surely secure your keys. With renewed verve, you pat your hair more neatly into place. The eager young woman sashays over to the window table. Time feels as fast as drying nail polish. You sigh, catch yourself, and breathe.

A couple is seated at your table. Engrossed in each other, they giggle and clink their glasses with what you think is exaggerated aplomb. The hostess gently interrupts their tête-a-tête. At this juncture you think, *Gosh, I just want my keys that I am sure are sitting there, and it would be so much faster if I went over there myself.*

You rein yourself back and wait. *What?*

Happy hostess is laughing uproariously, hand on her chest, joking with the interlopers at your table.

You stare. At the three of them.
You then stare at the parking lot.
You again stare.
Well, actually you have graduated to glaring at them as if you could concoct some mind mechanics to hurry the process along.

What on earth is taking so long?

Your legs start to move before your brain engages. You find yourself at *your* table, the unwitting couple and the waitress at your mercy. You see the hostess has something in her hand. Your keys, of course.

Icily deadpan, you say, "I see you have my keys." Finally, the laughter subsides. You extend your arm with purpose, narrowly missing their wine glasses. Three deer in the headlights stare at you. Three jaws drop.

"I'm sorry, ma'am. I'm afraid there are no keys."

You eyeball the hostess' perfectly manicured hands as she gingerly pockets the business card the gentleman at your table proffered her. A harrumph oozes from your pores. Using your best schoolteacher face, you give all three a patronizing glance. With one eye roll and a *tsk tsk*, you drip with sarcasm. Your words are clipped, crisp, and precise. "Well *thank* you all . . . for nothing."

Turning dramatically on one heel, you avert your eyes from any human contact. Your diva pivot morphs into a brisk march as you make a beeline for the impotent car. You do not care. They were clowning around at *your* table impervious to *your* need for *your* keys.

You are fed up with being accommodating, kind, and patient to all. You are dumping your purse!

You keep striding to your car with purpose. You reach the car, then slump against its locked door. Stress hormones light a frenzy in your blood. You open your purse wide and scream into it. You see your keys, attached to the actual key holder featured in your purse, hanging neatly above the zippered pockets.

You look to the left. You look to the right.

You stand a little taller, smooth your skirt, look around to see if anyone is witnessing your Purse Dump display, and detach the keys. You slide behind the wheel.

You scream, "Surely, it will be different with a NEW PURSE!"

Aaah, the New Purse

It feels good to purge and start afresh. Your mish-mash brain unwinds. While picking up batteries for your partner, royal icing cookies for your daughter's soccer team, and laxatives for Mom, you spy a new purse. You covet the notion of that purse. You walk around that purse sitting enticingly on the display counter. Your old bag droops on your shoulder, worn at the shoulder strap, one handle constantly dropping off. A baby wipe escapes from the folds of your sorry satchel and almost winks at the approaching salesperson.

You quickly push your offending purse behind your back while trying to smooth down the cowlick in your hair with the other hand.

And then she arrives. The salesperson. She knows how to do it. She could have sold you a house, a swimming pool, a fridge, and a car with her delectable, seductive sentencing. "It's beautiful, isn't it?"

You nod like an annoying bobblehead doggie in your grandma's rearview window. There are no words. You want that new purse. You decide to buy that new purse. You eagerly give the salesperson your credit card. You have that momentary Hasty Happy.

You know you won't let this happen again.

The Vow

With hand on your heart, you commit to you.

I will treasure my life and take time for me.
I will consider carefully before I let anyone mess up my life with their chaos.
My new purse and my new life will stay clear.
I can love others without messing up my innards.

You feel good.
You feel cleansed.
You embrace yourself.
You meditate.
You exercise.
You even say *No.*

You utter, "I am a loving, compassionate woman. I care about those I love very much. As I take care of me and my health, I am a kinder, more patient soul." Until—

Guilt

In a moment, the bloom on the rose fades. You try to pick up the pieces of the fiasco you spun. Shame, guilt, anger, and fear ensue as you realize people got hurt after being flung from your purse.

Uh-oh. Very uh-oh. *My bad.* You feel this guilt. It hurts.

How could it not? People are upset that you are not laser-eye focused on them. The dACC in your brain pings pain. You miss the dopamine rush in that moment. You ache to connect. Who cares that dopamine is designed to attract safe people? So what if these folks are rude in their Hasty Happies? At least they are here.

You miss the familiar routine sound of purse-opening pleasure.

Re-Stuffing

Purse restuffing begins innocently.

CLICK. The new purse opens. The loading of a life purse happens gradually. You savour the open acreage in your new life purse. You smile with glee as you effortlessly locate your keys, cell phone, and lipstick. You remember with delight why a purse was invented—for the sheer purpose of holding your personal stuff.

Then you help someone dear to you. Make a little space for them. You even like sharing your life purse.

Some loved one asks if you can store something temporarily for them in your beautiful and handy purse. Walking to the restaurant, your significant other asks if they can put their keys or wallet in your purse.

You stuff extra snacks for a kid's soccer game in the place reserved for your cell phone. When the garage calls to say your car is ready to be picked up from its service call, you can hear the ring deep in the recesses of your purse but cannot find the phone.

Mom or Dad's appetite is on the down low. You pop in a protein drink.

Gosh, Sandy gave you that hard copy of a work project to edit. Fold and stuff that sucker in the side pocket. Don't forget the prescription for Fido's thyroid meds—where is your lipstick?

The Hasty Happy Purse Dump on Repeat

You open your gorgeous new purse and repeat the cycle once again. *Here, I have room for that bicycle in my bag. . .*

We become adept at loading up our purses, dumping them, and reloading them again. Little purse dumps, new vows, new purses— we restuff our lives and forget about ourselves. We cycle between dumping our purses to take care of ourselves and restuffing our purses to care for our peeps. When we take care of them, we mix with their energy so much we no longer know whose energy it is: theirs or ours.

We can do it over and over again, not realizing how we are impacting our bodies. If we do know, we don't see any way to change it given our life circumstances.

Heavy?

It ain't heavy. It's my purse.

Like so many women, we were accustomed to the heaviness of our purses. Just as we do with our real purses, women showed us how we carry both our lives and others' lives in our bodies, minds, and emotions. It seemed natural.

With our physical purses, the extra stuff we put in often affects us over time, taking a toll on our bodies. Unaware of our constant, busy movements throughout a typical day, we shift the purse from left shoulder to right shoulder. We switch the purse from our left hand to our right hand. With nary a thought, we seek momentary bodily relief as our purses begin to bulge. We get creases in our shoulder from the heaviness, but we rarely notice.

Your shoulder has gotten used to this weight you carry—this uncomfortable comfort, a lumpy and known appendage.

We Carry On

We get used to carrying the burden as if that is the way our purses always felt. We forget that once our bag was new. A new purse has a particular scent of freshness and possibility, a pretty purse with compartments for this and sections for that. Empty pockets await one person's keys, cell phone, wallet, and makeup. We carefully place our items in the correct new purse places. The purse remains light in weight. After all, it was designed for just one precious person.

You love how light it feels—sashaying on the sidewalk, swinging your purse freely, hair blowing perfectly in the breeze. You hardly notice your purse at all as it plays softly on the wind. So, when a loved one asks if you can carry one tiny, little thing for them, you say, "Sure, just pop it on in."

And you do it one hundred and eleven more times.

And then you start using the new purse like the old purse. Despite its new, make-sense features, you revert to restuffing and overstuffing and ignoring the sensible, newly streamlined features. You cram. You swear, *It ain't like my old one!* as you rummage, trying to find your keys in the innards of this new, foreign model.

You try to like the purse. It is so pretty and supposedly functional, lighter on your shoulder, so it has your chiropractor's stamp of approval. And now, exhausted, you fling that newfound freedom of a purse across the room and grab your old go-to bag. Your shoulder heaves under the familiar weight, but like an old mare on a farm path, whinnies a sigh of *Okay, I know this*, and your shoulder takes on the burden again.

You tried, but this is known. Your Hasty Happy has become a habit. Your heart finds it easier to look out for others, your head returns to worrying and making plans for other people, and your hands reach for the easiest and quickest thing to eat. You eat something high in carbs and comforting just this once. You don't go for your walk because you must visit someone in the hospital.

Your self-talk heightens to *At least I can walk, not like so-and-so who is bedridden*. Others are grateful or not. You are running around so much doing for others you deserve that nap. A new heavier burden digs a rut into your shoulder.

Hearts that beat so well when unencumbered, start to beat a little faster as we carry more. Our purses sag, and according to McCraty, our hearts jaggedly beat to this new normal.

The New Normal

Of course, that's what you carry in your purse! *Other people's stuff.*

Then you continue comfortably uncomfortable until the next personal crisis hits again—a scary blood test, an invitation to a school reunion, a crying jag. And in a Hasty Happy moment, you go out and buy another new purse. Then, you start all over again by opening your purse and gradually carrying it all.

Inevitably, their hijinks are all too much, and you need a happy—even if it's hasty—so you dump your purse. You feel guilty, so you open your purse once again and continue to carry everyone's stress. As we write this, imagine us thigh deep in our different years of new purses. We know about this because we do it. There is no judgment here.

The Purse Drop

The purse dump on repeat eventually leads to the purse drop.

This purse dumping can go on for years, but then you end up dropping your purse altogether from sheer exhaustion and overload. You are so tired the bulging bag just falls open off your lap. You don't even know how others' lives are entangled in yours. You can't carry your purse with everyone all mixed together in your purse anymore. You have nothing more in you to give. You are done.

When Leslie closed her practice for what she thought was a short sabbatical, the toll caught up with her.

As her husband observed, "You helped everyone get into a lifeboat, and once they were safe, you were left with a collapsible dinghy. You got in it, and it overturned."

Gulp. Leslie was taking on water and didn't even know it. As Leslie rested, it became very clear that she was the very audience this book is about.

We can pour energy into our people and the causes we care about:

For 365 days a year.
A grand total of 3,650 days for 10 years—doing the same thing.

Caring Women

It's more than enough to figure out our own outside and inside messages. When we are so close to other people, it can become a real information overload. It's hard and downright complicated to tell the difference between our outside and inside messages and other people's outside and inside messages. It gets really messy.

Another thing, memories of times we needed protection, including our life experiences, are glued inside us like little Sticky Notes. These Sticky Notes can skew our sense of who is safe and who is not safe to us.

Remember the purse dump is a Hasty Happy—not a sustainable one—that eventually leads to the purse drop. Everybody in the stories you read, including yourself, has marvellous caring intentions as they—and you—connect and then carry so many.

Margie just wanted Judge and her family to have a nice day. In her various attempts, she discovered that her kids, her dog, and even herself were annoying. In the modern stories, *you* simply wanted to show care at the nursing home, share a chuckle with a friend, or help your child get to the next step in their life.

Instead, quite the hijinks ensue as Dad bites your head off, Marcy's *sorries* poop you out, Abbey's texting tears your heart in two, sister Janice's superwoman caring mows over you, Wilma's frostiness chills you to your toes, husband Ed's helplessness incites your fantasies of saying *Grow a . . .* , and good ol' Georgie's lumpiness makes you want to sell the house with lumpiness included.

We hear you and Margie saying: *I am caring for everybody, inspired by VeeVee's first instinct to reach out. I am going the extra mile, and they treat me this way? My VeeVee, mirror neurons, dopamine, and oxytocin hits—as well as all the messages I receive—inspire me to bring people together, to connect and to carry, all in an effort to survive and feel good. Then, those I have cherished, chastise me, chuckle at me, and chuck me out. Really?*

Uh-hum. Yes. That can happen.

But wait. These are not nice things to do and say. If I do a Hasty Happy, do parts of me get into a Hasty Happy like Margie, Dad, Marcy, Abbey, Janice, Wilma, Ed, and Georgie did? Have I gone to the other side and joined them?

We hear your agony.

I use the same Hasty Happy they do? What kind of nincompoop am I? I judge others to the point of abandoning them. I give up or push away or run away from my loved ones?

I can't believe it!
I didn't mean to.
I couldn't help it.
It's just not me.

Racoon Alert!

You turn to your friend on the commuter train and say "You have a bit of makeup up by your nose. Looks like eyebrow pencil?"

She smudges it quickly, and it's gone. She thanks you for the heads up. Then she says to you, "Raccoon alert," as she hands you the unused half of her tissue.

The constant tears of allergy season have culminated in a black riverbed of mascara below both your eyes. You had carefully applied a full makeup for this morning's talk you are giving at the bagel breakfast. You had thought you looked swell. Were it not for a friend's intervention, your audience would have been looking for Halloween treats to accompany the smoked salmon.

The Last to Know

Women, we simply do not look at ourselves first. With our oxytocin stores, our VeeVee nerve curiosity, as well as all the messages we have ingested, we check on those around us first. It is hard to see ourselves and difficult to believe we, too, have Hasty Happy habits, especially with people we love. We are often the last to know.

If Margie and I have social VeeVees, don't other people have them too?

Well, of course, they do. Until they don't. Oh no! Just like Margie with Judge and her family and you enduring your dad, spouse, kids, family, and friends, you have a front row seat to the Hasty Happy habits of the people in your lives.

They also have a front row seat to your Hasty Happy habits. Yup. Take out the compact in your purse. If you can find it.

Who is this madcap, critical, careening, over- or under-the-top woman? In the words of Miss Piggy, "C'est moi?" Oui.

C'est what? I thought my VeeVee made me a smiley, welcome wagon type. Where is my VeeVee? Where are other people's VeeVees?

So quickly you almost miss it, VeeVee waves goodbye. When VeeVee vets that you may not be safe in any single moment, and particularly, that no one safe is near you, she toodle-loos and says *goodbye*.

Well-intentioned, VeeVee knows that her sisters, SpeeDee and DeeDee, have survival skills her social self does not. When VeeVee bids goodbye, SpeeDee directs your nervous system. Then, if SpeeDee's talents are exhausted, DeeDee takes over. SpeeDee and DeeDee can be the queens of rude. They urge you to be abrupt to save your butt. This strategy is effective. It's best to be rude if you can only count on oneself. It's even scientific. Dr. Porges coins the term for such self-preservation, "biological rudeness" (Porges 2017, 8).

Biological rudeness is efficient. Rudeness keeps you from fraternizing with the enemy. If you are alone, you don't know who to trust. When you don't entice, you can't make nice with unsafe sorts who could harm you. By judging others and making comparisons, you grab your competitive edge.

It takes a lot of time to say kind words, listen well, and offer understanding. What a time waster when danger is afoot. Being biologically rude saves you time and energy. You stare, glare, ignore, grovel, snap, shout, mumble, say nothing, or even simply up and leave.

Don't fret. Social VeeVee loves to come back to join SpeeDee and DeeDee, especially when she hears a sincere *hello*.

Next: Get to know your nervous system Purse Sisters and how they affect your life performance.

CHAPTER 8

Meet the Purse Sisters: Your Nervous System Trio

All the world's a stage, and all the men and women merely players.
—William Shakespeare

When a Queen is out and about, her security entourage is stealthily invisible, whispering orders and insights consistently, ready to redirect her movements at any time should danger appear. A Queen's duty roster requires her to be safe enough to sparkle, be warmly engaging, present and clear at all important functions. Sparkle is de rigueur. Safety sets the stage for her to Sparkle.

We are all such royalty. Your Purse Sisters seek your safety. Just like the security entourage encircles a Queen, you have a team of three Purse Sisters that remain invisible when all is copacetic and yet can jump into royal protection formation at a hint of danger.

As Shakespeare penned, we star on our own life stages. With a nod to the bard, your performance in life is orchestrated by the Purse Sisters: VeeVee (ventral vagal nerve of the parasympathetic nervous system), SpeeDee (sympathetic nervous system), and DeeDee (dorsal vagal nerve of the parasympathetic system). A grand centre stage, your nervous system is the foundation that supports you. As these nervous system sisters sing, dance, and perform, they set the tempo of your life.

These sisters are fuelled by both the energy in the room and the energy in you. As if they had microphones and ear mics, each sister picks up these energy cues. Like a stage director's voice in the ear mic of your favourite morning talk show host, the sisters feed you your lines and movements. If energy flows, it's an all-star performance. If energy kinks—in the audience or in you—your show hiccups.

Stage Settings

These sisters set your nervous system stage at:

- **Safe to Sparkle**: Your energy flows effortlessly. You connect. Your Life Purse is gloriously light, and stuff is easy to find. The three sisters perform in harmony together or VeeVee teams up with either SpeeDee or DeeDee.

Or

- **On Guard**: Your energy kinks. You are in defence mode. Your connections turf. You carry everybody's stress—yours and your peeps. Your Life Purse is tediously messy and heavy. SpeeDee and DeeDee perform solo.

Which stage setting will it be?

Everything depends on Baby Sister VeeVee.

VeeVee's Performance

Purse Sister VeeVee

VeeVee On Stage

You are Safe to Sparkle. Whee. Glee! VeeVee promotes support and harmony at the base of your existence: your nervous system. She takes the *nervous* out of nervous system. Social VeeVee, using her braking ability, never appears on your stage alone. Team player through and through, she always co-stars with both or one of her sisters. VeeVee inspires such social pizzazz. You become a team player. She helps you reach out to others for support.

When VeeVee stays on your stage, she moderates SpeeDee and DeeDee. In her quest to connect with safe people, VeeVee's talent rocks with her neuroception and face-heart path. She helps you team up with people who can connect and be there for you. VeeVee reveals your open-heartedness to others in your warm voice, expressive eyes, and listening ears. In times of stress, VeeVee helps you try to connect with people first.

VeeVee Off Stage

VeeVee waves goodbye?

VeeVee also uses her same face-heart path to neurocept if people around you are safe for you. VeeVee checks to see if people look you in the eyes, listen to you well, and speak in warm, kind ways. Alert to even the most minute change, agile hoofer VeeVee keenly senses when something is off.

A twinge, a tension, a softness—these are the Energy Kinks that grab her attention. With her lengthy agility inside of you and her face-heart path targeted to check out the kindness—or lack of—in others, she is super-equipped to seek out clues about people and from you, deciding how you should respond to events and people you encounter.

If VeeVee's neuroception senses one iota of danger, she experiences **Stage Fright**.

The Goodbye Girl

Stage Fright makes VeeVee the Goodbye Girl.

She does not pause. She acts in haste. She gasps *goodbye* and hoofs off your stage. Her sisters must then take over. When she neurocepts there are no safe compadres to help you weather the storm, girlfriend, VeeVee knows this is truly dangerous.

VeeVee has a ginormous job when it comes to looking out for you. Like a reptile, you must check in with your body sensations, but honey bun, you got way more info for VeeVee to vet. Your Emotion, Mind, Body, and Connection Energies are human doodle add-ons.

Your VeeVee must vet people and stuff that are safe. Your VeeVee has to vet people and stuff that are not safe.

It's an outside and inside job. VeeVee must look for both stuff that connects you and stuff that protects you.

VeeVee's neuroception senses enviro danger in the here and now, such as:

The props, the lights, or tipsy ladders on your physical stage.
Snakes, bears, or some other threatening animal.
Someone who might hit you.
A car veering toward you.
A hurricane on the horizon.
A robber trying to steal your purse.

VeeVee's face-heart route is adept at scouring for Hasty Happy in others, from your audience and their camera angles, other people's faces, voices, and body postures, such as:

Someone who does not look you in the eyes.
Or says nothing at all.
Or ignores, stares, glares, bares their teeth, growls, shouts, snaps, mumbles.
Or physically harms you.
Or someone goes back and forth between being lovely and being horrible to you. So confusing.
Or you cannot find anyone at all.

Or you scare VeeVee yourself.

This is a biggie because energy whisperer VeeVee vets all the juicy energies within yourself about your current responses to events and people. She also scours your ancient history and past experiences, giving herself the most up-to-date data for her safety report.

These are the worst possible things as far as social cupcake VeeVee is concerned. VeeVee is aghast. Vetted and concluded: no safety or no safe person to be found, not even you. SpeeDee and DeeDee cannot play together without VeeVee, and they certainly do not play well with people.

You are socially gonzo. You only focus on signs of threat in others' faces, postures, and voices. It's hard to think clearly or at all. You can easily misread what is really going on. These changes are felt in your insides. Your emotional energy feels downright uncomfortable. So uncomfortable, your Mind Energy jumps on board, trying to label this Emotion Energy, this feeling, so you remember it in hopes you never experience it again.

Without a good blood flow, delicious nurturing oxygen is so low that your Mind Energy creates mountains out of molehills. Mistakes in labelling feelings and thoughts become something you believe to be absolutely true. In the same way VeeVee believes your Energy Kinks, SpeeDee and DeeDee continue to believe you are scared.

Mic Drop

VeeVee drops her microphone and hoofs it to the wings. SpeeDee and DeeDee direct you to be On Guard. Oh my!

VeeVee lets her sister team members do what they do best, help you on your ownsome. SpeeDee and DeeDee engage a protection protocol for you. Various parts of you are fuelled by SpeeDee and DeeDee as these two queens of rude try desperately to protect your Sparkle. Without VeeVee's brake, SpeeDee and DeeDee are left to their raw talents and swoop in to secure your survival. Your brain blesses you with a bias to notice the negative scary possibilities in life, causing effervescent VeeVee to hoof off your stage even more often.

Your caring intention believes you are reaching out to connect, but without VeeVee, you are *sparky* not sparkly. If life's upsets are uncomfortable but not deadly, SpeeDee and her toe-tapping, high-kicking bursts of energy concoct your escape. If all her frantic antics fail, only then will reluctant, droopy Deedee take over.

SpeeDee's On Guard

Middle sister SpeeDee's **On Guard** secret sauce is a high energy solo act.

Purse Sister SpeeDee

When people think of stress, they tend to incriminate this middle sister. SpeeDee literally has your *back*. A spinal network originating in your brain stem, SpeeDee runs down your back from your neck to your waist (Rosenberg 2017, 22–26). When SpeeDee is in the driver's seat, she puts pedal to the metal.

The showboat of the Purse Sisters, this devilish showgirl's high falootin' energy inspired us to call her SpeeDee. SpeeDee's zippy energy directs your body to move fast. You are like an ambulance— siren screaming, careening through red lights, rudely disrupting traffic. You are devilishly quick, affecting you and fellow motorists.

When SpeeDee is in charge, your energies are askew. Super-fuel hormones *adrenaline* and *cortisol* flood you and dopamine plummets. You breathe much faster. Your heart goes a mile a minute. Your blood vessels narrow, blood pressure goes up, and blood pumps to muscles and away from your brain. You sweat more, feel cooler, your pupils are widened, and digestion decreases as blood is diverted from the regular mojo of life: eating, sleeping, digesting, sex, and general maintenance. Rerouted blood and energy superpowers your muscles so you can fight, flee, fawn (Walker 2013, 12), or mightily impose your power with a revved up frosty stare (Rothschild 2017, 42).

SpeeDee's Mottos

"I Like to Move it Move It" by Reel 2 Reel (1993)

Every person for themselves.

No time to be polite.

Not safe here? Move.

The cues SpeeDee puts in your ear mic are no longer the splendid lines that VeeVee fed back to you. Feeling on your *ownsome*, whom can you trust? With no one safe to converse with, SpeeDee inspires you to talk to yourself. But the lines she feeds you are old, stale, and out of tune with the present situation. She is reading your Sticky Notes back to you. With help from SpeeDee, you are quite the artiste at coming up with Sticky Notes about yourself and the people in your life. You embellish, exaggerate, pontificate, minimize, ignore, or negate all the reasons you are on your ownsome.

If you are alone, you rely on yourself, no one else.

Comparing

You *must* compare.

You make yourself more or less than other people. It must be your fault or someone else's fault. If you figure out whose fault it is, maybe you can get to the source of this alone misery. SpeeDee tries to help you by listening to you about how you are better than others, so you know your survival strengths (and their weaknesses). SpeeDee tries to help you by listening to you about how others are better than you, so you know their survival strengths (and your weaknesses).

You made Sticky Notes about all these memories, and SpeeDee reads them back to you. Then oopsie, they come out of your mouth or show up in your actions. Others cannot see all these Energy Kinks inside of you. But boy oh boy, do they see your outsides.

No one experiences your caring intentions towards them. Instead, you have desperate, though well-meaning, intentions for yourself in these goodbye moments. You intend to have somebody around somehow, even if you have to carry their burdens.

Why? You are born to connect. You don't want to be alone. It feels so awful.

But without VeeVee's brake, you can't connect in a real way. You come up with strategies so a person will at least stick around. Half-baked plans. They are lousy solutions to connect in a meaningful way, but maybe somebody will at least stay.

Five Hasty Habits

With SpeeDee's fuel, these five Hasty Happy habits try to help you not be alone.

Too Bossy

You hope: If people will listen to you and do what you say, you will be okay, and people will stay with you. You won't be alone. Instead, you go from endearing to jeering.

Remember dear old dad at the nursing home, snarling at his devoted daughter? Adrenaline bursts through your limbs and voice, *I'm right. You're wrong. Don't argue.*

You blame, cut people off, tell them what to do, yell, call people names, critique people's moves, thoughts, and feelings, or even hit. Everybody else is wrong. (You may or may not say it, but you sure do think it.) You compare. You know better than they do. Too busy being bossy, you do not see or hear anybody.

If you really are unsafe or your family and or friends are unsafe, you need this brave energy to clearly set your energy border. Yet, you are soap opera ug-lee when you tear a strip off the barista for a minor coffee infraction. You don't carry a purse. Your minions carry it for you.

Too Pleasing

You hope: If you are what people want you to be, surely they will stay with you. You won't be alone. Instead, you go from pleasant to pleading.

SpeeDee inspires you to exalt others: *You're the best and I'm a mess.*

You turn on the charm and throw yourself under the bus. SpeeDee's adrenalin and cortisol compadres supercharge your self-effacing tirade. Like Marcy at lunch who could not hear her friend's genuine concern, your Too Pleasing talk has you sorry for this and sorry for that. According to you, it is your dreary mood that caused the rain, the dollar to drop, and the cat's furballs.

You are sorry you are a bother or even exist. Too busy talking to yourself in guilty shame land, you can't hear anyone else. You spitefully blame yourself as you compare yourself to others. Simply sorry for everything, you believe that everyone's feelings, thoughts, and actions are all your responsibility.

A Too Pleasing woman is brave when she reads the room and negotiates a way to get out of a sticky situation. But that same self-sacrifice is brutal to witness when she attacks herself and apologizes ad nauseum. She can't even see the load she carries. She slings a big backpack behind her to carry everybody else's stuff.

Too Escaping

You hope: If you avoid doing anything to make anyone upset, people will want to stay with you. You won't be alone. Instead, you go from here to eternally gone.

SpeeDee boosts you to *runnnn. You can't catch me.* Like Abbey, the teenager in our prior story, you skedaddle without putting on a track suit. You'd leave the room, the subject, the country if you could. You escape by changing the subject, talking too fast, or checking your device. Maybe you joke too much (or drink too much or stay at work too much). You never hold still for a minute, let alone stay around for a meaningful conversation. You *Go Girl,* but not in a pro-active way.

A Too Escaping woman is brave as her escape artist skills are used to evacuate her gang tout de suite from the hurricane but is downright infuriating when her *it's been fun I gotta run* gig leaves her acting clueless to herself and to others. Exasperated and ignored, her peeps tire of the same old show. All she needs is a tiny waist pouch for her essentials, no one else's. Any extra items are in the car for her quick escapes.

Too Helpful

You hope: If you fix everything and become indispensable, people will stay with you. You won't be alone. Instead, you go from caring to overbearing.

You run roughshod over the very people you love. Even when you don't say it, people know *I am helping you whether you like it or not.* Always prepared to help, your peeps are Number One on your endless to-do list. Janice, the sister in our previous tale, may have meant well, but her do-gooding efforts had deleterious effects.

You take that energy surge and fix, fix, fix. You clean house, paint, and straighten out drawers and everybody else. You help the little old lady across the street even when she doesn't want to go. No one can stop you (or talk to you); you are just too darn busy. Instead of feeling helped, your loved ones feel helpless or just darn irritated.

A Too Helpful woman is brave when she knows how to save a baby trapped in a burning building, yet so annoying when she gives advice you don't want or need and says, wait for it, *I was just trying to help.* Her bag? An oversized rolling wheels suitcase.

Too Frosty

You hope: If you use your logic to figure it out and make sense of things, people will want to stay with you. You won't be alone. Instead, you go from nice to ice.

Like Wilma sipping from her glass with a glare-y stare and no offer of a glass to you, you too can be the queen bee of frost. Cool, calculating, condescending, unavailable, and sometimes sarcastically cruel, *Yes? You wanted something?* Your emotional engagement is nil. Your empathy metre is stuck at zero, and you feel sorry for no one. With slate-coloured eyes, you go about your business, ignoring and willfully dismissing others with nary a word. You know you are chilling. You. Don't. Care.

Calculating, unavailable, and even coolly cruel, a Too Frosty woman is brave to use her stealthy logic. Emotions and niceties can nix lifesaving logical action. But in everyday life, her icy stare bores into your core. Feelings are tsk-tsk ignored. Everybody gets the chills! Her purse of choice? A very smart phone in a sleek case with just enough room for a vivid lipstick. All the better to shush you with!

If using all your supercharged mojo has failed and your SpeeDee has exhausted her bag of tricks and there is still no safety, you gotta go old school. This is bad. It's so bad, you feel like you will die. With a shudder, SpeeDee reaches out in flailing desperation to stoic DeeDee, dropping the mic in DeeDee's hands.

DeeDee

Oldest sister DeeDee's On Guard secret sauce: low or no energy solo act.

Purse Sister DeeDee

Terrified, DeeDee cradles the mic. It's you and DeeDee, baby. More shy, less showy, DeeDee is expert at staying under the radar. A one note, soft shoe kind of gal, there are no disco moxies or fanfare energy for her.

DeeDee was around way before your Little Doodle was even a thought. SpeeDee, like a young pup, bounces, while DeeDee snoozes like an old dog and directs your body to be very still. We lovingly call her DeeDee because she is *death-defying*. She knows how to feign death when your life is being threatened.

DeeDee's energy dips low and slow to get you out of trouble. She sloowws the whole enchilada down, like lower than a limbo stick at a luau. DeeDee's close-to-death schtick is meant for those times you are in dire trouble. You freeze and sometimes faint. You feign death. Chemical messenger *acetylcholine* comes in to soothe you. Your tense muscles slacken; your heart rate and blood pressure take a dive. Your breathing grows slow and shallow. Super-duper endorphins help you numb out so you don't even realize how just how bad the situation really is—and so it might not hurt so much (Scaer 2007, 16–18).

DeeDee's mottos:

"Alone Again Naturally" by Gilbert O' Sullivan (1971)

Every person for themselves.

No time to be polite.

Not safe here? Do not move.

Even though she is unlike SpeeDee—an ambulance with a siren—DeeDee has just as powerful an impact if you are in her path. When Florida had a big chill, so did iguanas. Their reptile DeeDees slowed them down.

They looked dead.

They acted dead.

The iguanas were fully alive, just chill enough to reserve energy during the cold snap. Frozen in action, unable to grip the tree limbs they called home, they fell by the dozens, bonking people on their heads.

In the animal world, DeeDee helps potential prey stay still so that a predator may not find or bother them. If seen? Fussy predators often don't like dead meat. They either ignore the lucky stiffs, or if they do grab them, might spit them out. The would-be dinner morsel, frozen in time, saves enough energy for a quick escape. They might get pawed around a bit, but they shake it off and make a run for it later. Finally, if the prey is not so lucky that day, and a big brute picks him for an entree, the numbing freeze of DeeDee takes the sting out of the chomp. Gruesome, basic, and effective (Levine 1997, 96–97).

In our human world, DeeDee helps so you don't at first feel the physical impact of a trauma endured in a car accident or a fist fight. You can momentarily numb out in the face of bad news, sparing you from emotional and mental pain. DeeDee keeps you unseen and frozen from the pain of terrible situations and terrible people.

You detach from what is going on inside and around you. You may not even see faces, hear voices, or understand what is being said—no Connection Energy anywhere. You are not connecting on your insides. And on your outsides? Well, you are iguana-like, so helpless you stay very, very still.

Maybe this danger will pass, and you will be ignored by the dangers that be.

Or maybe you get
So still
You. Look. Dead.
No one will bother you then.

SpeeDee urgently calls you to act.

DeeDee instructs the opposite:

Do not do.
Do not think.
Do nothing.

Icky, we know, but you have seen how gory the old days were? Ever watch *Game of Thrones*?

You use DeeDee's help more than you realize. Although SpeeDee may be a more well-known sister, DeeDee has been a big protector for you as well. You had to protect yourself from so many things right from the get-go. As a Little Doodle, you were always learning about who was safe and who was not. Sometimes the very ways you were cared for emotionally and physically harmed you. This is terrifying and feels deadly because you couldn't choose to leave or fight to take care of yourself. Your only option was to live with it the best you knew how. Just like Diana Ross and her famous Supremes, DeeDee implores you: *Stop! In the Name of . . .* Life.

With DeeDee at the helm, all attempts to connect remain futile. DeeDee slows you right down. Others do not see all these Energy Kinks inside of you. But boy, oh boy, do they see your outsides. No one experiences your caring intention.

Just like SpeeDee, DeeDee feeds back to you your Sticky Notes and urges you to compare yourself to others.

DeeDee's Two Hasty Happy Habits

Too Helpless

You hope: If you can't do anything, then people will see how much you need them, and they will stay with you. You won't be alone. Instead, you go from cuddle to puddle.

Like the husband Ed in our story who was petrified by work, Too Helpless sucks all the air out of the room. You feel helpless, like you have no control. Everything is an unmitigated disaster and is too much. You sigh a lot and tell anyone that will listen about how you can't handle anything. Caught in your personal soap opera, your energy dips so low you cannot muster a smile, an eye glance. Loved ones feel empathy for you, but your inner drama drains them and pushes them away. No one gets near you unless they help you.

A Too Helpless woman is brave when she finds a good hiding place during a home invasion, but her constant sighing is so trying. With no sense of how to meet her own needs, she hopes someone will notice and offer to carry her old used canvas shopping bag because she just can't.

Too Iced Over

No hope. You are alone: You don't move or feel anything so people will stay away and not hurt you. You won't feel the pain when you are alone. You go from graceful to glacial.

Like Georgie, beyond helpless can dip into total frozen. Not the Frost that SpeeDee fuels. This Antarctica ice is deep. This is not SpeeDee's Hasty Happy habit of a purposeful and superficial layer of frost awaiting a sunny afternoon.

No eye contact.
No kind words.
No smiles.
Nothing.

When others are on the receiving end of this frozen ice routine, they are not seen, known, or heard by you. Nothing inspires you.

A Too Iced Over woman is brave not to feel anything when what is happening to her is life threatening, but her frozen demeanour keeps her hopelessly alone and saps the gusto right out of you. Trying to connect is useless when you get nothing back, so leave her alone. Her handbag is steely and closed. No one gets in. Things simply slide off her Teflon purse.

VeeVee's Stage Fright Persists

Thar she goes. Sparkle to On Guard, then On Guard to Sparkle, over and over again. Both these events happen on autopilot and under the radar. On Guard and Safe to Sparkle happen at the drop of a hat, all the time. It is inevitable that you will try to get people together even when your stage is set by only SpeeDee or DeeDee. Eek.

With either SpeeDee or DeeDee in charge of your stage, VeeVee must hoof it. It's not the way you caringly intend, but with either of these sisters running your Stage, *Be abrupt to save your butt* reigns supreme. You are biologically rude. You don't mean to be.

Wow, you can easily get upset with these Purse Sisters. VeeVee's hoofing on and off your stage is dizzying. SpeeDee and DeeDee's rude repartee is annoying in others and embarrassing in you.

SpeeDee and DeeDee—who just want to keep you alive—fuel your Hasty Happy habits. In a moment's notice, they divert your energies from regular growth, healing, and repair to save you, their damsel in distress. To SpeeDee and DeeDee, you are their hero, their go-to gal who must be protected at all costs.

These two sisters drip with drama because danger demands quick and out-of-the-ordinary intervention. They relish their antisocial cahoots because they know that once VeeVee has said goodbye, you are in enemy territory, the *Alone Zone*.

Your Purse Sisters truly believe you are alone.
You cannot be social.
You cannot be kind.
You must be selfish.

That is the biological reality. You will be selfish and self-centred even though it's the last thing you want. The funny thing about being on your On Guard stage? You can still believe you are being kind and caring. Because being rude doesn't fit with how you see yourself, it is harder to notice your own rude (Tavris and Aronson 2007, 18).

With only SpeeDee and DeeDee, you continue to try to connect. You can't. You carry.

Caring intentions to connect are hardwired in you, but on a stage set at On Guard, your immense desire to safely connect and protect yourself and those in your circle of care, compels you to keep opening your purse to carry other people's stress. These two gigs, Safe to Sparkle and On Guard, feel messy because both stage settings are working within you, all the time.

When you and others are on stages set to be On Guard at the same time, all VeeVees have said goodbye. Safe to Sparkle is a distant memory. Appreciation or hope for the good times to roll again? Fuggit about it. Even so, connection tugs at our hearts. You persevere to connect and then carry everyone's stress, including your own. Carrying everyone else's stress, including your own, is exhausting.

Welcome to **Care-y Stress**.

CHAPTER 9

Care-y Stress and Its Sidekick, Tricky Guilt

Caring for and loving people when your biology thinks you are unsafe creates a secret tug in your heart, mind, and gut. When you deliver caring intentions from your On Guard stage, you create the unique stress cluster, Care-y Stress. Carrying people and their stuff in your purse puts you directly in harm's way.

Valiant trooper, you are walking in mucky territory. You started your caring intention from a sparkly, hopeful place within you. Then, peoples' Hasty Happies gave you Stage Fright. Even though your VeeVee said goodbye and your stage is On Guard, your caring intentions bring Care-y Stress on, putting you right in the thick of things. In this murky mess, everyone has memories and Sticky Notes. Everyone's energies get mixed together.

Whose energy is it? You don't know. You usually don't know what their stories are. You just see they are unhappy; you want to make them happy. The Care-y Stress six show up.

The Care-y Stress Six

You see a loved one hurt. You hurt. Your VeeVee says goodbye. An emoji with hearts for eyes, all you see is that someone you love is in a sticky wicket. You empathize with their hurt; you feel it's yours. You don't just feel for them; you feel their pain within yourself.

You are with a loved one in a bad situation. You hurt. Your VeeVee says goodbye. You are exposed to the same situation they are in (a hospital, a nursing home, their heartbreak). It can bring up your Sticky Notes of situations you have faced in your life.

Your loved one does a Hasty Happy. They hurt you. Your VeeVee says goodbye. Guess whose purse they are in and who they take it out on? Yup. Now you must protect yourself from them.

You are upset because they hurt you. Your VeeVee says goodbye. You gotta protect yourself to take care of yourself. You Hasty Happy them back.

Then, you get upset with yourself at being upset with them. **Tricky Guilt** gushes throughout you, giving you Stage Fright. VeeVee says goodbye loudly. You become upset with yourself. Ouch, that hurts!

Finally, you compare yourself to your loved ones and belittle your own pain. You minimize, even ignore, that any of this hurts you. You abandon yourself. You hurt yourself.

Your purse is stress-full.

All these people you let into your heart—your purse—are either turning on you or leeching on to you. At On Guard, your VeeVee is gonzo. You feel all alone. As Care-y Stress envelops, you hear yourself exaggerate or minimize yourself and those around you. Everybody feels alone.

As if this weren't enough, Care-y Stress changes your insides. In a weird way, you are used to the adrenalin and cortisol overload. Carrying people becomes comfortable. Your heroic heart beats way too fast or way too slow. This urgent beat becomes your new baseline beat. Your brain and heart egg each other on, and VeeVee responds as if there is danger, even when there is not. Your brain wants to help. It brings together all the sensations your body creates and designs a neural pathway called conditioning. Your brain is hopeful that this combo pack of experiences can be used for you in future times. Your brain creates a path you can revisit over and over again. It's habit-forming (Graham 2013, 11–12).

Particularly when you have been on high alert, due to a crisis or an overwhelming schedule, SpeeDee's heart rhythms are constantly in a whirling Zumba mode, rarely slow dancing to a ballroom grace.

When life calms down, you notice you still rev high. Strangely, some of your parts like this abnormal crazy beat. You are so comfortable with this uncomfortable baseline that when you try to relax, be healthier, and allow your heart rate to come down to a more reasonable, copacetic baseline, you wriggle and squiggle and feel it's not right.

If your SpeeDee has tried every which way to help you, DeeDee may slow you down to endure your crazy world. Your heart beats slower. Your blood pressure is low and slow. You can get used to this listless, lethargic, slow jam too. You create a new baseline that is erratic and jumpy or slow and sleepy. You forget that you are meant to have a nice long break between heartbeats and nice long even breaths, clear thinking, enjoyable emotions.

It's just easier to seek Hasty Happy. Hasty Happy drama, so well-rehearsed, becomes your Hasty Happy habit. When you are stressed out, you need something badly. You need a reward.

A Dopamine Hit

It's harder to try something new. Your nervous system knows a quick dopamine hit could soothe and renew you, at least for a moment. It's hasty, fleeting, but effective in the short term. You Hasty Happy back at people. Ah! Sweet dopamine bathes you inside as you recognize this familiar replay.

They are Hasty Happy.
You are Hasty Happy.

You easily slide right on into the ways you have rehearsed. You are Too Bossy, Too Pleasing, Too Escaping, Too Helpful, Too Frosty, Too Helpless, or Too Iced Over. Like Judge, who ached for his familiar doggie biscuit, you reached for the reward that was tried and true.

You Carry, Not Connect

The connecting you desire turns into carrying. You carry everybody's stress, including your own, and then the chances are high that everyone, including you, will be biologically rude. When no one feels safe, nobody reveals their hearts, their vulnerabilities, their joys, or their fears. Being vulnerable feels like shame. Happiness seems like something you grab. You continue this same old carrying with nary a thought for a rich and real connection with people. Your imagined celebration party becomes a deflated balloon for one.

Most pressing, as Margie encountered all her loved ones performing their Hasty Happy habits, she did not want her precious VeeVee exposed to the hurtful behaviour flung her way. Margie wanted her VeeVee to stay tucked away in the wings, thank you very much. Leaving her own VeeVee out of the equation, she enticed the people around her to *do the work of getting their VeeVees back*. Then perhaps, she could feel safe again. The people around Margie, their stages set to be On Guard, did not like this at all. They wanted Margie to get *her VeeVee back on her stage*.

The nerve. Mmm-hmm. A standoff.

She tried in vain to get Judge and her family to get their VeeVees back on their stages. This was impossible. Margie had Care-y Stress, a malady that always leads to the **Care-y Stress Mix-Ups.**

The Care-y Stress Mix-Up

You pick the wrong VeeVee.

You and Margie make the critical error: you urge *them* to get their VeeVees back on their stages. You think you have the perfect solution: The Purse Dump. Surely if you ditch them and dump them out of your purse, they will stop their Hasty Happy hijinks. Surely such a big move by you will knock them into action. You insist they get their vamoosed VeeVees back. You think this will help both you and them. Tender-hearted and caring, you want them to get their VeeVees back so they can swirl on stages set at Safe to Sparkle. At Sparkle everyone can be their awesome best.

Nice try. Can't work. You are welcoming the wrong VeeVee. The only person in charge of their VeeVee's whereabouts is the person who owns the VeeVee. You are right about something: there are no VeeVees anywhere.

Biologically reset and wired too high or too low, you feel these kinky results. You don't think as clearly; you judge yourself and others. Full of Care-y Stress, on a stage set to be On Guard, those beautiful caring intentions of yours get all mixed up.

Mix-Ups by SpeeDee and DeeDee

If your stage is run by SpeeDee, Care-y Stress Mix-Ups are fast and to the point. You frantically declare: *Not with my VeeVee you don't.* You have had it. These people need to get their VeeVees back. Your VeeVee vets how unsafe these hooligans are. You dare not expose yourself and your sweet VeeVee to this unsafe lot.

Your exasperated caring intention knows *I care for you; I see trouble ahead*, but with a glare, you bellow, "Smarten up, act your age, shut up, and listen to me. Just do it." In other words, get your VeeVee back here pronto.

Ugh, *Too Bossy*.

Or

Your sincere caring intention knows you have an idea that might help, but with a pleading look you quiver, "Well if you think that's okay. You know better. I would hate to upset the apple cart. Whatever you want, we will do." In other words, if I please you, maybe your VeeVee will return.

Sufferingly, *Too Pleasing*.

Or

Your super-fuelled caring intention knows you have many ways to help them avoid a problem. But you say, "Forget about the big stuff. Let's just enjoy life." In other words, what's the use? Their VeeVee is never going to show up, so I will forget trying to use mine.

Madcaply, *Too Escaping*.

Or

Your efficient, caring intention knows it hurts to see someone not be able to do something you can do easily, but instead you shake your head and utter, "Tsk, tsk, tsk, I know what's best. Here, let me do that," as you take over with what you think is aplomb. In other words, I will help you with your VeeVee so you will always need me.

Gaggingly, *Too Helpful*.

Or

Your precise caring intention is to review the facts in a practical way to get through the trouble, but with a sip of your iced cappuccino, and an up-and-down stare, you drop, "Is that what you are wearing? That will hardly do." In other words, your VeeVee is out of whack, not mine. Get it back on your stage.

Brr, *Too Frosty*.

Or

If your SpeeDee has tried all the high Hasty Happy energy she can muster, or if the situation and your Sticky Notes advise this is deadly serious, your stage is managed by DeeDee.

You are exhausted. Your VeeVee is tuckered out. I need your VeeVees back on your stages. Your worried caring intention knows life can be difficult sometimes. You wish you had more ideas right now. You slump into a puddle and sigh, "Help! Can you do it?" In other words, give me your VeeVee.

Swooningly, *Too Helpless*.

Or

Your overwhelmed caring intention knows how bad the pain of this situation is and there is nothing that will change it. But if you could say anything you would say, "Just. Leave. Me. Alone. No. Can. Do." In other words, "Do not show me your VeeVee."

Chillingly, *Too Iced Over*.

Sheesh. It's a Hasty Happy hoopla. No one wins even though your good intentions are so caring. Wha' Happened? You meant so well. You eventually feel terrible about your behaviour. (Unless you really are Miss Piggy who thinks remorse is overused and ho-hum boring.)

You say to nobody in particular, "We have to stop meeting like this," and then you try again. Guilt says hello. Maybe guilt is an organ in the body. Our hormones and chemistry and all the messages we receive about doing the right thing morph into our feminine systems from an early age.

Gobs of Guilt

Guilt can put Margie in a corner. Just ask Margie.

Margie loved kindergarten despite her propensity for shyness. Kindergarten was a place of structure and discipline. Kindergarten was also colour and loud voices. She so loved her teacher. Her teacher had a presence in her coordinating necklace and earrings and her coral lipstick, framing her bright smile. Teacher loved guiding tiny people.

The trouble was Margie also loved Rocco. Rocco had curly brown hair and blue green eyes. Margie was mesmerized. Despite all the distractions, Margie was a very, very good little girl. She tried to colour inside the lines, line up straight going in and out for recess, and nap at the appointed hour in class. And she never talked during class, never. Both mom and dad had said how important it was to listen to her adored teacher. Margie always put up her hand and spoke only when she was called upon.

One day, all the tiny people were abuzz. The weather spoke of running on the hill. The clouds were a canvas for little heads' big imaginations. The teacher had a chore ahead of her that day. The sun shone through the main floor windows. Five-year-olds love the play of light and refraction. They see rainbows.

The sun danced on Rocco's hair, and Margie stared at the glow. The room percolated with energy. The truth was everybody wanted to be outside. Margie's mind wandered. She had trouble concentrating on anything other than Rocco. Sitting in front of her, Rocco did not follow the rules. He leaned forward and poked Michael in front of him. Rocco had something in his hand he wanted to show Michael. A few other boys were jostling and squirming too.

Margie's thoughts kept drifting off. A small detective, she perused the scene and concluded that these boys were not being good. That made them *interesting*. She did not know that there was any other way to be other than good. *Uh-oh!* she thought. *Someone will get in trouble, whatever that is.* She had avoided trouble so successfully all her five years; maybe she would finally get to see it.

A hubbub of sound, she could barely hear the teacher. Margie wondered what it would be like to talk while the teacher spoke. Rocco seemed to have no trouble. Even Mary in her two ponytails seemed to be watching Rocco and looked like she might talk too. The room was busy. The rainbows now landed on top of Rocco's head. Margie thought, *Oh my, that is beautiful.*

The teacher, usually even toned and calm, had a curt, sharp ring to her voice, "Whoever is talking, and you know who you are, stand in the corner right now. I have had enough of this."

Margie froze.

How did Teacher know that Margie was more enthralled by Rocco's rainbow halo than the picture of the cat on the board? Margie had wanted to see trouble. She did not want to be in trouble. Margie had not said a word, but she had been thinking of talking.

Then Teacher said, "You know who you are."

It had to be Margie.

Margie's bottom lip trembled. She knew the tears would follow. She felt like all eyes were on her. She could not look up. Guilt shrouded her as if to protect her from all the looks from the sea of five-year-old faces. Biting back tears, Margie slid her little bum off her chair. She scuffled to the back of the room. Feeling the heat of the stares on her back, she dutifully found the corner. She stuck her nose right into the green wall and hoped that not seeing what was behind her would make her disappear. Her minuscule chest heaved with the sobs she tried unsuccessfully to still. Snot and tears ran together willy-nilly. How could she ever have done this? Her knees shook, and she told herself that she deserved this corner. She had thought about breaking the rules. She should be punished. She was guilty as charged.

Just as she was wondering how long this would last, she felt a touch on her right shoulder. "Margie, what are you doing in the corner? You weren't doing anything wrong. Now, go back to your seat, please."

Teacher's hand gently lingered for a moment on Margie's shoulder, as if to whisper, *there, there.* This lovely teacher sensed the little girl's unwarranted guilt. She had been a little girl once herself. Teacher patted her own hair into place and took a breath. She turned, faced the class, and in the no-nonsense voice reserved for such occasions bellowed, "Rocco, Michael!"

Her coral fingertip pointed to their respective corners at the back of the room. The little lads had not offered themselves up willingly, yet somehow justice prevailed.

Tricky Guilt

As Teacher declared, Margie was not guilty. The little munchkin had another experience entirely, a magic trick. The guilt that Margie owned was not real. It sure seemed real, but it was just a name she gave to all her body pings and pangs. Her body parts' sensations reflected the delight in her own being, and the delight when she connected with people.

Her body had parts that rewarded her for connection. Her face-heart path sought connection with the boisterous boys and the terrific teacher. Feel-good oxytocin flowed within her in as she connected with both the new friends and the lovely adult woman. Mirror neural pathways in her unawares replicated the actions of the boys and of the teacher in her insides. Her body had parts that gave her pleasure when she enjoyed time connecting with herself dreaming, thinking, creating. Feeling connected to all these people boosted her dopamine. Her insides grinned.

Her body had parts that sent out ouchies within her when people rejected her, as real as the pain on her skinned knee from her fall at recess.

Her mind parts chimed in too. She had a heap of messages from religion, family, media, and school. She had numerous messages about being a responsible woman she received from her mom's cells. She carried within her all the things she was told on TV, in the media, and in her fairy-tale princess books. Her Emotion Energy wanted to convey all this information to her.

Guilt became the word of choice when she felt this way. All these stirrings merged within her, giving her sensations that her cells and society loved to falsely label as guilt. Margie believed **Tricky Guilt**.

Margie was a good, obedient student. But even *thinking* about something that could give Margie delight made the sweet girl believe she was bad.

It might not have been guilt, but it was a trick alright. *Tricky Guilt tricks us into taking responsibility for things that are not our responsibility at all.*

Tricky Guilt tricks us into taking responsibility for things that are not our responsibility at all.

Margie adored the kids and the teacher. On this Crayola bright day, Margie sensed if she took one for the boys, they would be happy. And the teacher would be happy too! Margie wanted to play and enjoy the rainbows in the class. The kids wanted to joke around. *Margie wanted to connect with them.* Margie wanted Teacher to be proud of her and to think good things about Margie. Margie sensed Teacher wanted quiet and order. *Margie wanted to connect with her.* An absolute cluster-fest of people's wants faced Margie. Both the boys she liked and the teacher she loved seemed to want something. Their somethings were different. Margie knew one other something. Margie wanted—*Margie needed*—to stay connected to both the kids and the teacher.

The need she felt took shape within her. Kinks appeared in her small body. A gooey, tingly, prickly tummy-tugging replaced the sparkles throughout her being. Margie's VeeVee detected her teacher's abrupt change in vocal tone. Teacher frowned and narrowed her eyes. Teacher wanted someone to take responsibility.

Margie was gobsmacked that the boys she so admired seemed oblivious to Teacher's needs. Margie noticed the boys glancing at each other. She felt their angsty *uh-ohs* in her own insides. Margie had butterflies and not the good kind.

How could she make this ache in her go away?
How could she connect with both this adult woman and these kids?

Tricky Guilt knew: *Go to the corner.* Give Teacher the order she desires and take one for the boys.

Putting herself in the corner solved Margie's big dilemma.

At five years old, she shouldered responsibility; it just wasn't hers to shoulder. She would do whatever she could not to feel alone. If she had been bad or if her teacher thought she was bad, she needed to do something to repair the break in the connection that had occurred with her beloved teacher. The boys would surely thank her for her ruse on their behalf. Tricky Guilt propelled her into action. She bit her lip, took a deep breath, stood tall, and Margie took—

The Tricky Guilt Trip

On her SpeeDee fueled legs, Margie marched to the back of the room. Margie thrust herself into the corner. It's a Tricky Guilt trip she took. And you take that same trip, right back to carrying everybody in your purse. You believe at some cellular level that taking emotional responsibility will bring you connection. Your needs and others' needs clash within you. You take the fall and choose connection with people.

The trickiness doesn't stop there. The results of your self-sacrifice are often not what you want. Look at Margie. Margie did not get the connections she craved. The boys thought she was plain silly to hurl herself in the corner. The teacher, though kind, still told Margie she had done the wrong thing. Margie's butterflies remained. She felt misunderstood. She felt alone.

The Glue of Tricky Guilt

At the tender age of five, Margie mistook the bodily stirrings within her as a call to be responsible, even when she was not. Sticky, gooey, and glue-y emotions and messages about being good and others' needs twisted and twizzled within her. Her needs and other people's needs collided. What delighted Margie smooshed together with what she thought would delight others.

Clever, brave little peach, Margie could barely print, but she made a note. She called this kinked energy sensation, *guilt*. She did not know it was a trick because it felt so real—so real she knew she had to glue this note to her very innards. It stuck. Margie and all caring women share this.

Tricky Guilt Sticky Note: *Their delight only. Ditch me.*

Tricky Guilt Sticky Note: Their delight only. Ditch me.

At age five, Margie already had so many sticky notes. Some she remembered. Many she did not. Some notes were downloaded before she could talk, let alone print. If the prayer book at church said turn the other cheek, she did. Stick a note. If her dad said be quiet while he read the paper she did, even though it was hard to play with her Barbies without having them talk. Make a note.

Some notes said:

> *Feel guilty for even thinking about doing something bad.*

Many notes advised her to play by rules, so she would stay connected to other people. And if she wanted to do something for herself, she had this note:

> *Do not for a moment stop thinking about other people.*

Many of the notes concluded with staunch opinions written in red crayon:

Margie, if you do this, you are guilty.
Margie, if you don't do this, you are guilty.

Margie also made notes about being selfish, even when she was not. She stuck these pseudo selfish notes smack dab on top of the Tricky Guilt ones. Like a stack of syrupy pancakes, the pile of notes grew higher and stickier. As Margie grew older, she made more and more Sticky Notes.

As Margie feverishly made notes, here's how tricky and sticky the pile got:

- I am pulled between people all the time.
- I feel guilty because I cannot meet everybody's needs.
- I can't have my own needs. That would be selfish.
- I feel guilty because, for a moment, I thought of having a need of my own. That would be selfish.
- I feel guilty because not only did I recognize my need, I tried to take care of it. That's selfish.

And, to top it all off, Margie got older, read self-help books, and made this note:

- I know it is important to meet my own needs too. Meeting my own needs could help me love others without burning out.
- Burnout would not help me or them. I feel guilty when I forget about me. Sheesh.

Creating Sticky Notes

What does any enterprising smart woman do to remember something important? Make a note and stick it in her purse. Brilliant.

Margie started making notes and sticking them in her life purse right away. A Sticky Note about an Energy Kink could jog her memory. Though it's only an opinion, she believed it to be true. If an Energy Kink happened to her, she could look at one of these old Sticky Notes to come up with a plan. Her VeeVee could read her Sticky Note and say, *Oh, I've been at this rodeo before,* and act even quicker to say a goodbye.

Then Margie's SpeeDee or DeeDee could help her out. A rough plan perhaps, but still, a plan.

After all, you put a tissue in your real purse *just in case.* You plop a Sticky Note down inside of you just in case it could happen again. But as tissues accumulate, so does your litany of Sticky Notes. As Margie had encounters with people, she made notes and stuck them in her purse. She carried people with their stress, and she carried the notes.

Margie, frustrated, dumped her purse many a time. Margie, like you and all caring women, continued to feel Tricky Guilt and pseudo selfish as her life unfurled. Naturally, she did what she did best. If she had only known that her Tricky Guilt and all her other Sticky Notes were simply a gorgeous alert to know who she was and what her needs were! Instead, Margie pulled up her big girl panties and opened her life purse, again, without noticing what got her in such a dither in the first place.

Margie and you stuff your purses with all your Sticky Notes. You toss them in your purse to join all the Care-y Stress stuff people hand to you from their On Guard stages. The people and the Sticky Notes that you and Margie carry are weighty and scary. Just like a Hasty Happy doughnut or extra glass of wine, this Hasty Happy purse dump may provide immediate relief, but it cannot solve the real problem.

The more you stuff the purse and dump the purse, the more guilty and alone you feel.

CHAPTER 10

Purseonal Baggage:
You Carry Yesterday's News

You have baggage, and it's purseonal. A beautiful bag can hold both people and your memories. A reptile cannot hold on to a handbag. Well, at least a shoulder bag. They seriously cannot have purseonal baggage. You, on the other hand, have been connecting or carrying people since you were knee-high to a grasshopper.

A Hasty Happy historian, you made copious notes about your various social meetups and stuck them in your purse. The situations, people, and experiences that have touched you make the baggage you carry extremely purseonal, er, personal. Reptiles don't need to hold on to memories of closeness to others. Reptiles rely only on their body's sensation of the present environment. Memories mean nada to a reptile.

Save your breath about yesterday.
Feelings? Nope.
Mind and thoughts? Miniscule at best.
Connect? Ack!

A reptile is solely solo.

A reptile cannot feel alone, but we can.

For a cold, awful moment, Margie felt so alone. She had tried so hard to connect with the teacher. She had tried so hard to connect with the kids. She tried so hard that she holed herself into the corner. When she did that, she got the very thing she was trying so desperately to avoid. She was Alone.

If she made a note of this time, perhaps she would remember never for this to happen again. Margie needed to remember her *stuck in the corner* story. She never ever wanted to be alone.

I can't be alone.

Ever since your Little Doodleness came into being (yes, even while you were renting the womb room), you had this ability to mark important moments. Whenever something important happened—especially something that could affect your survival in your precious world—you did it: you slapped a note onto your insides to mark the occasion, and it stuck.

What occasion?

The Alone Zone

The *I am all alone and I hate it* occasion. We call it the **Alone Zone**.

So awful was the possibility of being alone, you needed to recognize the ickiness of it, so you would remember not to go there again. As a baby, being alone was not just a social gaffe. Being alone was literally life or death.

Before birth you were mixed together with Mom's energy. You two were one and the same. You grew in that energy. Then, birth! For the very first time, you were separate from Mom. Your energy started to take its own form and define from hers. *Boo* and *scary* do not even cover the sensory terror that birth ripped through you.

Wonderful day, you entered the world.

Terrifying day, as all that familiar mixed-together energy you experienced in the womb room was unceremoniously terminated. That Alone Zone experience signalled your abrupt break from the familiar mixed-together energy that had fuelled you for hopefully forty weeks.

This initial Alone Zone memory must remain intense for you. You gotta remember it so you can continue to seek out others who will help you.

Today, your aware adult self does not remember the drama of your birth or clearly remember your younger years. But your Energy Kinks remember, and when they do, you enter the Alone Zone. No one is with you, or no one safe is with you. If you don't recognize someone as safe, there could be a kazillion people around, and you will still feel alone. You could be with your closest buddy, spouse, family member, or co-worker. Doesn't matter. You feel the Alone Zone.

The Alone Zone is chill, stark, and gripping in your biological core. Even among a sea of familiar faces, you gird yourself. *Every person for themselves.* Birth is a necessary process. This alone time every human feels as they say goodbye to the womb room is not about blaming moms or nature. Please, we have enough on our plate. The fact is: at birth, there is only one way to go—out.

VeeVee, always looking out for danger, knows that this exit from the womb room is as big as it gets. VeeVee, using her neuroception, sensed that your Body, Mind, Emotion, and Connection Energies kinked as you slipped into the birth canal. You had all this new movement and inner acrobatics. You felt it and were trying to make some meaning of it. The VeeVee in your mom knew that her Emotion, Mind, and Body Energies were whirring way over tempo. Both of you were preparing to do the unfathomable: break this connection-carry capsule, this energetic mixing you two co-created, and, of course, your own VeeVee had to say goodbye.

Well, that is something for VeeVee to remember.

Bye–Bye VeeVee

At birth, VeeVee bid you goodbye. Your sparkly world fell apart. You were born to be in and stay in relationship. You did not want this to ever happen to you again. Ever. Hopeful Little Doodle, of course you opened your purse to people and to your memories. You believed this purse opening practice might prevent you from entering the dreaded Alone Zone.

You carry on:

- You cannot be alone, so you *carry people* in your purse. Energies get smooshed together, but at least people are around.

- You will not repeat that lonely history, so you *carry your purseonal baggage*. You become adept at creating and stuffing Sticky Notes into your purse. You remember and store all the times you were thrust into the Alone Zone. Reading a Sticky Note from before might help your VeeVee know even sooner that this could be trouble, and, bonus, your Sticky Note might include how you got through the icky Alone Zone before. It's an old note, based on old facts, but hey, at least you got a plan.

You and Margie make Sticky Notes.

You turn little summary safety reports into Sticky Notes. An info cluster, you put together Body, Mind, Emotion, and Connection Energy Kinks and mix them together at the time you experienced an unsafe uh-oh in your life. You sum up the note with your opinion about what helped or could have helped you survive the uh-oh. It sticks inside you so you can recall it should a similar uh-oh recur.

Energy Kinks

As a Little Doodle, you had Energy Kinks before and after birth. The drive for safety spurred you to always seek connection. This drive continues today, but connecting and carrying simultaneously exposes you to danger.

You meet a person in a Hasty Happy. Stage Fright. You experience an Energy Kink. Someone in a Hasty Happy cannot attend to you. Their VeeVee has lifted her foot off the brake. They simply cannot use their face-heart path. Your face-heart path cannot connect, so your VeeVee's neuroception gasps, *Alone Zone.*

People's Hasty Happy actions—attacking you, distancing you, minimizing you, or neglecting you, even for a moment—terrorize your Purse Sisters. The dreaded lonelies of the Alone Zone reverberate within you. You need to connect. You are powerless to make it happen. You tingle with the terribles at the mere sense of the Alone Zone: not imminently dangerous, but horrific all the same. Energy Kinks make your VeeVee say goodbye.

Better make a Sticky Note: Upsetting Energy Kinks happen all through life. Especially when you are with people.

Energy Kinks happen all through life. Especially when you are with people.

Your Mind Energy

Your magnificent Mind Energy creates parts of you. You try to navigate the world through these separate characters who all reside in your one being. You experience life's excitement, chills, thrills, and spills through various parts. Part of you loves the sun. Part of you loves the rain and the rainbows that might come with it. Parts encapsulate the vastness of your Body, Mind, Emotion, and Connection Energies.

Any of your parts can come to your rescue and make Sticky Notes about kinks in these energies. Each part within you tries to help you get through the Energy Kinks. Remember the times you believed you were in the Alone Zone and had to rely on only yourself? These brave parts took each Energy Kink as stress you had to carry. Parts carry the age and stage in life when you experienced an Energy Kink (Schwartz 2021, 36–37).

Every time you enter the Alone Zone due to an Energy Kink, a part—or parts—of you captures your memory of the events as you see, hear, feel, smell, touch, or taste it. The part(s) jots down shorthand details: the physical event itself, who was or was not there at the time, the emotion you felt, and the thoughts you had.

Your part captures how your body's nervous system was On Guard at the time too. The SpeeDee fast moves or DeeDee slow grooves you experienced to help you out are included in the Sticky Note. Years later, even in a completely different situation, your parts can reexperience the SpeeDee or DeeDee way it felt a long time ago (Anderson 2021, 32).

The Sticky Notes wrap your Body, Mind, Emotion, and Connection Energy Kinks into a cluster for VeeVee's convenient recall. Your parts sum up how you conquered Stage Fright and protected yourself. Your parts jot down their conquering Stage Fright *opinion* and finally stick the note in your innards. The details of the Sticky Note and where it is stored in your body depend on your unique Energy Kink. The

Energy Kinks give you clues about the Stage Fright you and VeeVee have endured.

Energy Kinks and the Sticky Notes

Your Energy Kinks and Sticky Notes you have about them show up in each of the four energies:

Body Energy Kinks

These kinks show up physically because you are moving with Stage Fright (SpeeDee is in charge), or you are staying too still with Stage Fright (DeeDee is in charge.) Body Energy Kinks include aches and pains, the tummy tingles, the terrible tireds, and illnesses.

Mind Energy Kinks

When creative and joyful thoughts aren't flowing, it's often because parts of you are filled with negative thoughts that stick like glue in your mind. Like weeds, these negative nellies plant in your mind without any help.

Mind Energy Kinks appear as the *if onlys, what ifs, I should haves*, and *I wishes*. They are in the past or future, not in the here and now. These naysaying thoughts can overtake a part of you quickly and powerfully.

Emotion Energy Kinks

Girlfriend, your parts can get so judgy about your emotions.

I should not be mad.
I should not be sad.
I must be strong and suck it up.
I can't be happy when everybody is miserable.
I am ashamed to get help.

Judging stops your energy flow. If you keep critiquing your emotions, they can become so backed up that you don't have a clue about what you are experiencing in the here and now. You end up using old emotions from your Sticky Notes. That is just confusing for everybody.

You might even get so stuck that the info your emotions have for you is unreachable, frozen in a big ice chunk you can hardly chip away. You might go the other way, spewing out your emotions with no rhyme or reason. Who cares if someone gets hit by a flying swear word, relentless pleading and crying in situations that are not so dire, or giggling and laughing when it really isn't funny? If you judge, ignore, or exaggerate them, you don't get the goods you need.

Connection Energy Kinks

You feel disconnected and alone, cut off from yourself, nature, and Love beyond time and space. Your actions puzzle you. All your parts confuse you and can seem at odds with you. You do not enjoy solitude. Or you might take over conversations and be left gobsmacked with actions that keep you away from people or distant from yourself. Meaning and purpose elude you.

The Sticky Notes You Know and Don't Know

You experience Body, Mind, Emotion, and Connection Energy Kinks at all different ages and stages in life, even before you were born. That means you are at varying heights and mobility to view events. That means you understand some words or don't understand words. These stages mean the Sticky Note you created was locked in the time frame you were experiencing when you made it.

Sometimes you can easily remember and picture the little written Sticky Notes your parts made. But often, these Sticky Notes are stuck in your unawares. Your Sticky Notes are felt and known by you even if there are no words on them. Your nervous system Purse Sisters pick up both types of Sticky Notes.

The Purse Sisters directly connect to your heart as well as to your emotional and survival brains. Your emotional and survival brain were in full bloom before birth. You craft Sticky Notes way before your ability to speak or analyze has blossomed. Up to around the age of six or seven, with the help of delta and theta brain waves, you ingested data. You downloaded and accepted information as fact without a way to challenge it (Dispenza 2012, 185–186). Your thinking brain, which uses language and memories you more easily recall, takes a longer time to develop—usually into adulthood (Blakemore 2018, chap. 6; Graham 2013, 6).

Survival Brain: You and Reptile

As a human doodle, your survival brain is connected to VeeVee and DeeDee. DeeDee extends deep into your gut. Information is taken in through the skin to the spinal cord that acts as an antenna to the survival brain (De Beauport 1996, 207–208).

Your survival brain doesn't house emotion or thought. It can't feel or analyze. Instead, your survival brain—like the reptile's entire brain—learns by sensation, repetition, and routine. Your survival brain is the hub of *routine*, both the things you like to do and the things you don't like to do. You just do stuff like breathing without thinking. Also, many of your routine habits happen because your survival brain is doing its job (De Beauport 1996, 227–228).

The Purse Sisters directly access your survival brain. When VeeVee says goodbye, your link to your thinking brain is compromised. Instead, Hasty Happy habits happen routinely and without thought.

Now Add Emotions

Unlike the reptile, you are emotional.

VeeVee links to your emotional brain through your five senses (eyes, ears, nose, taste, touch), which include your face-heart path. Your emotional brain area houses the highest concentration of receptors that accept emotion (Pert 1997, 130–142).

Timing is everything. Your emotional brain receives inside and outside information a quarter second before your thinking brain can think about it. Your part's Sticky Notes can give you Stage Fright. If that occurs, VeeVee bids goodbye, sending you into a Hasty Happy habit immediately.

Bit Player to Scene Stealer

Crucial to VeeVee's neuroception of safety or danger are two small almond-shaped structures in your emotional brain: the *amygdala*. Without your amygdala, you would be too fearless, unable to protect yourself when real threats appear (Van Der Kolk 2014, 60). Also housed in your emotional brain is your *thalamus*, which gathers all your sensations (Graham 2013, 17).

These sensations are sent to the amygdala and the thinking brain. Most of the information is received by the thinking brain, but about 5 percent travels faster to the amygdala. If the amygdala gets spooked, it vetoes your thinking brain (Baker and Stauth 2003, 133–134). Then, you act without thinking.

Miniscule amygdala may look like a bit player in your emotional brain's survival roster. But one drop of Stage Fright exploding through your system can thrust her into a powerful grandstand performance. The amygdala alerts you to new dangers. The amygdala alerts you to past dangers.

Here is where it gets interesting. Like a barcoding system, your amygdala codes all your Sticky Notes as dangerous—whether you remember the event or not.

Grocery Store Convenience

A grocery store sells a gazillion items. It is a lengthy process to pick up each item and punch the price in as if it was a new event each time someone purchased a loaf of bread. A barcode system streamlines life for both the checkout person and the customer. The barcode is scanned. The item is matched to the store's massive inventory. Bingo. The price appears.

Imagine that your amygdala barcodes all your Sticky Notes. Many barcodes in your human store will be different than the bar codes in other people's stores because of your unique experiences, chemistry, and history.

Sticky Note Barcodes

You have an automatic chemical, electrical *oomph* that sticks when Stage Fright roars through your system. The pain you feel causes you to glue this fear-filled event to your insides. Remembering your favourite ice cream cone is lovely, but that memory won't save your life. But the pain of a hot stove burner or the heartache of not being invited to a birthday party is painted in neon within you.

Your amygdala runs your Sticky Notes through this scan, asking: Is this event *now* like an event in your Sticky Note inventory?

Tiny mighty amygdala scans all your Sticky Notes that have recorded your Energy Kinks. You probably made a kazillion Sticky Notes about your Energy Kinks since the threat of being alone goes to your survival core. Your scanner finds a prior physical danger or a kink and the Alone Zone angst you experienced before. Your amygdala matches a new event to the past one. The danger alarm is set off.

Amygdala says *Boo!* This SOS call from inside of you gives VeeVee Stage Fright. Oh gosh. You know what that means. VeeVee says goodbye. SpeeDee and DeeDee are left, and you, my dear, are

On Guard.

We all make Sticky Notes, different ones. It all depends on those purseonal Energy Kinks.

If Lynda and Leslie were to open their purses right now and dump them upside down, some of our items would be similar. A wallet, a brush, keys, breath mints.

But some would be different. Some would be different for obvious reasons. Leslie wears hair elastics, so a bunch of these would be found in her purse. Whereas Lynda more often wears her hair down, so no elastics. Other items would be inexplicably different.

Why does one woman carry a special saying written on a worn-out piece of paper while another woman carries around an old movie ticket? Emotional flavouring. Your Emotion Energy spices all your experiences.

Both our life experiences and our emotional energies differ.

Lynda's Apple Barcode

Never offer Lynda a golden delicious apple. With deep respect to apple growers everywhere, this type of apple has been barcoded in Lynda's amygdala. For most of us, apples seem to represent wholesome nutrition: *an apple a day keeps the doctor away*. Not to Lynda. Why did this Sticky Note get barcoded by Lynda's amygdala and end up in her purseonal baggage?

To know Lynda's amygdala story about golden delicious apples, we take a trip across the Atlantic. Just nine years old, Lynda travelled with her family across the Atlantic Ocean in that most unfriendly seafaring month—December. On sail from Southampton, England, to Halifax, Nova Scotia, the sea took a vicious turn midway in the journey. The waves bounced wildly. The crew scrambled to chain down the furniture. The ocean rocked the ship without mercy.

Lynda felt the swirl in her little body with each crest of the wave through the tiny porthole. As the sea rolled, Lynda rolled. She held on for dear life in her top bunk. And there they were, lovingly placed by her bedside by the steward, a gigantic bowl of golden delicious apples. With each heaving of the ship, all Lynda could see, all Lynda could smell, were these yellow sickly sweet-smelling apples. She was so nauseous.

As her body felt more wretched, she wanted her mother. She felt so alone. The scent of the apples and the connection kink of wanting her mother were paired:

Golden delicious apples = Being alone

Her nine-year-old parts put an item in her purseonal baggage.

The barcoding of Sticky Notes acts immediately. If a scan is made and you do not check out your Sticky Note, you can re-enact how you acted way back when—to an old event you may not remember. The amygdala assumes that this event is exactly the same as the past. Your amygdala never wears a watch. With no sense of time, your amygdala believes this old event is happening right now, unless you intervene.

Imagine you are at the grocery store and the wrong barcode is printed on the bread wrapper. The cashier scans your bread, and it comes up lima beans. You tell the cashier, "It's bread, not lima beans." But, unless the cashier intervenes, those dang lima beans will be on your bill.

This scanning is awesome and a necessary system for avoiding actual scary events. It's good to remember that a stove burner is hot without needing to touch it every time you cook. These Sticky Note matches to your past experiences happen fast. VeeVee hears the amygdala's clarion call and tries to connect with people who can help you. If VeeVee cannot find a person who can help you, or goodness, finds a person who could hurt you, your first line of defence is turfed. VeeVee must vamoose. Hasty Happy ensues.

But barcoding your Sticky Note is a broad system. Mistakes in matches are inevitable. You NeuroGoof. It's quick. The speed with which the amygdala receives info from all aspects of a Sticky Note, such as smell, touch, and taste, means amygdala acts in haste. The warm caress of the sun on your skin or the familiar scent of hot asphalt might be enough for you to remember.

So, when Leslie offered Lynda the yellow apple—Sticky Note barcode match. Everyone sees an apple; Lynda feels *alone*.

If Lynda didn't recall this event or make the connection between this memory and golden delicious apples, how might this purseonal baggage play out in Lynda's present-day life?

Suppose Lynda is visiting Leslie. Leslie is excited to share the golden delicious apples she just purchased at the farmer's market. Lynda, seeing the apples, turns green. Quicker than you can say *Johnny Appleseed*, Lynda's amygdala barcoded a Golden Delicious Sticky Note. Her VeeVee vamoosed.

Lynda's SpeeDee energy, with her Too Bossy habit says, "Why on earth would you choose those kinds of apples?"

Leslie feels a knot in her stomach. Leslie's VeeVee vamooses. Leslie sheepishly blames herself and says from her Too Pleasing habit, "I'm sorry. I don't know." Leslie has a Sticky Note barcode around accusations.

Both are On Guard.

Instead, what if Lynda had wonder and compassion for that part of her that was alone in the stateroom? Lynda is visiting Leslie. Leslie is excited to share the golden delicious apples she just purchased at the farmer's market. Lynda could see the apples and instantly feel nauseated. At the same time, she could notice her body reaction and pay attention to how this could be connected to her apple story. At the same time, Lynda is aware that Leslie is excited about what she has bought and had a loving intention of sharing.

In that moment, Lynda experiences Stage Fright, but, as we will talk about later, she can choose to return to Sparkle.

Your Sticky Note-Taking Career

A smart woman always has an opinion. Early Sticky Notes are based on the way you experienced something as a baby or very young self. It's so climactic you mark it in your cells. These notes are important since they were recorded at the time of an Energy Kink, but they are often distorted and unreliable if used now. A Sticky Note can be like your favourite high school sweater: once cherished, yet if you try it on now, toe-curling.

An Energy Kink Story
as penned by Little Doodle

You are having a fun day, cooing and laughing with your parents or caregivers. Charley the family pup is playing too. The adults look you in the eye, speak in harmonic tones, fascinated by your every goo-goo and ga-ga. Everyone is chuckling. Charley's tail is wagging. All the VeeVees in the room are having a grand old time. You feel deep love throughout your Little Doodle self. Love tickles through you from head to toe.

Then, a crash!

They no longer look at you. Their voices are high-pitched and agonized. Their eyes dart over to Charley. Too tiny to move without help, lying on your back, your view of the room is limited. Your little VeeVee's neuroception senses Alone Zone.

Where are they? It had been so grand.

Stage Fright oozes through you and VeeVee hoofs it. Clever you, you use what resources you can. You raise your little arms to seek out bigger arms. Your eyes grow larger trying to take in more of the room so you can lock a gaze with your parents, caregivers, or maybe even Charley.

No go. Your insides tell you, *No one is here. I am alone.* Stage Fright rushes and floods your insides. You cry. Loudly.

Charley was a very good pup. He was just so excited, so gosh darn happy he backed into the table behind him throwing the table lamp afar. You were lying on the couch as everybody fawned over you.

Crash, bang—broken china chaos.

You were so tiny you could not see the table, the lamp, the surprised Charley. You only had baby bytes of info. You could not see the whole event. From your vantage point, the only reality you could mark for posterity was that they were all gone. You were never truly alone, but what other sense could you have made of it?

How might this story unfold? Depends.

The All-Was-Well Ending

And then something wondrous happens. One of your parents or caregivers picks you up right away. They whisper to you in soft muted tones, "There, there. All is well. Ooh that was scary, huh? Charley was so happy to be with you that his tail went wiggly waggly and hit the lamp."

They smile and coo at you. The delight in their voices and eyes makes your eyes dance. You wiggle your arms up and down with glee. Charley licks all of you. Your VeeVees all meet. A cluster of calm and happy people, doggie, and the broken lamp swirl into one glorious memory.

You love dogs to this day.

Your possible opinions:

> *If it's scary, I might cry.*
> *I ask for help. Someone will come.*
> *I love dogs!*

During this puppy palooza, people responded immediately to your cries.

They sparkled. No Hasty Happy. You had a moment of the Alone Zone. Quick and loving responses repaired your lonely heart quicker than you could say *woof*. Later in life, you meet a dog. You don't know why, but a familiar warmth licks your insides. You smile and run up to the friendly fella.

What if the same crash happened the same way, but people acted differently?

Different Endings

People no longer look at you! Their voices are high-pitched and agonized. Their eyes dart over to Charley. From your vantage point, they are all gone. No one is attending to you. Where are they? It had been so grand!

No Sparkle. Stage Fright oozes through you. Your Purse Sisters are On Guard.

One possibility

They pick you up right away, but no one is smiling or talking in soothing voices. They say anxiously, "That's a terrible thing that happened to you. You are fragile. You can't be around dogs anymore. That's a bad, bad dog. I'll make sure you won't ever have to deal with that again."

Your possible opinion:

> *I will be rescued; I don't have to help myself.*

Or

No one comes for the longest time. You cry louder. Your face is red. Your arms are pumping. Finally, somebody comes to you. They think you are too over the top. (You are a baby, for crying out loud. That's what a baby does—cries out loud.) Anyhoo, they minimize how scared you are. They don't look at you directly, and they swoop you up and laugh, and say "That's just Charley."

That's confusing. All that ado with no explanation and no attention to your scaredy feelings! You don't feel better or soothed.

Your possible opinions:

> *Nothing to be scared about. I have no fear, even if it's dangerous.*
> *I won't have any feelings.*
> *I will tell a joke and laugh it off!*
> *No one cares about me.*
> *I must work really, really, hard at being seen.*

Possibilities are endless when you are minimized.

Or

Someone bellows at you, "Stop crying! It's just the dog."

Or worse, they give you a slap because you cried. Their eyes are narrow and intense. Their body is constricted. You see the hand coming at you. You cannot run as you are a baby, but your little arms and legs churn in the air. So fast. SpeeDee tries to help you, but she leaves and DeeDee helps you freeze so you won't feel the sting.

Your possible opinions:

> *I hate dogs. I get hurt when they are around.*
> *Don't cry; bad things happen if you do.*
> *If I feel scared, I am bad.*
> *No one should be scared.*
> *To be safe, I can never be scared.*

There are so many possibilities when abuse answers your innocent plea.

Or

No one comes at all. They attend to the broken glass, the dog, but not you. DeeDee must take over.

Your possible opinions:

> *What's the point of crying?*
> *All on my own. I'm not going to tell anyone what's going on for me.*
> *People let me down when I need them.*
> *This is too much work to ask for help. I just won't ask in future.*
> *No one wants me. I'm worthless.*

Later in life you meet a dog—

You draw back a bit and shudder even though it's a tiny dog with a pink bow, wagging its tail, wearing a goofy smile, eager to play nice with you. You don't know why this sudden dread drenches your insides. Or you feel nothing at all when other people seem happy to see the dog.

Not Just Kids' Stuff

Leslie once had the honour of coaching real *Your Honours*. She desperately wanted this connection to the legal elite to be a game changer. Invited to provide mediation training to provincial court judges, she was excited and humbled to present to such an esteemed entourage.

It was the 1990s. Flowing midi dresses were in style. As Leslie was glad-handing, she felt something happening around her midsection and upper thigh area. Engaged in repartee with a judge, some inner judge of her own cried, *Leslie Ann Gillespie, your underwear is falling down!*

On the loose, the wild drawers hovered above her knee. "Would you please excuse me for a moment? It has been so lovely chatting with you. We are about to start in a few minutes, and I really should powder my nose."

Leslie shuffled to the washroom, about 360 kms away, hoping against hope that the offending panties stayed locked at knee level. Just as the dangling drawers reached mid-calf, she hurled herself into a stall and whipped those suckers off. Examining the precarious panties, she assessed the damage. Acute. No elastic, shoelace, or safety pin could help. One choice: commando.

Commando, too, is how Leslie felt. This was 9:45 a.m. Leslie discussed areas of common ground, nonconfrontational techniques, and active and empathic listening skills with one hundred judges all day until 5 p.m. wearing absolutely no underwear.

So, what is the point of sharing this humiliating ditty? Aren't you supposed to imagine the audience naked and not yourself when it comes to curing stage fright jitters? What possible kernel of educational insight can one garner from this tale of knickers malfunction?

Loose underwear happened to Leslie as an adult. We continue to make Sticky Notes throughout life, and they replay so much they get stuck even more. The exhilarating opportunity for a professional gold star was now paired with the familiar Alone that coloured this memory with embarrassment not excitement. For almost two years after that embarrassing incident, a part of Leslie always double-, triple-, and quadruple-checked the situation of her knickers—to the point of obsession, to the point of being late for meetings, to the point of pantie panic. Her amygdala was stuck on high alert when it came to her undergarments.

The Sticky Notes from childhood and adulthood pile up. Energy Kinks are not limited to one Sticky Note. You create a bunch of Sticky Notes for one event. Energy Kinks continue throughout life. You keep writing Sticky Notes. You create new Sticky Notes from parts of you that are older and have more resources to understand this event. That's a lot of Sticky Notes any way you slice it.

Try not to get worked up. Please don't make another Sticky Note.

A Note About Sticky Notes

You make Sticky Notes to help you solve problems in the future, but Sticky Notes are not always correct in the moment. You can mismatch this moment *now* to a before-time energy cluster. You NeuroGoof. These notes are created from a part of you that had the perspective of your actual age and accompanying resources you had at the time of the connection. Uh-oh.

What if you found old notes from before as you were going through stuff?

Legal case in point. For a brief (brief, get it?) time, Leslie practiced law. If Leslie looked now at a Sticky Note she made some thirty years ago, she might find this:

Tort=P.I., remember APPL for Leave

A tort is the name for personal injury. To initiate a tort claim, sometimes you need an Application for Leave. Leslie found this note, thirty years later as she cleaned out her basement.

She thought: *Tart or Pie?* What should I make from the apples this fall? It can be very confusing. It might not be helpful. It might not apply. Or you might even derive another meaning entirely.

VeeVee Gets Stage Fright from You

Your purse opening practice is well-intentioned, but there is a glitch. You collect **Yesterday's News**—real past events you might have made Sticky Notes about. You give yourself Stage Fright.

When an event occurs that affects your physical safety or there are no safe compadres to help you weather the storm, girlfriend, it is truly dangerous. If a stage light is about to crash, or an audience member is heckling and violently flicking popcorn at you, or if memories of past connections kink your normal flow, VeeVee—rivetted with Stage Fright—says goodbye.

But whether your biggest critic is *actually* in the audience, or you *imagine* they are there, Stage Fright doesn't care. VeeVee's neuroception picks up your Stage Fright, and you are On Guard even if nothing unsafe is there. VeeVee NeuroGoofs. VeeVee thinks your purseonal baggage containing Yesterday's News is happening to you in the here and now.

Stage Fright, energetically experienced in the here and now, always errs on the side of safety. Whether a danger is truly present or you have a memory of a danger from before, you can experience it the same way as an allergy (Gordon with Frandsen 1993, 239). Yet, so often, Stage Fright can also be inaccurate, and, well—not real.

Care-y Stress happens as you get close to people and their stress. They stress you out. You carry more than stress happening in the here and now. There's also stress from your past that you have stuck in your purse for eons. Sticky Notes. That old stuff you carry scares you too. You believe that old stuff is happening to you now.

Did you notice how people in both the Margie story and the modern-day tales acted over the top when their actual safety was not threatened?

There may even have been helpful sorts around—like yourself—and their VeeVees still said goodbye. When VeeVee gets Stage Fright, she says goodbye and heads to the wings, creating a Hasty Happy in us and in others. NeuroGoofs create Hasty Happies because Stage Fright sticks. VeeVee believes your opinions about imagined past or future terror as if they were happening now. Your parts want to remember in case you experience anything like it again. Sticky Notes become part of your Energy Kinks.

Now VeeVee vets that dreaded Alone Zone feeling that her social self will not, and cannot, abide.

Unless you advise VeeVee that this Sticky Note of old is not really happening again, she will faithfully go by your Sticky Note memory. Real or NeuroGoof—it doesn't matter to VeeVee. VeeVee hoofs on and off your stage with each Stage Fright cue. Stage Fright, if left unexamined, is plain old scary. *Safety first*. She errs on the side of caution. VeeVee, like an ever-ready referee, calls the play unsafe. Poof. VeeVee lets go of the brake and drops her microphone.

VeeVee trembles in the wings. VeeVee knows you need help, and she knows that she is not the one to give it.

Don't worry. VeeVee has not abandoned you. A devoted performer, she stays in the wings, furtively glancing around for both danger and safety. Could VeeVee get less Stage Fright and perform with SpeeDee and DeeDee more often?

But what if VeeVee, with her little microphone feed meant just for your listening pleasure, whispered, *All's safe to Sparkle, baby. Don't get your nervous knickers in a knot.*

At Sparkle, life can be less auto tragic. At Sparkle, you may even make magic.

CHAPTER 11

Set at Safe to Sparkle:
Your Sparkle Birthright

When VeeVee is free of Stage Fright, she dances seamlessly on your stage, joining SpeeDee with her energetic moves and DeeDee with her scintillating stillness. With VeeVee's braking subtlety, these three sisters set your stage at Safe to Sparkle.

A beautiful backup band on stage, imagine your Purse Sisters how you like:

Glitzy tapping Broadway babes
Down-home country crooners
A folksy mojo
Hard-rocking women
Motown mavens
Jazz pizazz
Classical
Hip-hop chanteuses

You can't see them as you face the audience, yet you are strong in the knowingness that they are backing you up. VeeVee's dancing prowess sets the tone in three glorious teams. When all three Purse Sisters are dancing as a duet or trio, your stage is set at Safe to Sparkle.

The Trio

VeeVee, SpeeDee, and DeeDee just purr along.

Free of protecting you from threat, all three cue you in life as they jointly bedazzle your stage. SpeeDee and Deedee complement each other with breezy ease, percolating towards the common good of your health and your connections with people. These three sisters harmonize and so do you.

You are Safe to Sparkle as you look for people to help you survive and thrive. You rest and repair as you reverberate with calm zest. You heal all the time. You are your heathiest. Your organs, blood, and lymph flow operate at Goldilocks-just-right.

As long as VeeVee has no Stage Fright, she brakes SpeeDee and DeeDee just enough, so you purr at the right pace. Neither jingly-jangly or mopey-dopey, you are approachable and able to connect. Your jewelled ear mic assures that you receive support and guidance from your Sparkle. VeeVee reports back to you this zesty calm that radiates within you. Your face-heart path is welcoming and engaging.

The Duets

Duet # 1

VeeVee and SpeeDee inspire without Stage Fright.

Get moving, girl! It's playtime or worktime. Sometimes VeeVee and SpeeDee do a little cha-cha as DeeDee gently rocks on stage behind them (Rosenberg 2017, 35–36). You move with zest, not fear. SpeeDee's high energy boosts your movements in life. You engage your life audience with zesty ardor, belting out tunes, trusting your faithful team. Her zippiness lets you run, walk, pick up objects, move at just the right pace, and *ooh la la*—you enjoy sexy times too. You arrange dinners and plan events. You are creative, getting work projects done with ease. You dance Zumba, carry babies, dogs, and laptops, and wear a smile (all at the same time, of course). Your faithful heart and lungs both zoodle at higher energies in exhilarating, not exhausting ways, thanks to fearless SpeeDee. Your face-heart path is welcoming and engaging.

Duet #2

VeeVee and DeeDee inspire you to be still without Stage Fright.

Chillax. Be still girl. This moment is here for you to savour. At times, it is Sister SpeeDee who hangs back a bit, snapping her fingers while Sisters DeeDee and VeeVee run your show (Rosenberg 2017, 35–36). Still and soft, you purr in deep relaxation or intimate moments. You're all slowed down, all fun and no fear. Your breath and heartbeats are enjoyably softer and slower. DeeDee's lower energy keeps your slow jam rich and sexy, or soft and cuddly. You enjoy a massage, a meditation, a nap, or mmm, a deep and intimate encounter. Your face-heart path is welcoming and engaging.

In whatever team combo, your Purse Sisters headline your stage, freed from guarding your existence. Your Sparkle bubbles forth and you sense Sparkle.

Your Sparkle is always, always there.
You do not make Sparkle.
Even VeeVee, SpeeDee, and DeeDee together do not make Sparkle.

But, when VeeVee helps SpeeDee and DeeDee refrain from their On Guard gig, Sparkle is revealed. Like the tireless frontline worker with the tender soul, the protective equipment is removed, and your natural Sparkle can unfurl on your life stage.

What is Sparkle?

Sparkle is the core essence of wise compassion that is always within you.

Sparkle is the core essence of wise compassion that is always within you.

Life experiences can diminish or obscure your Sparkle, but it is waiting patiently to be known. Many thoughtful philosophers, counsellors, poets, and researchers have devoted their life's work to describing this magical birthright essence within you.

How do you name this sense of graceful connection within that delightfully wraps you in connections with all your parts and people and with all living things and the Love beyond time and space?

Sparkle has been described as:

- Innate purity and goodness (Brach 2021)
- The inner pilot light (Rankin 2020)
- The true self (Rohr 2013)
- The core self (Schwartz 2021)

As we described in Chapter 3, you arrived at life's party preset with Body, Mind, Emotion, and Connection Energies that, when flowing freely, are the juice that both sustains and energizes you at *just right*. When your energies are flowing, you experience Sparkle. Flowing freely inside, you sense a cool combo of zesty-yet-calm connection with yourself and with people. Energy flows within you, kink free.

The grounding comfort of Sparkle makes Vee Vee safe to stay on your stage. You can notice and bring kindness to all your parts who respond to Sticky Note warnings of past or future energy kinks. Your kindness for all parts of you flows out of a caring that doesn't get caught up in your Sticky Note warnings.

You can't imagine comparing yourself as smaller or bigger to anyone else.
No inner critiquing of you.
No outward critiquing of another.

You do not compare yourself as better or worse than the person with whom you are connecting. Your Sparkle can guide all the unique parts of you that have celebrated and protected you during your lifetime. You are gloriously present.

Sparkle can access your energies to give you info at so many stages of discovery. Your energies hold Sticky Note memories of thoughts, actions, and feelings you used to muster through life's Energy Kinks and surprises. You notice aches, twinges, or pains as well as soft comfort. You accept the ebb and flow of your varying emotions and thoughts without labels or judgements. Sparkle can hang out with all parts of your Mind Energy with appreciation and wonder about your feelings, sensations, observations, and thoughts.

There is a genuine warmth and respect for differences, as you kindly wonder about the thoughts, feelings, and actions of all your parts. You use this same noticing and kindness toward other people and their parts. You create meaning that is life-promoting and soulful-celebrating.

Happiness sustains you throughout. Happiness is not based on an event, a person's mood, or who is with you or not with you. It radiates. Happiness naturally expands, touching others effortlessly. This happy is truly heartfelt. Heartwaves flow from your heart engine without spiky jarringness or numbing flatness. You know this as gracious happiness that abides within you and is there even in the darkest of times. It is not a quick fix, but an internal knowing essence that you share with others.

Sure, a Hasty Happy can give you a momentary boost. But Hasty Happy has its price: a guilt hangover or a ruptured friendship, to name a couple. Resting in Sparkle, you have a heartfelt happy. This happy makes your caring intentions clear.

Your Sparkle

Your Sparkle just happens.

You don't have to fret about it. You don't have to will it. You don't have to conjure it up.

Although, we all seem to do these things because we love Sparkle so much. Prior to birth, you sensed Sparkle moments when all was right in the world. If Mom's nourishment nourished you, you could feel warm and snuggly, playful, and kicky. Literally tied to and in total relationship with Mom, her energy fed you. After the drama of birth, you longed to return to that familiar connection.

As a child, before you got bigger and created a zillion Sticky Notes, you might have had genuine moments when your stage sparkled. You simply noticed—full of wonder. Remember?

You played.
You dreamed.
You made your toys act out stories.
You purposely jumped in puddles.
You made snow angels.
You sat on the dog, not beside the dog.
You slept like a log.

The uniqueness of all your parts came sparkling through. You luxuriated in the here and now.

Snowflakes

We are just like snowflakes.

No flake is like another. Their uniqueness allows a coming together to create something different. As they fall softly, drift madly, or dance saucily, snowflakes bask in individuality, alighting on eyelashes and tongues. Each snowflake's purpose is separate and distinct. Yet their combined efforts create a snowy blanket to kiss the sleeping buds, a laugh-filled trail for tobogganers, a soft place for children's arms to pump angels into the landscape.

As the snowy stars fall to earth, one by one, a transformation takes place. White abandon turns green lawns into frosted cupcakes. For a moment, we hold our breath at the miracle of change. We feel transformed.

Human existence needs all these unique parts of us to Sparkle. People will die out if they stop dreaming, creating, learning, and enhancing.

We need all of us to share our snowflake uniqueness.

We need all of us to share our snowflake uniqueness.

At birth, you started to take shape. Your unique natural abilities for math or cooking, communication, problem-solving, languages or music, art or management, poetry or science, and organization swirled throughout you.

Our gifts, talents, and interests are diverse. Artists allow us to feel and see what is beyond us. Engineers help us find resources and allow us to traverse our planet. Entrepreneurs create beyond the expected, and our world abounds with never-ending innovation. Businesses and laws provide structure and order, so chaos won't destroy. Poets, writers, singers, and dancers play with the beauty of untamed energy. Health care providers tend to us and help our bodies use their wisdom to heal. People who care for our homes, who clean, and who make sure our roads are safe, allow our VeeVees to rest. Teachers expand our minds. Kind and patient souls care for children, our tiny sparklers.

Your Sparkle is real.

But it's not all sunshine and roses.

Sparkle is not nirvana. It is not a panacea of perfect bliss in which you transcend and hover above everything and everybody. Sparkle is not lofty. Sparkle is not an escape. Your celebratory show in this world is genuine, no matter the circumstances.

Life can be picnic perfect in one moment and a grand feast covered in ants the next. When you Sparkle, you can be in the chips or down for the count. The circumstances do not determine your mood or actions. Your ability to resource the gifts in your Body, Emotion, Mind, and Connection Energies allows a buffet platter of possibilities and helps you remain engaged and focused, steady in the face of others and your life events.

Like a Dorothy in the *Wizard of Oz*, who withstood cyclones, flying monkeys, green wizards, and wicked witches, the Sparkle courage to get through anything has always been within you. Dorothy was flummoxed by tornados, broomsticks, falling houses, and three lovable but needy companions—replete with their own Hasty Happies. As any good witch would do, Glinda illuminated what Dorothy had within her. Glinda's kind demeanour and her wand turned a spotlight on what Dorothy already knew but had forgotten amid the Yellow Brick Road hijinks.

Just like Dorothy, this beautiful Sparkle essence is always yours. Life may be full of moments where you have no sense of Sparkle. You can feel empty. You can feel that even if Sparkle was ever with you, it's somehow been banished. Although life happens in a myriad of joys and devastations, Sparkle remains, undaunted, a connection beyond each separate us to the connection of a bigger us.

And no, sweet you, in all your woe and all your worry, you have not damaged it. Sparkle is there for us, for you, always ready for you to rest into it. We are not saying that the challenges, illnesses, abuses, hurt, betrayals, and the storms of your life do not exist.

Yes. They do. So does Sparkle.

It fills you in your own sense of your world. It can appear in your favourite colour, in the face of a cloud, and it can soften your face to a smile as a song lilts throughout you.

For Dorothy, ruby red signalled her Sparkle. Three clicks of her heels emanated from Dorothy's innate sense that she could find home. She trusted not only Glinda. Dorothy trusted her own knowingness that sparkled throughout her. In that sense of home within, Dorothy's energies flowed freely. Though far away from Kansas, she was not alone. Glinda did not get Dorothy home. Dorothy did. Dorothy's Sparkle birthright guided her like an inner GPS. Glinda did not cajole Dorothy to click her heels. Sparkle that lined Glinda's *good witch* insides shone out beyond Glinda, encouraging the Sparkle in Dorothy to dance.

Glinda was a good witch, but she wasn't a saint. Glinda, like you, like us, like Margie, had to work through her On Guard when a house landed smack dab in the middle of Munchkin land. A girl in gingham and a dog in a basket whomp from the sky? Part of Glinda wanted to say, *Gosh, girl, you think you got problems? I must calm down the Lollipop League. You have an adorable dog, and you got the shoes. Stop snivelling!*

Glinda Used Magic

Glinda acted as if her VeeVee was on her stage, even when her VeeVee was not.

She did this by resting into her Sparkle. She let it do its Sparkle thing. She could imagine times she had VeeVee with her and not in the wings, and from that place, she could give this girl and dog a proper *hello*. Infused with a steady resolve, Glinda was grounded in her own Sparkle and filled with kindness for herself and for this lost young girl. Glinda could notice her own body as she flinched from the lady on the broom yet leaned towards the girl who trembled. Glinda could sense the fear of Dorothy, the anger of the Wicked Witch, the giddy jubilation of the Munchkins. Glinda's mind received and sorted all this data. Creativity, clarity, wonder, and brave tenderness spun within Glinda.

Present on her own stage, Glinda could offer true assistance to Dorothy—and her little dog too—when she inspired Dorothy to act from her Sparkle stage. Her Sparkle, the simple act of letting Sparkle imbue her, made Glinda's stage safe enough for Glinda's VeeVee to return from the wings. Glinda's VeeVee swirled on her stage, quelling her Stage Fright—created both outside of her by the Wicked Witch of the West and within her from Glinda's own Sticky Notes: her history of sibling angst with her Wicked Witch sisters.

Glinda's VeeVee softly braked the influences of her SpeeDee and DeeDee. With all three sisters on her stage, Glinda could Sparkle. Glinda emanated her own energetic calm even in the midst of mischievous Munchkins, a dead sister under a misplaced house, and another sister careening around on a broom. Dorothy's own insides sensed the energetic calm beaming from Glinda. Dorothy sensed her own Sparkle in the presence of Glinda's Sparkle.

Sparkle was Glinda's birthright. When she set her stage at Safe to Sparkle, she inspired Dorothy to click her heels, a golden moment of Sparkle magic.

Your Sparkle Power

You have Sparkle Power too.

You began life with the aid of another's nervous system showing you the ropes. We can be like Glinda and show our unique Sparkle. The magic of Glinda the Good Witch sprung from Glinda's gentle smile and kind eyes. The wand? Merely a pretty prop every fairy tale needs.

Like Glinda, in the face of your own dishy drama, you, too, can teach others—with your stage set at Safe to Sparkle—how to set their own stage at Safe to Sparkle. You are both a Dorothy and a Glinda. One woman's wand is another woman's pair of ruby slippers.

You come alive. You remember you have all you need inside—your Sparkle. You can endure. You can figure it out, even if you can't figure it out this very minute. You know you will get through. You sense there is an opening at the end of the current long, long tunnel.

You can say to yourself even during times of turmoil and loss:

- *I am with my unique self, separate yet connected to all parts of me and you.*
- *My heart's electromagnetic field connects me to others, all living things, and the Love beyond time and space.*

Create Magic: Embrace your Sparkle Power

Pause, breathe into your heart, rest in your Sparkle, and choose to embrace your **Sparkle Power.** Your parts can count on you to be there. Sparkle can be with, and get to know, the parts of you that are in a Hasty Happy. SpeeDee, freed from fuelling Hasty Happy habits, activates you with zest and clarity. SpeeDee combo-packs the messages from your Body, Emotion, Mind, and Connection Energies so you can act in ways that are genuinely helpful to both you and others. She juices up your mental, physical, and vocal power. SpeeDee fuels your Sparkle Power to choose actions.

You can say yes to what you can do and no to what you can't. Yup. Sparkle Power can border up your energies. You are no longer Too Bossy, Too Pleasing, Too Escaping, Too Helpful, or Too Frosty. Deedee is also free from fuelling Hasty Happy habits. She is at her relaxing best, helping you be genuine in the moment. You enjoy getting your needs met. You don't rely on the drama of Hasty Happy to hopefully get what you need. DeeDee can nix her protective icy vibe. Too Helpless or Too Iced Over are not in demand.

You connect graciously with people, free of your Hasty Happy habits, even when others are in their Hasty Happy habits. You kindly express genuine interest in others. You are responsible for you, and you know when to be responsible to care for others.

You speak from what you feel, always with compassion and not with apology.
Your pace and cadence are just right, not too fast or too slow.
You are engaged in the moment without a hidden agenda.
You can ask for help.
You can give help.

Instead of relying on Sticky Notes, creative ideas blossom. Free of judgements, you create new ideas or possibilities, fresh actions, and incredible connections. They become actions that help both you and others heal and Sparkle. Actions that cause pain or cramp growth do not emanate from Sparkle.

You connect just as you are, with people just as they are, not how you imagine either you or them to be. You care without losing your own sense of you. Whether you are by your ownsome or in meetups with people, you never feel alone. A delicious connection to life, a hope prevails, even among sadness and challenges. You are aware of the energy of other people and the energy of you.

You can Sparkle even when—sigh—others cannot. You easily share the spotlight with your fellow cast members. You neither hog the stage nor mix up your energy with others. All parts of you can rest into your Sparkle when your Purse Sisters are all on stage. Basking in Sparkle, you can feel for, or feel with, other people without Tricky Guilt or Care-y Mix-ups. You feel such a comfortable ease on your insides. People find you a drama-free pleasure.

Love. Pure, pure love.

See what happens when in that doorway moment, Margie embraced her Sparkle Power.

CHAPTER 12

Margie Owns Her Sparkle Power

After the Hasty Happy hoedown, Margie, like all of us women who carry instead of connect, found herself sighing, *I had the best intentions, really I did*. But intention is a hope, a wing, a prayer. Remember how hard Margie tried to make Judge happy? Margie went to so much trouble, all over a woeful, slobbering dog. And her kids. And her husband.

And even though that tale took place in the 1960s, women continue to sidestep themselves repeatedly.

Imagine though, if Margie's caring intentions came from such a bright spot within her that she didn't feel tired or used. What if Margie's parts got along just swell with Sparkle? What if Margie didn't act like she was better or worse than those around her? Then, Margie could care for herself as well as for Judge and the family with a happy energy expanding from her heart—a type of happy that was enduring and health-promoting, not hasty and health-demoting.

People around her might have their own Sticky Notes about Margie, but Margie knew she could never change their Hasty Happy actions. Margie might no longer refer to just her Sticky Notes. They had some good info, but the data was often out of date. Aglow with heartfelt happy, Margie could create a separate space for herself and a separate space for those she loved. Maybe it was a simple thing Margie did to make her caring intentions clear, so her family and others, even a dog, learned about this heartfelt happy.

The Doorway Moment Do-Over

Hand still on the doorknob, Margie paused and chose to review and think. Funny enough, it took hardly a second to turn this around. Margie noticed her inner tizzy. She breathed in, then out. Margie held a kind wonderment for her VeeVee. Given the present turmoil, Margie guessed her VeeVee might be saying goodbye and allowing her SpeeDee to drive her actions.

At that, she said a warm hello to her VeeVee. She smiled at Judge. Margie's VeeVee sensed safe with this warm welcome. When VeeVee sensed safety, Margie's Sparkle could shine. Her Body, Mind, Emotion, and Connection Energies signalled that all was swell. Margie connected with her insides and connected with grace on her outsides.

As if VeeVee had a little mic with a direct feed to Margie's insides and to Margie's beautiful ears, VeeVee fed back to Margie what VeeVee sensed from Margie's true Sparkle insides:

VeeVee Message

Lovely, your emotions gift you with up-to-date data. Your mind ripples with meaning and creativity! Joyfully connect, girl: with yourself, people, all living things, the source of Love beyond time and space. Sweetness, you have courage to choose thoughts and actions both loving to you and to others, without sacrificing you or those you love. You have a body that can grow and heal. You are just right—not worse than, not better than, anyone else. You are rocking life in this very moment.

Whether Margie chose to stay or leave the house, she owned her Sparkle Power.

Margie Stays Home

Margie felt Judge's eyes and heard his whimpering plea. Her heart softened. The VeeVee running between her heart and head lit up with caring love and warmth. Margie's eyes met Judge's eyes. She smiled inside her very self. Margie playfully chided him at his invitation to stay home.

On earlier occasions when Judge did his doe-eyed routine, Tricky Guilt compelled Margie to stay home.

This time felt different. Before she removed her hat, coat, and gloves, she took the doorway moment to check in with her parts. Margie realized it would be better not to rush around that day.

She still had half the dishes to do, and her favourite show was on TV. Margie did a quick inventory. She had all the ingredients for the supper meatloaf and more than enough clean shirts for Bert. The better time to get the pork chops was not today. Tomorrow, Wednesday, the butcher's weekly specials would dance in neon on his whiteboard.

With kind wonderment, Margie paused to check on her nervous system. Margie put her hand on her heart and said, **Hello VeeVee** as a way to encourage VeeVee to stay on her stage. She imagined her breath going in and out through her loving heart. Inhaling for four counts, exhaling for eight, she did a quick body scan and let herself notice the pulled strain in her neck. It probably would be a good idea to take out the ice pack.

"C'mon, Judge, or should I call you Dr. Judge?" Margie tosses Judge a treat as she gets her ice pack from the freezer. "Thanks for reminding me to rest my neck. Although I think you had this in mind."

They both settle in to watch the last half of the show. Rested up, Margie gets ready for the kids' return from school. Excited to hear how Bobby did on the test and how Elizabeth made out with her presentation, Margie feels energetic, full of wonder, and ready for the next part of her day.

Margie Sparkles.

Margie Leaves

As Judge continued to whine, cry, snort, and raise his brown eyes woefully upward, Margie noticed her breaths growing faster. With kind wonderment, Margie wondered where her VeeVee was. Oopsie, was SpeeDee running her stage? She simply said, *Hello VeeVee.*

She took even breaths, counting four inhales and counting eight exhales, about five times. She sat down on the steps by the door and took his loveable mug in her warm two hands and kissed Judge on the nose. Using her VeeVee, with full awareness she looked into the beautiful dog's sweet eyes and said, "There, there you big gob of goodness. I have it all set up nicely for you in the kitchen where it's cool, and your big water bowl is full."

Saying these words helped Margie more than Judge. Judge, after all, was just doing what a dog does. Margie's words helped calm her own racing heart. She reviewed her plans and knew that she would be out for just a few hours. Whether or not she was home, Judge would be doing the same thing—napping. If she didn't go out today, she'd be behind the eight ball, which would affect everybody. She needed to get her hair washed and set. Even the thought of the head massage yet to come relaxed her. On the way home, she could pick up the notebook for Elizabeth and a few things at the store, including dog food.

Although Judge still barked and sighed, she winked at him as she closed the door and said, "Ciao for now, big fella."

In both scenarios, Margie made a space for her and a space for Judge. Margie owned her Sparkle Power on her separate stage.

Margie arrived at life's party primed for the best survival gig, getting a bunch of safe people together. She was also bio-designed to feel comfy safe when she was with other people whose stages were set at Safe to Sparkle. That's how humans roll. When Margie's caring intentions were clear, she stayed on her stage, not Judge's, or anybody else's. No Care-y Mix-ups. Safety for her loved ones.

Margie's Energy Border

Amid caring for those she adored, she knew there was a place and space for her and a place and space for those she loved. Her Body, Mind, Emotion, and Connection Energies were separate yet connected to parts of her and to others. Sparkling, Margie did not mix together her energy with Judge or her loved ones. She knew where she left off and others began. Margie had an **Energy Border.**

Even with her heart's large electromagnetic field that reached out so lovingly, Margie was grounded in her own marks on stage. She kept her nervous system where all precious items should be—in her very own purse. Margie wanted to care for both herself and those she loved. If she kept her purse open just to herself, not only would her purse be far less messy—she could also best respect and encourage others to care for their separate purses too.

Margie noticed how one scoop of ice cream on a sugary crisscross cone does not look quite right. When she saw pictures in a children's book or saw ads for Carla's Cream Confections, she didn't see one lonely scoop sagging in the cone container. Put all the sprinkles on it, all the gummy bears or cookie crumbles, and one scoop still looked like a prom dress with running shoes, unfinished and out of place.

When she splurged for ice cream, she got two scoops: a foundation scoop and a topper scoop. Margie loved how all the accoutrements stayed on better and looked better. She even thought about getting two different flavours. They could be distinct and taste good. She imagined swirling both flavours with her tongue. Maybe combining the chocolate with the pistachio? Or eat them separately, savouring the sweet possibility of each unique flavour?

Like two separate scoops on a cone, Margie and her loved ones could Sparkle and celebrate both of their unique flavours. She really wanted both herself and her family to Sparkle. When Margie's family sparkled, she was genuinely happy for them because she knew when sparkly people got together, they each would gain healthy benefits. They would grow, restore, and heal in the closeness of people who twirl on stages set at Safe to Sparkle.

Margie wasn't selfish for wanting a Sparkle system near her. The more people who Sparkle, the better for all. Margie hummed a line from a Cole Porter song, *It's de-lightful, it's de-licious, it's de-lovely.*

Change

Margie knew that both her love and her clear thinking could change DNA. DNA strands swirl prettily in test tubes. To measure the effects of feelings and thoughts, scientists asked three groups of people to hold test tubes of DNA. They then gave the three groups different instructions (Dispenza 2012, 19).

The *first group* was asked to hold the tubes and at the same time sustain feelings of happiness and appreciation. The *second group* was asked to hold the tubes and do two things at the same time: sustain feelings of happiness and appreciation and concentrate their thoughts clearly on changing the shape of the DNA sample—winding or unwinding the swirly strands. The *third group* was instructed to focus only on concentrating their thoughts on changing the shape of the DNA sample. They were told not to sustain feelings of happiness and appreciation.

And then, magic really did happen.

In the test tubes of Group #2, DNA danced and moved and changed. Appreciation and intentional thoughts together altered DNA. The DNA changed shape when feelings of appreciation and specific thoughts about the desired change happened at the same time. Only when feelings and thoughts worked together did change occur.

Appreciation on Purpose

Appreciation on purpose makes you think clearly.

When you actively appreciate something or someone, you can create an alchemy within yourself. You engage your heart, brain, and body rhythms to blend into a pleasing harmonious rate. Your heart is in the loop. As the brain and heart dance, you experience a greater capacity for thinking clearly and using your intuition (McCraty, 2022, chap. 4).

Margie knew thinking and wanting the best for her peeps was essential.

When Margie played out the above healthy caring scenarios, she kept this in mind: someone must hold the test tube with appreciation and clear thinking. That someone can't fail. That someone must be alert and clear and able to concentrate to make change happen. Margie knew if she was cheerleading others, she had to hold up her pom poms with exciting energy. It was best to wonder about what was going on inside her and what she might need to shake those pom poms.

Her caring intentions for Judge and her family could now be clear. If she kindly wondered about both Judge and herself, Margie must have been set at safe to Sparkle. Margie's VeeVee needed to be on her stage. It was VeeVee who showed her kind and safe concern. It was VeeVee that calmed SpeeDee's exuberance. It was VeeVee that provided DeeDee with zest.

Margie's ice cream dreams gave her an idea. Sure, it was truly fantastic to enjoy the uniqueness of each person she adored. Those different coloured scoops of creamery confection compelled her to connect.

Ice Cream and DNA

Then, she remembered a misadventure. The kids were at school, and Margie was out and about. Quite busy, Margie forgot to have lunch. Boy, she was hungry. She pondered, *Oh dare I do it? Well, it's not like I do it every day.* Margie splurged. She bought the ice cream cone. And wouldn't you know it? There was a triple scoop sale. Three scoops for the price of two. That cinched the deal. Margie could get a scoop of each kid's favourite flavour plus her own. At least she was thinking about them. Chocolate on the bottom. Pistachio in-between and strawberry on top. Gorgeous.

If she lived in the here and now, this was an Instagram moment for sure. Margie's tongue played with each flavour, but then—well, it was a warm day, so very soon a goopy mess appeared—pink ran into green, green ran into chocolate. Was that a strawberry or a pistachio caught in her tooth? And then the overstuffed cone just toppled—a grey, sloshy thing on the gravel. There was something to be said for separate cones.

Once again, the life source DNA came into play. On Margie's DNA were little end caps akin to the plastic ends on shoelaces. Just like real shoelaces, these end caps must be intact, not frayed. If you have ever tried to put a lace through a hole without a plastic end, you know you usually decide that it's game over for the lace and toss that old shoelace in *la garbage*. Or do you recycle it? Hmm, that decision is stressful too.

In any event, the shoelace had a shorter life because the plastic end wore out. DNA's plastic ends are called *telomeres*. If Margie's telomeres wore down, got shorter, she couldn't throw out the DNA like she could a shoelace. Age and its wear and tear shorten DNA—and shorten life. On the other hand, caring for others and being kind counters some of the biological aspects of stress and slows down the shortening of telomeres (Blackburn and Epel 2017, 11). Yay!

As Margie reached out kindly to people, she made more oxytocin, called the "molecule of kindness" within her (Hamilton 2017, 54). Ah. This increased oxytocin encouraged her to keep reaching out with kindness. The more she gave kindness, the more oxytocin she got, and the more oxytocin she got, the more kindness she could give. The comfort she gave through oxytocin inspiration raised the oxytocin in the people she nurtured. Her loved ones turned on their own oxytocin taps when they received Margie's kindness.

Nature wanted Margie and her loved ones to keep producing this huggy-type hormone because oxytocin is good for hearts. As oxytocin swirls into the bloodstream, its friendly nature attracts nitric oxide to join the fun. Nitric oxide floods arteries, parting the artery walls wider and lowering blood pressure. As if that were not enough reason to cuddle up and make oxytocin, increased oxytocin levels in Margie lowered her inflammation, boosted her immune system, and helped her heart stay strong (Hamilton 2017, 43–70).

Margie didn't pet and nuzzle Judge because she knew both their oxytocin levels would skyrocket and help their health. She did it, and then Judge nuzzled the cuddles because it felt good. Touch can soothe. A caring, attentive touch bonded them (Linden 2015, 19). Both woman and dog felt *safe*. Parts of Margie's brain lit up excitedly in the presence of Judge, inspiring her to care for him and the people she loves (Buczynski and Simon-Thomas 2019, 10–14).

Too Much?

On the other hand, too much caregiving could hurt Margie.

Caregiving can shorten telomeres (Blackburn and Epel 2017, 77). We know, seriously? At this point Margie might have thought that the only answer was to run off to Bora Bora. That Polynesian drink with the little umbrella in the big coconut sounded pretty good. Margie gave her head a shake and came up with—

This answer: Margie could care for herself and others too. These two types of caring are not mutually exclusive. Her telomeres that protected her DNA, her longevity, needed a good mix of caring for herself and caring for others. Of course, when her loved ones were okay, Margie felt happy, but she also knew their happiness did not entirely depend on her. Throwing herself under the bus for them to feel happy would only provide short-lived happiness for them and for her.

She needed to do her part by finding her delight so she could delight in caring for them. The amazing thing is when she found her own source of delight, it gave those she cared about the opportunity to find their own delight. Margie was doing what nature inspired, to care for her loved ones and herself from a stage set at Safe to Sparkle. At Sparkle, she could care for herself and her loved ones at the same time.

Both = Double Delight.

To create her own Double Delight, Margie knew choosing one thing could make all the difference. She chose VeeVee. Margie opened the clasp on her own purse and said, *Hello VeeVee*. She knew life would be different with a new purse—her very own.

CHAPTER 13

The Mighty Power of Hello

Adult Margie recalled her Grandma Irene's words from when she was a little girl: *Margie, kittens are born skittish. They need to learn how to feel safe. Hello is a great beginning.* During the times her VeeVee was offstage, Margie was reminded of the barn kitten she met when she was six years old. The little kitten was as wild and skittish as Margie's own VeeVee. The barn kitty hopped on and off her Grandma Irene's porch as often as VeeVee hoofed on and off her life stage.

The Barn Kitten

Little Margie adored a kitten at her grandmother's farm. Big blue eyes framed in total fluff, the little gaffer hopped and jumped and played—by itself. Margie wanted to play with the little kitten, not just watch its antics. Margie gleefully scooped her up in her little arms. Whoosh! She scurried right out. Undaunted, Margie tried again, "You are so cute!"

"Ack!" This time, the kitten swatted Margie with a tiny, but aggressive paw. The tangle of limbs and battle of wills continued until Margie threw the now nasty little beggar across the porch. Scratched and bedraggled, Margie limped into Grandma's kitchen.

"My, my, my. Margie, you look like something the cat dragged in."

Ugh. Now Margie was miffed with her grandma.

"Well child, what happened to you?"

Between sniffles and nose wipes on her sleeve, Margie shuddered and stammered out the porch drama, ending with, "But I love her."

Margie had Care-y Stress at a tender age. On the porch, six-year-old Margie could never have won. Margie kept bellowing *hello* to the kitten's Vee Vee without saying hello to her own Vee Vee first. Grandma Irene knew her Margie well. She sensed both the excitement and the disappointment that rippled within her granddaughter's six-year-old body. Margie, such a feisty and kind spirit, was downtrodden.

She had so much love for that kitten, it burst through her. Margie was convinced that her love would flow through to the little cat. Margie's love, so very large, felt so electric it must be magic. It must heal. It must help. She was sure this love would quell all the scary heebie-jeebies in the tiny kitten. Margie was gutted when the kitten rebelled and rejected all this love. Gutted.

With all the loving might within her, Margie tried so hard to show that kitty love. An achy awfulness drenched Margie's inside. One part of Margie was stomping mad. *Bad Kitty!* she wanted to scream. Another part of Margie swiftly put the blame on her own small innocent soul.

Margie quickly made a Sticky Note about the porch disaster. She scribbled out: *I am lousy at loving. I must try harder and harder.* Margie stuck this note in a place close to her heart so she would never ever have a kitten run away from her again. Margie no longer saw the beauty of the kitten. She plum gave up on the furry fella as she yanked its claws off her throat. She chose herself over the ferocious feline. In that moment, she really didn't care about Kitty. She was no longer the caring, sweet girl she thought she was supposed to be.

Tricky Guilt oozed through Margie.

Grandma knew all this about this little girl she adored, making her adore her even more.

Margie's Hasty Happy actions tugged hard at Grandma. Grandma's own VeeVee could easily hoof it:

- One part of Grandma wanted to grab Margie, fetch the kitten, and reunite them.

- One part of Grandma feared for Margie's safety and longed to implore Margie to be careful and just stick to house cats.

- One part of Grandma longed to chastise the little girl for her angry, ugly outburst.

- One part of Grandma wanted to ignore Margie's six-year-old woeful pleas.

- And one part of Grandma had to bite her lip from declaring, "What a drama queen, Margie!"

All these parts tempted Grandma. One of them reminded her of Margie's grandpa, and boy did she have Sticky Notes about his antics. She knew her own VeeVee had Stage Fright. If VeeVee said goodbye, SpeeDee and DeeDee would go gonzo, making Grandma's stage unsafe. More Stage Fright for VeeVee. Her VeeVee would have no desire to hop back on her stage. Despite the whir of Margie and the Kitty energy, Grandma sought her VeeVee so she could own her Sparkle Power. Grandma knew she must love this little girl from her own separate space, a space energetically calm and present. Opening her life purse and letting Margie's upset in would only increase the odds of the Hasty Happies for her and Margie.

Kitty and Margie needed safety.
Their separate spaces deserved respect.

Grandma knew that good fences make good neighbours. Grandma, Margie, and Kitty needed friendly borders between their nervous systems. She knew that in every moment she decided one of two possibilities: *Do I say yes, or do I say no?* This survival reality could get confuse-y and all mixed together in Grandma's insides. Grandma carried all the messages about being a responsible caring woman. They swirled inside her. She could feel all this stuff as Tricky Guilt. This pseudo guilt could trick her if she did not make a choice to do something different.

It would have been easy for Grandma to ditch her delight so she could delight Margie and the Kitty. Grandma could have carried on in a Care-y Stress way and do the Care-y Mix-Ups. She could have focused on their nervous systems, their VeeVees, not hers.

Grandma knew if she did not do something different, she would forget her own VeeVee and try to get Margie and Kitty's VeeVees back on their nervous system stages. Impossible. On top of that, if she carried Margie and Kitty in her purse, their nervous systems would get mixed up with her nervous system. Inevitably, Grandma would try to tell Margie and Kitty what they should do or not do without listening at all to what was important to each of them.

Not because Grandma was bad. Only because she had tried to love them by carrying them inside of her purse.

She knew she had to say hello to her own VeeVee if she was going to help Margie. Grandma made a choice. Before she did anything else amid the angst of her granddaughter and the genuine caterwauling of the kitten, Grandma Irene paused. From this purseonal space, Grandma championed Margie's caring intentions for Kitty. Grandma wiped her floury hands on her apron, grabbed the iodine and the gauze, and with all the tenderness she could muster said, "Margie tomorrow, we say hello. It'll be okay."

Margie, reaching for one more bandage, said, "Grandma, I think I would like that very much."

The next day, the two of them went to the barn, armed with a bottle of milk and a bowl. Margie was so excited. She ran ahead of her grandmother, flew through the barn door, and at the top of her voice yelled, "Here, Kitty, Kitty. I'm here!"

Margie didn't want to be patient and allow the kitten to take its sweet time. Margie wanted to rush in and make the love happen, even when Kitty had different ideas.

Grandma, trying not to roll her eyes, said, "Let's try something different. I'm all out of iodine, Margie." She motioned Margie to come back to the barn door and stay put. Grandma poured a little milk into the bowl and placed it near the first horse stall, a good twelve feet away from the open barn door. Margie dashed up to the bowl and squatted on her little legs. With one strong arm, Grandma scooped Margie up and returned her to the barn door opening. Margie sighed loudly, her anxious breath making her bangs jump up.

Grandma encouraged Margie to hold back and watch. Each day she sat beside the little girl. She showed Margie how being still and breathing deeply softened the flying butterflies in Margie's tummy. Margie felt a peaceful purpose as she waited each day with her grandmother. She learned that she could stay quite still. This gave her a quiet pleasure that her running legs and busy voice had not known. Margie could feel solidness in her legs and an opening in her heart

They did this every day for a week. With one adjustment. Each day, Grandma moved the bowl of milk a little closer to the barn door. By the end of the week, the kitten drank milk at the barn door opening. Margie said, "Hello there," as Kitty, with closed kitten eyes of bliss and purrs of happiness, swished beneath Margie's chin. Margie's smile was as broad as the beams in the barn.

Grandma grinned and wiped a tear from her eye. Grandma chose to say hello to her own VeeVee, which helped Margie's VeeVee stay on

Margie's stage, which helped the kitten's VeeVee stay on the kitten's stage. Years later, Margie would use this choice too.

The sense of wonderment and love Margie had originally felt for the kitten whooshed within her. Her spirit was touched, not irritated, by the cat. Their Sparkles met. Margie, basking in her own separate self, saw Kitty with new eyes, not a reflection of what she had needed the cat to be. Kitty sensed safety, and with a deep purr and a playful pat, leaned into Margie. Each one listened to the others needs and wants, their Energy Borders unique to them.

Margie had Double Delight.

Adult Margie, warmed by this memory, allowed Grandma Irene's wisdom to help her now with judgy Judge. Margie's VeeVee could dance on her stage and help her avoid SpeeDee and DeeDee's Hasty Happy. A loving hello to VeeVee made sense.

More Than Hello

Grown up Margie loved her VeeVee. It was the kind of love she felt for Judge. Whenever Margie returned home, she'd call out, "Where are ya, old fella? Yoo-hoo, Judge. Hello."

When Margie knew that VeeVee might be hoofing off her stage, she yoo-hooed, *Hello, VeeVee*—because she loved her VeeVee. The only one who hoofed on and off Margie's stage was VeeVee. SpeeDee and DeeDee stayed put. VeeVee loved Margie just as fiercely as Margie loved her. VeeVee never rested from being on the lookout for Stage Fright. VeeVee always tried to protect Margie. She kept tabs on VeeVee, not with anger or frustration, but with love.

Just like her beloved Judge, Margie thought of VeeVee almost all the time. She wondered, *Where are ya, VeeVee?* when she sensed VeeVee was not around. If Margie did not readily know where VeeVee was, she would seek her with earnest. She wondered what could nourish

VeeVee and give her sustenance. Margie wanted to be close, to cuddle VeeVee. She wanted VeeVee to rest if VeeVee had done too much. She wanted VeeVee to play and to have regular exercise. She was not perturbed with, or jealous, of VeeVee.

Cherishing VeeVee: Purseonal Safety

Adult Margie loved VeeVee. She just had to keep her safe. Margie remembered Kitty. *When you really love something so very much, you keep them safe.* Margie's Grandma Irene designed a safe space for Kitty. Kitty stayed around Margie a lot that precious summer. Skittish, vibrant VeeVee also deserved safekeeping. Margie's life purse was perfect for safekeeping VeeVee and her two sisters. Margie trusted that Judge, her spouse, each child, and each friend had their own types of purses encasing their nervous systems. Whether they were doggie bandanas with a place for treats, big brown briefcases, schoolbags, or princess pocketbooks, they all tenderly held each loved one's nervous system. Margie made a space for herself and a separate space for Judge. Loving her loved ones and loving herself were not mutually exclusive. Delightful.

Sometimes safe seems the furthest from love.
We fall in love.
We are mad with passion.
We can be thrillingly obsessed.
We count the days, the hours, the minutes until we unite again.

The object of our affection can fill our minds and hearts and infuse our tissues. The whole world glows. How does everyone not see it? Romantic love has great press. It's so darn poetic. When we are in those moments of grand romance, we want to stay in that bubble-wrapped moment, safe and happy.

Love.

Love is not only kisses, stolen moments, and happy trills. Love is also for a friend, a child, a grandchild, a pet, a parent, a grandparent. Bliss. Love fills us with wonderment and compassion. Love wraps us deep in tenderness with another. We see the rich hue of their eyes, not the tubes in their body, as they endure illness. Love envelops us through the deepest anger and times of separateness. Love allows our wonderment to hold a space without judgment.

You long for your loved one to be near you, to play with you, to work with you through tough times. You want your loved one to stay. At one time before you ever met, you said, *Hello*. It is good to say hello. Too many marriages and friendships have been lost to the neglect of a current hello. Love is present. Love is fluid. The invitations to stay with each other can be fresh in each moment.

You hope their stay is joyfully warm. You do not want to hold people in a way that binds—not that kind of staying. You want them to play, savour all their feelings, and see the stars with you. When they are out of sight, you wonder about where they are and how they are doing. You wonder how they have been while they were away. If they are tired from doing too much, you offer rest. If they have been still and alone, you offer ways to pep them up. You attend to them easily because you love them.

You want them safe. Always, safe.

So it is with VeeVee. Your love for VeeVee inspires you to have her with you as often as you can. And when she is not on your stage, you can kindly wonder, not be judgy, about her whereabouts. Like your brain and heart, you are gifted with one precious, glowing VeeVee. VeeVee does not have a twin like your lungs or kidneys. Rare, precious, and essential, VeeVee is the only VeeVee you have. VeeVee is the sole performer of her multitasking feats. Far-reaching inside of you, she has a huge responsibility for your total health. VeeVee, social and engaging, also reaches outside of you, encountering people and events. These meetups affect VeeVee, an incredibly sensitive type, to her core. VeeVee deserves TLC. VeeVee will lap it up and stay.

A View From the Bowl

Kitty loved the milk. Her sandpaper tongue lapped it up as fast as Petunia Pig snorfled through the trough. Kitty drank so fast. Milk sprayed everywhere, coating her eyebrow feelers and dancing into her nose. The familiar smells of the barn calmed her tingles. Kitty paused from inhaling the milk and sat down. Her paw flicked the excess milk from her eyebrows. She stood and gave herself a shake. Dust from her fur flew up and caught in a rainbow shaft that came from the barn door opening.

Kitty turned her head towards the open door, hoping to see the source of this sunburst of colour. She saw two faces, those of a girl and an older woman. Kitty noticed how the rainbow came from behind the little girl, landing on her head and illuminating the girl's big green eyes. Kitty liked these eyes. They were just like her own mommy's.

Kitty took a little breath and stretched way out in the same sunbeam that caressed the little girl's head. Mmmm. Life is a bowl of milk, a cool floor, and a rainbow ray. Kitty's VeeVee and Kitty purred. The little girl with the big green eyes seemed a lovely addition to a purrfect moment. The barn and all its kitty-enhancing features made Kitty feel safe. Once safe, the feral kitten's nerves untangled, and she loved up that little girl as if she was a big bowl of milk.

Kitty's VeeVee was safe inside the tiny cat's skin.
Margie's VeeVee purred inside her little girl body.

In that sun-kissed week spent crouching at the open barn door, Grandma Irene showed Margie how to say hello to her own VeeVee. That week and the ones that followed showed Margie how to make her caring intentions sparkling clear to enjoy Double Delight.

CHAPTER 14

The Summer of Love: Margie's Purse

The cat and girl may not have truly understood each other, but they loved each other. The city girl was a bit loud for the kitten's liking, and she could get so wound up. Kitty did not see how alike the two of them were.

Rather than get snarly and paw-patting about it, the kitten remembered to go to the barn for a catnap when Margie was rambunctious. Kitty could snuggle nicely in the mare's stall. Those times were few and far between though because the kitten adored Margie.

Margie would stare at her and purr back, unlike their grabby first meeting. Margie would scratch Kitty behind her ears in just the right spots. Margie rubbed her belly and sang to her. Sometimes they both stretched out in the sunbeams on the porch, enjoying warm rainbows on their faces. And Margie was always up for a game of unwinding the wool. Grandma didn't seem to like this so much.

Sometimes Kitty just licked her paws and watched Margie with tender interest. Kitty wondered what it was like to run on two legs—not four—and how Margie's eyebrows didn't seem long enough to help her navigate distances in tight corners. Kitty was flabbergasted that Margie hated her own favourite thing in the whole wide world: milk. It didn't matter. Unlike the first day they met, their differences were just *different*.

On that fateful day on the porch, Kitty had been initially intrigued by Margie. But the more Margie held her and cuddled her, the more Kitty felt miffed. Kitty had wanted to like Margie, but Kitty was so hot and uncomfortable. Kitty went from snuggly to snarly. Kitty had to teach this girl a lesson, *Calm down there, Missy*. Now Kitty realized that she could never calm Margie. If Kitty stayed chill, she also noticed Margie did not seem to stay in wild-girl land as long. She licked her paw, stretched, and did a lot of noticing that delightful summer.

That summer, between playing and cuddling with her new best friend, Margie learned a ton of great things. She learned how Kitty loved the barn and loved to stretch and understood how holding her too tightly made Kitty too wiggly. Seeing Kitty in the barn that week helped her know that Kitty needed the barn. Kitty wasn't leaving Margie when she slipped into the barn to rest or explore. Kitty would always show up on the blue green summer days and swish around Margie's legs. She would crawl into Margie's lap and snore while Grandma read Margie a story. Kitty scratched on the tree as Margie swung in the big tire on the tree limb. Margie loved Kitty without the angsty urgency of their first meet-and-greet.

Grandma taught Margie about the horses, which ones were for riding and which ones were for plowing. Grandma showed her wildflowers that were fine to pick and weeds that were not. Grandma showed her how to take the green peas out of the pods and pop the peas at Kitty.

Margie loved these Grandma-and-Kitty-soaked days. She longed to hold these memories snug within her.

Grandma knew that soon Margie would go back to the city. She hoped she could help Margie remember the week-long barn vigil and how Margie could love herself, and kitties, and people, in a connected, not mixed-up way.

When Margie got mad because a butterfly flew away or sad that Kitty was down for a nap, Grandma looked kindly into her eyes and said in a sweet, clear tone, "Okay Margie, purse rehearsal time. When you rehearse your purse, you will own more and more of your Sparkle Power."

Grandma and Margie placed their hands on their hearts and breathed into their insides, imagining Sparkle. It's the sense they had when they watched clouds or heard tinkly bells or felt a breeze. "Breathe it in, Margie. Hold the Sparkle, whoosh it through you, and blow out the jangles."

They sparkled out the cobwebs of Stage Frights. Each of their Vee Vees came back to their nervous system stages.

Purse Rehearsal

Purse rehearsal became the evening ritual that helped them both.

These night time tales put a goodnight kiss on the end of each day. Just before bedtime, Margie received a nice hug from Grandpa and a tweak on her nose. Grandpa pretended he caught Margie's nose and put it in his pocket. Then he would take it out and place it in his palm and ask Margie if she would like it back.

Margie always said, "Yes, please."

Grandpa jiggled her nose back on after a few clowning gestures of putting it on sideways or upside down.

Grandma took this time for herself. She washed and sometimes curled her hair. She massaged the white cream in the blue jar on her face and elbows. As she did so, Grandma sang or hummed, filling the farmhouse with gladness.

Every second night Margie had a bath in the big tub. Kitty did not attend. Kitty, who seemed to spend more time in the house as the summer unfurled, curled up on Margie's bed each night. She'd stretch and lift her tiny bum into the air, roll over twice, and end with three circle turns before plopping into Margie's lap. Margie loved all of this. It never grew stale.

The first story night, Grandma picked up the purse Margie had brought with her. "Margie, this will do nicely." Although the girl's purse may not have been used during these weeks of climbing, petting ponies, shelling peas, and walking cow paths, it was perfect to embrace the summer of love lessons.

On Margie's purse was a gold clasp in the shape of a heart. It made a nice CLICK every time Margie opened and closed it. A beautiful lining in Margie's favourite colours graced its insides. Margie loved the look, feel, and scent of the gorgeous lining. Whenever she saw the swishy insides, she felt goose-bumpy good. Margie felt very grown up with her purse, though she was not quite sure how to use it.

Grandma had Margie look at her purse with the heart clasp and told her that this purse would remind Margie that she was Margie. No one else could ever be Margie, even if they had the same name. The first stories helped Margie remember the week when Margie and the kitten were frenemies. Grandma asked Margie how she thought Kitty and her became pals.

Margie said, "I put Kitty down and let her be in the barn. It was hard to stay at the barn door and wait."

"I remember, Margie, but you did wait, and look what happened." Grandma petted the kitty snoring in Margie's lap. "You made magic that day, Margie. You had Sparkle Power, and you owned it."

The two looked each other in the eyes. Grandma placed a finger on Margie's just right nose. "You breathed right into your heart as you sat down. You had to think to do it for just a pop of a moment."

"You mean like this?" Margie asked. With that, Margie snapped open the heart-shaped clasp and breathed into the gorgeous lining of her purse.

"Yes, Margie. Just like that. That moment is real, even if it seems like magic. As quick as it is to turn on your heel, bite your lip and think before you talk, or open your fabulous purse, you can make the next thing you do count. You can decide to do something different. It was different to sit and stay by the barn door, huh?"

The little girl nodded.

"Why did you do something different that day, Margie?"

"Grabbing Kitty didn't work. I felt better, too, when you fixed me up. You said we could both try something. I guess I wondered what could happen."

"You, my girl, have been wondering. That's a good thing. You know what happened when you stayed at the door? You felt your insides, and you felt such love for Kitty that you let Kitty take its time to drink the milk. Seems to me, Margie, you and Kitty each had your own spaces."

Margie touched the heart-shaped clasp on her own little purse and smiled, "And then, Grandma, we got together!"

"Yup Margie. You are a very smart girl indeed."

Grandma's Purse

Grandma brought out her purse too.

They rehearsed their purses a lot. Some nights, they both stood up and drew one leg behind them and breathed into their hearts.

One hand on a heart and one hand unclasping their separate purses, they looked at the Sparkle linings inside, inhaled, and giggled. Grandma and Margie placed their hands on their hearts and breathed into their insides, imagining Sparkle. Margie knew she had Sparkle Power when she looked at the sparkle lining in her purse.

Other nights, Grandma told tales about how to keep the Sparkle Power going. Depending on how the day had gone, some nights it was easier to see their Sparkle. If Grandpa had not put Margie's nose on exactly right, or if Kitty was frisky and not willing to sit in Margie's lap, parts of Margie were edgy. Her VeeVee said goodbye.

As the nights carried on, Grandma encouraged Margie to use her sparkly wonderment to explore her purse. Grandma gave Margie a gift. "Margie this is a good thing to put in your purse." She placed a compact mirror in Margie's hands. "Look at your face, Margie, when you get upset. Let me show you."

Grandma pulled a compact out of her own purse and made all the faces her own Hasty Happy could display:

She knitted her brows together and bared her teeth.
She feigned helplessness and played the victim.
She bobbed her head up and down and pretended to talk nonstop.
She put on her know-it-all face.
She put on her goofy face.
She made her head go from side to side saying, "Na na na, I can't hear you!"
She put on a gasping, scared face.
She even did a freeze face.

Margie tried them, too, and put in a few of her own.

"Margie, listen to me talk when my face does one of these." Grandma then sounded too angry or too confused or too sad or too scared.

"I don't talk my best from here, Margie. I always carry a compact to check my face and bring it back to this."

Grandma looked gently into Margie's eyes and smiled right from her heart. Margie cherished the compact and vowed to use it often.

One evening, they chatted about the Sparkle lining and how its immediate visibility boosted Sparkle Power. Grandma explained that if you stopped, opened the clasp, looked in your purse, and had trouble seeing the lining because it was covered up, your Sparkle Power would have far less oomph.

Margie opened her purse. Grandma noticed some stuff stuck in the lining. "Margie is that pink glob what I think it is?"

Margie looked down at the bedcover, "It's old gum, but it's not my old gum."

Grandma did not think that was a better alternative. Opening her own purse, and breathing through her heart as she recalled her own Sparkle, Grandma said, "Whose gum, Margie?"

"Rocco's."

"Rocco's, I see. Anything you want to tell me about Rocco's gum being in your purse?"

"He was chewing it, and he just stretched it way out of his mouth to show me and the teacher came. Rocco looked at me and he has green eyes and . . ."

"Margie, take a breath."

"And Rocco said, 'Here. Put this in your purse so I don't get in trouble,' and that's all there is to it."

"Honey, school was over awhile back, right?"

Margie nodded.

"What happens now when you see this gum in your lining? Anything?"

"I get sad or mad."

"Okay. . ."

"Sad, because I thought Rocco would think I did a nice thing and he'd ask me to play and everything, and he didn't even ask for it back."

"That does sound sad, honey. And the mad?"

"He makes me so mad. I carry his gum, and he plays with Janet."

"This all happened before the summer, right?"

"Uh-huh."

"You look like you are feeling it happen right now." She handed Margie her compact mirror. "Margie you just gotta get this old gum out of your purse. Unpacking old junk that no longer helps is a very good thing to do."

With tissue, and some manoeuvring, the offending old gum was removed. "Look Margie, more Sparkle, see?"

They unpacked a few more old things: the gum, a key to an old music box, a dog bone, and a crayon. Grandma placed them in a separate Yesterday's News box. Together, they said, "Thank you" for each item unpacked. Margie and she would chat about where each came from—whether it was scary, mad, or sad stuff—from home, school, friends, other people, accidents, or how boys or girls are supposed to be or not be. They talked about how it once helped Margie to put it in her purse. After that, some items were kissed goodbye and tossed away. With more room, Grandma helped Margie repack her purse with reminders of all the good things Margie, Kitty, Grandpa, and she had done that summer—pictures of pawprints and wildflowers, special little notes to remind her to Sparkle, and a few other things that boosted the Sparkle Power Margie felt when she opened her purse to herself.

Near the time Margie was to return to the city, Grandma put the purse on the nightstand and said, "Margie, isn't your purse beautiful?"

Margie bit her lip, "It is Grandma, but if I keep my purse closed to other people, do I close myself off from everybody else?"

"Oh Margie, no. With all your Sparkle Power that comes from taking care of your purse, you are so loving to everyone. You can check out that you are not too rude with your compact. Your rehearsal cues will fill up your insides with happiness. You can all love well—without Hasty Happy—when everyone has their own separate purses. They and you would get all tangled up otherwise."

Misplaced Basketballs

This made Grandma remember a time when she was Margie's age. Grandma had a childhood, too, as a girl named Irene.

She grew up on a farm before she married and raised her own family. Irene's history with wild kittens started back then. She was not always as calm as she was during Margie's summer of love. Irene's older brothers teased the curls right out of her hair. The boys pushed and prodded her with nudges and words. One day, Irene stomped her little feet and marched into the kitchen. "That Randy makes me so mad. I could throttle him!"

Irene's mom had just made herself a cup of tea, grateful for a moment. Devouring her cuppa, Mom looked at Irene, "Do you know what throttle means?"

"No, but I would. He said I can't play with him and Jess because I can't keep up. I run faster than both of them."

Mom tried to keep her smile inside. She had been at this old-fashioned rodeo before. *Men and their legs.* "Honey, it sounds to me like what they say about you is not true. Do you think running in the house or yelling back at them will make them believe you?"

Irene squirmed, "Noooo, I guess not. But it feels good."

"I will show you a little trick I use when someone is trying to get me going. Let's go outside."

The two went out back to the basketball net. "Irene, stand over there near the net. I want you to pretend you are just like this basketball net. You have a basket, and you have a backboard."

Irene stood very tall.

"Wonderful, you look just like the net. But unlike the net, you have Sparkle Power."

Irene grinned and stood up even taller.

"Even in the ickiest times, like when the boys tease you, no one can take away your Sparkle. You own it. It is part of you. You were born with it. You feel Sparkle easily when you play with your doll or make cookies. But even when the boys tease you, your Sparkle is still within you. You just forget. This Sparkle power helps you know when a basketball is coming at you that is not yours."

Irene looked puzzled.

Her mom said, "Irene, if Randy said two years ago to you that you weren't fast enough, would it be true?"

"Probably. I would still be mad though."

"Yes, but I bet your insides would kind of know there was some truth in it. I mean, two years ago I wouldn't let you play with the boys because you could get hurt. But now you feel icky on your insides because what Randy said is not true and it's not yours."

"Not mine?"

Irene's mom continued, "Honey, I wonder if a part of Randy feels bad because you are his younger sister and can run faster than he can. But instead of saying all that, he just threw his feeling at you. He threw it like a basketball."

Mom's note to self: Have a gentle talk with Randy too.

Irene felt the power in her legs and thought this might be possible. At the same time, Irene felt a tinge of ick for being better at running than her older brother. The emotions of happiness and guilt all mixed up in her. It sure was tricky being an athletic and kindhearted girl.

"You, as the basketball net, can own your Sparkle Power. If you are not feeling sparkly, it's a clue this basketball could be someone else's, not yours. Unlike this real net here, you can imagine the ball coming at you, and then move yourself so the basketball hits your backboard. The basketball lobs back to the person who threw it. The way you use a backboard is firm and gentle.

"To backboard a basketball that is not yours, you say, 'Randy you are upset. That's too bad. I'm not sure why. I am bigger now and can run faster than I used to. I really like playing with you and Jess.' He might still not want you to play, but I think he might hear you better. Maybe he will think about it for a next time. Irene, you don't have to take in his mad. Whatever it is, it is his, not yours. You can love Randy without taking in all his upset."

Grandma Irene told Margie this story about herself and her mother to show Margie the importance of separating other people's Hasty

Happy parts from her own. Margie, a quick study, said, "I guess you can't make someone look in their own purse, huh?"

"A great question, Margie. No. But if we think back to Kitty in the barn, you did something that helped as you waited at the barn door."

Margie thought. And shrugged her shoulders.

"Well Margie, you started waiting patiently, and you stopped something else."

"I stopped yelling?"

"Yes, and then?"

"I smiled and kind of meowed, and then we said *hello*."

The summer ended too soon for Margie. She said goodbye to Grandma's summer of love and went back to the city. Did she remember her own purse with the heart clasp, her Sparkle lining, her compact mirror, her notes of good things for her, and her Yesterday's News box?

CHAPTER 15

Margie Went Back to the City

You might be wondering how on earth did Margie the adult get taken in by Judge's big brown eyes on that fateful shopping day? She had all these life lessons from her Grandma Irene. Many of us never get such attention from a kind mentor. Even so, Margie let Judge's sadness engulf her, and Hasty Happy habits ensued.

As a grownup, Margie revisited the kitten story. She had a quick tinge of upset and regret with her present self. Why did she still launch into Hasty Happy? After all these years, she was still enticed by the delicious purse dump.

Why did she still get Too Bossy, Too Pleasing, Too Escaping, Too Helpful, Too Frosty, Too Helpless, or Too Iced Over?

Why did she still try to care for people when her stage was set at On Guard, totally void of VeeVee?

She knew better. She was a grown woman. Besides, Margie was comfy-cozy in her Hasty Happy habits. Margie would ignore her needs as she carried people, only to become overloaded and dump them. Then once she had ditched them all to focus on herself, her brain alit in pain as Tricky Guilt engulfed her. She opened her purse and carried people again until she got fed up.

She dumped them. Then she had Tricky Guilt. Then she carried again until she would dump. She was a pro at the Care-y Stress Cycle.

Margie Cycled

This habit gave her quick hits of dopamine happy and brief relief from the dACC rejection pain. People were rude, but they seemed to stick around—even if it was conditional on Margie caring for them as she'd always done. With all the busyness of carrying, dumping, gobs of Tricky Guilt, and then carrying again, Margie just plain forgot. So busy carrying everyone in her purse, Margie forgot to rehearse the new, shiny lessons.

She forgot to use her clasp. She forgot she had a clasp.

Life happens. Margie wondered why she forgot. She thought way back. Even before the summer of love, she thought she probably had plenty of Sticky Notes she didn't know about inside her little Margie self. Then Margie wondered about what happened to her younger self after the summer of love when she left the farm with all its delights and returned to the city.

Oh, she remembered all right. When six-year-old Margie returned home, she had more experiences and, of course, she made more Sticky Notes. After all, she had demands and messages based on school, gender, culture, and people that encouraged her to open her purse and carry other people's stuff. She also had a built-in bias to remember the icky stuff. Any negative, unhappy, or scary events automatically downloaded within her. And when she got fed up, she would dump out her purse.

Tricky Guilt, so practiced in her life, came to visit, and she popped her purse open to others once more. And when she got fed up, she would dump out her purse. Simply a habit.

Adult Margie recalled times growing up when she rode her bike to the library and how hard it was to change the path she loved to take. Margie knew younger Margie wanted to remember Grandma's purse rehearsals. She really did. But she also knew it was easy for her to slide back into a familiar routine.

After that summer, she went back to the city. Old habits die hard. Young Margie cycled on and on.

The Library

The summer of love for Margie was also the summer of change. Margie loved the weeks with her grandparents, and she stored all the memories within her. She forgot to rehearse what she learned because life was full. As if that was not enough, a big change was about to rock Margie's world. Summer days gave Margie a chance to escape to the library. It was a private journey Margie could take on her bicycle. Once she arrived at the white clapboard building, the familiar walls became loving arms that wrapped her close, breathing the promise of newfound adventures into her awaiting heart. The smells of the old wood and the bindings and the hushed but important sounds of the librarian helping others comforted Margie.

She needed no help as the books called to her. Possibilities sat on the shelves, awaiting the curiosity of her outstretched arm. No judgment or expectations here. Margie was present and in tune with her home away from home. It was a lovely routine, safe yet exciting at the same time. Her parents approved Margie's weekly adventure. They knew the library was a safe bike ride away. They knew Margie was a good girl.

What they did not know is that the trip to the library was almost as important to Margie as the books. Margie loved the comfort of filling her backpack with new stories for the upcoming week. Pictures, smells, and sounds infused her thirsty brain. Her nickname, *The Book Reader*, was fine and dandy with her. But on her blue bicycle ride to the library, Margie transformed from bookish to brazen. She felt her legs pump the pedals and the breeze toss her hair. Skittish in gym class and harbouring some bad experiences playing team sports, Margie found this solitary endeavour *titan*. The route for the most part was direct through nice, lazy suburban streets. The few stop signs were familiar red buddies.

One part of the route was more rugged and rather secretive. Early into her literary forays, Margie found an abandoned parcel of land that was a more direct route to the library. The shortcut was more fun than two major, boring roads. Like the cow paths at her grandparents' farm, this trail felt magical and secret. Deeply shaped ruts defined the field between the suburban homes. When it rained, engraved lines from other bicycles grew more entrenched, and when the colder nights came, the ruts froze that way.

She loved the challenge of fitting her blue bike into the well-worn paths. She loved the comfort of staying in the grooves. Sometimes it was very rocky, but when she stayed upright and prevailed, she had a surge of physical success. The magical part was that whenever she took this route, she never met anyone else, despite the obvious wear and tear created by others.

She felt special to be the only one and, oddly, a little scared that she may one day run into someone else, invading their path. Or there could be teasing teenagers, who might make fun of her, or worse be holding hands and—yuck. These possibilities made her feel sassy, something her family would never attribute to good old reliable Margie.

Margie became an adventurer, traversing the path of other explorers such as she. The odd comfort of this rocky abandoned lot paired with the emotional pizazz in crossing its tricky terrain. Margie's brain thought this pleasurable route was so nice that it would be best to make it automatic. Then Margie's brain could have more space to enjoy all the new stories she devoured each week.

Her brain loved pleasure.
Her brain also loved efficiency.
This bike path became the only way Margie could get to the library.
At least her brain thought so.
A habit hatched.

Eventually, this path was not good for Margie to choose. Margie biked on the well-worn ruts with the deep rivets, and her knapsack hit her in the head. There was wire and junk in the lot. Her tires went flat. She fell a few times and skinned her knees. Other things happened too. It took a heck of a long time and a lot of mishaps before she let herself take a more efficient route to the library.

Change was afoot.

They paved the nice suburban streets and added a new road. The abandoned lot was no longer a shortcut. Still, Margie took the defunct shortcut with the familiar bumpy ruts.

Because it gave her comfort.
Because it represented freedom.
Because it was her *secret* pathway.
Because the path in her brain had carved this path out as the most direct and only way to the library.

Repetition, routine, plus emotional reward encouraged Margie to continue with the habit past its usefulness. The original reason she started the routine made sense. Her brain recorded it as a solution, even though it was a little-girl solution that had limiting options. It didn't make sense now.

One day, barbed wire stretched across her lot. Margie, intrepid explorer, climbed over the offending barrier, lifting the bike and knapsack too. Trips to the library now required bandages.

After these arduous journeys, Margie was pooped. Her backpack felt so much heavier because she had walked and held up her bike to get through her shortcut. When she arrived at the library, Margie had a task to do. Best not let anyone get in her way. She no longer took time to inhale the book smell she so loved. She didn't let her fingers trail over the book spines that sat at attention in the shelves. She did not dilly. Nor did she dally.

Margie would grab a few books, even some she'd read before, and dump her week's worth of books quickly onto the librarian's desk. She didn't notice the librarian's attempt to catch Margie's eye. She didn't hear the kind lilt in the librarian's, "Well hello, Margie. How are we today?"

One Saturday, a piece of wire pierced Margie's bike tire. Margie was starting the long walk home just as her buddy Rosie was arriving. Her backpack felt even heavier when she walked. Margie was bedraggled. Rosie looked as fresh as a daisy. She even had some daisies poking out of her bicycle basket.

A fudge-coloured spot graced Rosie's overalls but Rosie didn't seem to care. "Hey ya, Margie. I just took a new road. It goes right by this great park. They gave out ice cream today. I got chocolate. I got these flowers for the librarian. There were a whole bunch of wild ones. Gosh Margie. What happened to your bike?"

Margie mumbled something like *nothing much* and returned home on her old route, but the possibility of this new road seemed a little sunnier that day. That night, Margie had trouble sleeping. She had scratches from the wire, little slices on her legs. The sheets hurt.

As exhausted as she was, her mind was on fire. Margie's brain never seemed to stop thinking. That made Margie's brain swell with the *what ifs* from her Sticky Notes. But good news! It allowed her to think outside of the box. Reviewing her day, Margie did not feel proud of her snippy ignorance to the librarian and to Rosie. As she tossed and turned alone in her bed, a longingness welled up inside Margie. She had loved going to bed at Grandma Irene's because they did the purse rehearsal every night.

When Margie had left to go back home, Grandma Irene kissed her goodbye, handed Margie her purse, and said, "I love you, Margie. Try to do the purse rehearsals at home. It's easy to forget. Not to worry, each time you pick it up, you will remember our time together. That feeling will help you remember. Spending time with your purse is important, Margie. You will learn to like it."

Margie also forgot the big thing that Grandma Irene told her the night before she came home to the city.

The big thing: "Margie, some people might say that you do not need to take time for your purse rehearsals. You might believe them."

Margie, who adored the purse rehearsals each night, could not fathom this big thing. Margie's eyes bulged out with, "How could this nice purse time at night hurt anybody?"

"People might say, 'Margie if you spend time on yourself, that's not nice. You are selfish. You are unkind.' People just get mixed up. People mean well usually, but they are just so busy and used to carrying on. When people say this, they just make a mistake. They think taking any time for you away from them is not okay. The mistake they make Margie, and this is important, is not the time you take for you. It is what you do with the time that counts. Each time you take time with your purse, you clear your purse so your Sparkle lining is easier to see. Sparkle fills you with kindness. You are kind to yourself as you clear and stop carrying old Sticky Notes you don't need now. Be kind to yourself, like finding things that make you feel sparkly and popping them in your purse. As you are kind to yourself, kindness bursts from you, and others receive the kindness you shine."

Margie thought about when she took time and breathed and felt calmy-good inside. She was kind to the kitten, and the kitten stayed by her side a lot all summer. Margie's connection with the kitten transformed. She saw the similarities and differences between her and the kitten without upset. She didn't force herself on Kitty. She got to know and adore Kitty. When she changed her hasty tries at grabbing kitty, albeit out of love, and used the kind wonderment Grandma taught, loving got easy.

Margie thought back to loving that biologically rude kitty. Then Margie dumped Kitty. Hmm. *That was biologically rude too.* Margie now thought about today's library misadventure. She noticed how her stubborn decision to keep taking the old path made her rude. She was not nice and fresh. She was so tired. Her joy was dimmed.

Kind? No.

Perhaps, pondered Margie, an easier, happier route to the library did exist. Rosie seemed to think so. She fell asleep dreaming of Kitty.

The Newly Paved Roads

A crisis urged Margie to ride the newly paved roads.

Finally, there was no other option because the lot was gone. New houses filled the once empty space. Margie continued to veer towards the old lot, which was no longer there. *Oh yeah, darn, forgot about it.* The ruts in the old lot were no longer there, but the ruts in her brain that remembered the familiar routes continued to exist.

Margie wondered about the new route. Though scared and hesitant, Margie also felt a twinge of excitement. Dopamine tingled in her. Thinking about giving the librarian some daisies amped up her cuddly oxytocin. Maybe this new route could bring some fun.

Her bike hit the new road. Eventually, in the orange sky of autumn, the new route felt easier. Margie travelled to her library faster and in less pain and turmoil. She wondered why she had loved that dirty old lot for so long. Margie enjoyed her legs pumping, the breeze, and the smoothness of the fresh pavement. She flew on this new road. She inhaled the fall air. She discovered a new park with a shiny new fountain, perfect for Margie's parched lips. *This never happened on the old road.* The ease of the new route made her smile.

Emotional reward returned in technicolour. It became a lovely new routine. A new habit hatched. As Margie imagined the new path and then braved the new road, feelings came up.

Regrets

Regrets. She had a few.

The *I wishes* arose in Margie.
I wish I had stopped this old path.
I wish I had started the new road.
I wish I hadn't been rude to Rosie.
I wish I didn't climb the barbed wire and hurt myself.

The *if onlys* arose in Margie.
If only I went on the new road sooner.
If only I wasn't so stubborn.
If only I was kinder to Rosie and the librarian.
If only I was braver and quicker to change, sigh, like Rosie.

The *what ifs* arose in Margie.
What if I had taken the new road right away?
What if I had saved myself all these uh-ohs?
What if I had gone for ice cream?
What if I had been kinder?

All these were sprinkled with the finishing layer of *I shoulds*.
I should have known better.
I should have been smarter.
I should have been braver.
I should have been kinder.

As the *wishes*, *ifs*, and *should haves* arose, a dull ache licked at her. Little shadows gathered inside Margie. Her Sparkle lining, though there, seemed a million miles away. Tricky Guilt trickled throughout her. This pain was real.

The Winds of Change

Change itself, breaking an old habit that comforts you, will hurt. Wishing you had made the change sooner will hurt you too. But as Margie knew as she licked her ice cream cone one day, as she peddled easily, as she smiled breezily, *delight* happens in the here and now.

Margie reached a crisis—no lot left—until she changed. It would have been better for her to change earlier, sure.

Even if there is good reason to change a habit and start a new one, knowledge is not always enough. We often wait until crisis moments wake us up to exchange old habits for new. Creating a new path was more for Margie than just knowing it was faster and easier.

Any new path has to offer us something that's worth the pain of letting go of the old tried-and-true route. That old way, like Margie's old lot, assures a dopamine hit that soothes in the moment. For Margie, the old path was painful after a while. She felt weary, and it showed in herself and how she treated others. She thought about the possibility that Rosie advertised. Margie pondered all this.

She knew the two things she had to do: Say goodbye to say hello. Then, she could open her purse to herself.

The Good Goodbye

Before she could say hello to the new perfectly paved path, she stopped for one last look at the old lot. Margie appreciated all the joy the old lot had given her. She appreciated what she would miss.

Margie also appreciated—Margie. Margie bit her lip, took a deep breath in, and recalled what bravery it took for her to hang in with the old lot. Perhaps a celebration was in order.

Margie put her bike down outside the barbed wire, ignoring the flashy, New Homes signs.

- She stood and thought about the first day she found this shortcut.
- She smiled as she recalled how sunny that day was and how the shadows fell on the bike path. She laughed at the times she stayed upright and the times she fell.

- She recalled that despite whatever happened as she rode the familiar but rocky path, she would come out on the other side and see the library.

- Feelings of exuberance and accomplishment filled her up.

She bent down and put a marker where the path in the lot would have started on the other side of the barbed wire fence. Probably nobody saw the little paper bookmark amid the bulldozers and dust. She knew it was there. Margie thanked the old lot that gave her such pleasure. Then she recalled something from the summer of love.

The Night Before Margie Learned to Say Hello

Grandma didn't rush out to the barn the same day that Margie had tried to cuddle the kitten on the porch. First, she had to get Margie ready to say hello. She made space for her own love of her grandchild that night. She tenderly looked at Margie's *lion-taming* scratches and rebandaged them. She fed Margie her favourite meal. She washed Margie's hair in the farm kitchen sink and got her excited and ready for the day to come. At nightfall, she tucked the sweet girl in with a cherished stuffed toy and a story that helped Margie drift off to sleep.

Grandma loved up Margie's insides too. Grandma told the little girl how brave Margie was to try to be with a wild Kitty. She extolled Margie's virtues of the day and celebrated the exuberance and earnestness of Margie's kind heart. She applauded Margie's attempts without scolding or shaming her, "Margie, kittens are like little lions. They fear everything until they get used to the world. That was awesome and brave to jump in with all that love. There are ways that kittens and big-hearted girls can really have fun together. I can give you some tips."

Grandma winked, kissed Margie on her rosy cheek, and whispered, "Tomorrow the adventure begins."

Margie's caring intentions were wonderful, even if the urgent way she acted upon them may have scared an already skittish kitten. Margie deserved appreciation for what she had done so well.

After taking this long trip down memory lane, adult Margie realized it's really hard to remember purse rehearsals no matter how old you are. She also knew that she deserved appreciations for what she had done well in her life so far too.

And so do you.

Your Purseonal Celebration

Your purseonal celebration begins with a good goodbye too.

Before you consider rehearsing your own purse, could you appreciate your caring intentions even if they did emanate from your On Guard stage? How marvellous that you kept trying to connect with others even when they were, or you were, not your best sparkling self. That takes true guts.

How could you not do the Care-y Mix-Ups?

You may be berating yourself by thinking you should have known better:

- You just learned that you operate with VeeVee either on your stage or in the wings.
- You just learned that when VeeVee is on your stage, you are set at Safe to Sparkle and your Sparkle can be revealed.
- You just learned that when VeeVee gets Stage Fright, you are set to be On Guard.

You cannot act on what you do not know. Your caring intent, like Margie's, is pure. Take a moment before anything else. Please cherish the caring you that reaches out, waves the flag, flings her arm across the person in the passenger seat, kisses boo-boos, jumps in where no one else would dare, and so many other awesome loving things.

We have never questioned the loveliness of your caring intention.

It could seem like we are telling you to drop all the Care-y Stress you have carried and try a fast fix that was here all along.

Perhaps that is how little Margie first felt when her grandma told her to stop, come inside, and wait until tomorrow. Margie so wanted to keep on trying because she loved that kitten so much, until it scratched her and she flung it, and then she felt terrible. Grandma Irene saw when the terribles overtook her little granddaughter. Her tiny being could not feel the Sparkle-lit beauty within. When Margie felt that true Sparkle—and not the terribles—the kind love safely shone from her insides. Just what a Kitty would like.

Your Sparkle-Lit Beauty

Sparkle-lit beauty resides within you and hides within you.

Your nervous system naturally responds to the Stage Fright you experience when people are in a Hasty Happy habit. It happens. You are not bad, weak, or unenlightened. You are human. Like Margie, the Sparkle lining in your own purse is always there. Yet you forget. Sparkle seems to hide in plain sight. Sparkle, even thinking about your Sparkle, can frighten a part or parts of you into a full blown Hasty Happy habit, especially if you don't even believe Sparkle is possible for you.

Margie's brain was not a clear slate. Her brain had already created well-worn pathways. Margie was used to picking up kittens and puppies as if they were toys. It was a well-rehearsed habit. Then as Margie grew into adulthood, her brain continued to create new neural pathways from all her experiences and inevitable Sticky Notes. Margie's brain was neuroplastic. Margie's brain kept learning and growing good stuff, and it had the old ruts of Hasty Happy habits. Grandma's new ideas were embraced willingly by Margie during Sparkle time. Margie would need to rehearse them so they became a comfortable pathway to use often.

What if you first took a moment like Margie —who said goodbye to the familiar path with grace and gratitude—to thank your life purse? Appreciate all the times you opened it and all the times you dumped it all out with a Hasty Happy habit.

What the heck? Thank that old bag?

Yes.

We know this is a bit of a conundrum. Before saying hello to your own purse, the best way through this puzzle is to respect the old ruts your life purse has gotten into, graciously letting them go by thanking them for a job well done. Then you can rehearse the new routes you would like your brain to take, weakening the old paths and strengthening the new paths.

Margie changed her route to the library not only because the old lot vanished but because she saw the promise of something better. This got her thinking about the purse from the summer of love. If she used it like Grandma had suggested, her caring for others might be a lot more fun. When she used her Sparkle Power with people, it was wonderful too. This hope inspired Margie to find her VeeVee with the same kind wonderment. In her heart of hearts, Margie knew.

We bet you know too. Margie, you, and us—we've been using the wrong manual for years.

The Wrong User Manual

Ditch me. Delight them.

It could never work. As long as you ditch yourself, VeeVee stays off your stage, and you are automatically abrupt to save your butt. You must be rude. You insult and hurt people. With VeeVee offstage, not only are you socially gonzo, your VeeVee cannot help other VeeVees learn how to act safely. VeeVees teach each other the art of warm smiles, soft eyes, safe voice tones, and good listening.

No VeeVee? SpeeDee and Deedee are left alone to run your stage. Their expertise is crisis management. Your energy flow gets kinked. Your energy is rerouted to saving you, not maintaining you. Your regular health will always be detoured. Your body will be in emergency mode, running too high or too low.

The irony of it all. The very thing the user manual taught you all this time was the exact opposite of what would give delight to you and others. *It is selfish not to take care of you. It is unselfish to take care of you.*

It is selfish not to take care of you. It is unselfish to take care of you.

A Gut-Wrenching Opportunity

Change is a gut-wrenching probability. Change is also a promise of opportunity.

It is true that people are used to the way you were before. They can try hard to get you to be like you used to be. It's comfy-cozy for them, even if they want you to change. You also weirdly got comfy-cozy in ditching your delight. It does protect parts of you. Change can sometimes be painful even though it will be way better for you and the people you love. Like Margie, you might have your own *I wish, only if, what ifs,* and *should haves.*

You maybe wonder if it is even possible to make changes:

- *Is this something others can do, but not me?*
- *What if I don't have the energy it takes to change?*
- *Is everything I did before worthless?*
- *What if I deserve to feel guilty because of mistakes I made?*
- *Have I screwed up so much that I can't fix it?*
- *Will people get upset and want me to be like I was before?*
- *What if it's too much to face my Sticky Notes?*

You might feel hopelessly tired. The news, though, is grim if you stay in the cycle. In Hasty Happy habits, you grab a quick fix, ignoring others' feelings.

You are biologically rude.
You feel guilt.
You ditch your delight.
Your Sparkle dims.

Unkind to yourself? Stage Fright. VeeVee leaves.

Unkind people or no people? VeeVee vamooses, and your VeeVee dwindles without other safe VeeVee companions to encourage you.

Someone's going to get really hurt. And that someone is not just you.

Good News

The good news is there is hope for something more: **Double Delight.**

Double Delight is possible for you when you set your stage at Safe to Sparkle. It begins with kind wondering for you and the people you love. Margie knew too. If she continued to review the *I wish, only if, what ifs,* and *should haves,* Margie's energies would be locked in the past. She could scare her VeeVee with the Sticky Notes such ruminating would bring up.

Margie decided the delight of loving both herself and others was the promise that made sense. If she took care of her purse the way Grandma taught her, she could connect heart-to-heart with people she loved, like she did with the kitten. Carrying the kitty had been a scratchy mess.

Margie replaced her Hasty Happy with kind wonderment. As she focused on cherishing her Vee Vee, Vee Vee stayed. It allowed her to kindly wonder about both herself and the people she loved. She reduced the Stage Fight she gave herself, and her relationships with others shone. Cherishing her Vee Vee in the here and now was the kindest action she could ever do, both to the delight of herself and others.

Margie decided to rehearse her own new purse.

CHAPTER 16

Sparkle Power: Design Your Own New Purse

As we were completing this book, we often thought of Queen Elizabeth the Second and her commitment to her own purse. In a limo or a carriage, at a state event, and even in her own living room conferring honours or shaking hands, her signature purse dangled from her arm.

During her Platinum Jubilee, the Queen invited a famous bear for tea. A bit clumsy with tea etiquette but so sincere, the little bear chatted easily to Her Majesty, extolling her with tales of his everyday adventures. With her familiar warmth and charm that would put any guest at ease, the Queen opened the clasp on her purse. She revealed to Paddington Bear the marmalade sandwich she kept privately within the confines of her own handbag. As did her cherished guest, she carried a sandwich for *just in case*.

The monarch showed little girls and big girls everywhere that their purses were private, personal treasure chests, available only to each owner. A marmalade sandwich could perk up the purse owner in between her many events. During tea at Buckingham Palace, exchanging pleasantries with an imaginary bear, Queen Elizabeth revealed the duty we all have.

It is each of our duty to keep our purses full of what sustains us. In that way, we are energetically on our game, for us and the people in our world.

It is our duty to keep our purses full of what sustains us.

Grandma Irene knew it. When her stage was set at Safe to Sparkle—not On Guard—delightful safety billowed within her; delightful safe energy wafted outside her. To keep her stage at Safe to Sparkle, Grandma needed her VeeVee on stage as often as possible. VeeVee inspired and sustained Grandma. VeeVee needed Grandma's love. It was Grandma's duty to care for her own VeeVee.

Grandma, though not a neuroscientist by trade, was practical as salt. Her VeeVee needed security. Grandma's own purse could oblige. Her purse reminded her to set her stage at Safe to Sparkle as often as possible. That's why Grandma taught Margie how to create her own purse before Margie returned to the city.

Where do you keep your valuables? Your Purse.

Your actual purse is great when it holds delight. You put things in it to make you happy, to make life easier, to ease or repair the what ifs, or to be on the ever ready—so you feel delight. Having chosen the items in your purse—a picture on a key ring, your favourite lip gloss—gives you delight. In your actual purse, you pack for what you know you need. You carry your identity, keys, and a phone.

Depending on your preferences, you customize. One woman's lip gloss is another woman's hand cream. In your actual purse you pack for what you think you might need. You pack tissues, bandages, allergy pills, a sewing kit, an energy bar—a thong? You never know. An ounce of prevention is a pound of cure. If you forget your purse, you run back, you grab it—you keep that purse close. It's your portable safety.

Your Own Life Purse

Your new purse can be safe enough to protect VeeVee, portable enough to accompany VeeVee, and accessible only to you. You won't want to leave home without it. Nothing is more valuable than your VeeVee nerve with her face-heart path that connects all your important insides, modulates SpeeDee and DeeDee, and connects to people with kindness. As if this was not enough, she is your ever-ready sentinel looking out for danger. Always.

VeeVee is a valuable gem to be sure. Your life purse has room for VeeVee with all the great things that keep her safe. All it takes is kind wonderment. You don't need a barn and a bowl of milk. With the right purse—your own—VeeVee will want to stay on your stage as often as she can, like a purring kitty.

As Grandma reminded Margie, it's what you do with the time, not the time that is important. Grandma's barn lessons and purse creations may seem like a fairy tale, yet science supports Grandma's summer of love. A safe nervous system is good for you. A safe nervous system inspires other nervous systems to seek their own safeties. With your own purse, you can Sparkle with love without people taking up acreage in your purse.

You can't safekeep other people's VeeVees, but you can safekeep yours. By taking care of your own life purse, VeeVee can accurately alert you to true danger. You can rely on your purse to connect with those you love without carrying their stress. When you do that, you have the potential for delight for you and delight for others simply because you reduce the possibility of Hasty Happy habits.

Cherish VeeVee

Your life purse has one passion. Cherish VeeVee to keep her on your stage as often as you can. Your purse will be full of sparkling delight.

It is the most unselfish thing you can do.

The summer of love lessons were about one thing and one thing only: cherishing VeeVee often and in the wonderment of Sparkle. Like Margie and the Kitty, by cherishing VeeVee, you cement a beautiful friendship between you and your VeeVee.

Feline fear thrust Kitty into hijinks. Stage Fright makes VeeVee go to the wings, sending you into Hasty Happy habits. Kitty was not a cool cat to hang with in her caterwauling angst. In your Hasty Happy, you, too, cannot feel the Sparkle.

Grandma transformed Kitty's fears into bliss with a simple hello. A tender hello says, *I see you. I hear you. I would like to know more about you. Please stay.* From Grandma's stage set at Safe to Sparkle, she reminded Kitty of Kitty's Sparkle. Grandma spoke kindly and softly as she made space for the kitty in the barn. Grandma purposely placed things in the barn that a kitten would love, such as cream, kind wonderment, and a little girl's open, now patient heart. In one catnap of a moment, Kitty paused and sensed a whiff of safe. Skittish jangles were calmed within her. Kitty stayed.

Sometimes, Margie's VeeVee was just as skittish as that kitten. In their purse rehearsal evenings, Grandma taught Margie how to cherish her VeeVee. Cherishing VeeVee reminded Margie of all the Sparkle within her and how she could choose to own her Sparkle Power.

Just like Margie and Grandma, you can design your new purse. Grandma packaged these life lessons into Margie's purse. Margie's purse, which she toted everywhere, could now make setting her stage at Safe to Sparkle easy to remember.

Let's create.

Design Your Imaginary Purse

Your purse, with its unique flair, illustrates your Energy Border. It reminds you that your energy is distinct from others. You can be connected and not mix with others' energies.

It can be patent or vegan leather, denim, or tapestry, large or small, a handbag or shoulder bag, knapsack, or clutch. Bright in colour or earth-toned, you decide. Enjoy designing. What matters is that this purse speaks to you of safety and comfort. You feel good, knowing this purse will make a home for VeeVee and her sisters.

Your clasp illustrates your choice to own your Sparkle Power, to give and receive your heart-chosen love. Your clasp can be in the shape of a heart as ours is. If a heart-shaped clasp does not speak to you, design a clasp that represents how you experience your heart-filled Sparkle Power—a flower, a butterfly, a gem. Whatever you choose is just right.

Your purse lining illustrates your brilliant Sparkle core. Your resilient and loving Sparkle—your birthright essence of wise compassion—is always part of your design and will never leave you. Again, allow your creativity here. Is it cotton or velvet, pastel or jewelled-hued, deep and rich in tone or neon bright? Any lining you create is right. This lining is your unique lovely design: a colour, a scent, a feel that calms you and energizes you.

Two Purse Items

Now imagine two permanent items in your own purse: a compact mirror and a cell phone.

Your compact mirror. Imagine your compact flips open. You can see how you look to others. Your compact mirror is your immediate access to the state of your Purse Sisters team. You can also use it to look behind you and notice which Purse Sisters are on your stage in any moment or what Sticky Note made VeeVee flee to the wings. This handy mirror will also help you unpack the Sticky Notes that may have given VeeVee Stage Fright.

Design your imaginary mirror in any way you would like: plastic, pearl, glittery, wood, leather, heavy silver, or light as a feather. Bedecked and bejewelled or clean of line, this mirror reflects beautiful you. However you imagine it is perfect.

Your cell phone. It could be the one you own now. Perhaps it's the one of your dreams. Choose the colour, size, and keyboard you like best. Keep your phone safe in your purse and choose how and when to use it. You can choose to use your cell phone to create a voice memo or written note to help you connect to yourself and all your energies with care and delight.

But the most wonderful part about using your cell phone? You have choice over your calls. You choose to use your cell phone to connect with others from the clasp on your purse. You can stop carrying others and their stuff *inside* your purse. You decide if you can Sparkle enough to have a conversation with kind wonderment.

Outside Your Purse

Keep your Yesterday's News box in a place outside your life purse. Imaginary or real, this unique container is a holding place for your private Sticky Notes. Some you may know well and some you might just be getting to know. Choose your box with tender care. It can be tin, cardboard, wooden, glass, porcelain, leather, or woven fabric. Round, square, or rectangular. Deep or shallow. It can be multi-coloured or plain in hue, wild or mild. Choose colours, textures, and a shape that make you feel good.

You have braved so much in the creation of your Sticky Notes. The Yesterday's News box is to celebrate your strength. It should feel inviting for you to open. Some people have real boxes in which to put their Sticky Notes. You can place the box on your nightstand and put in any Sticky Notes that could interrupt your sleep. Do what feels right for you. Brava.

You now have your imaginary purse with a clasp. It opens. It closes. You have a purse with a Sparkle lining, a compact mirror, and a cell phone inside and a Yesterday's News box outside to hold your Sticky Notes. You have all you need for VeeVee to sense safety using her neuroception so she can hang out on stage with SpeeDee and Deedee. Placing these items in your life purse with fresh thought and kind intention will help prevent or repair the Energy Kinks that happen as life unfurls.

Your new and different purse has special care instructions.

Purse Care Instructions

Congratulations on the purchase of your new and different purse!

This purse is opened by you, for you. If other people's stuff is popped into this new and different purse, it will become *an old and not different purse*, and delight for you and those in your world will be at risk.

If you follow these guidelines and open your purse just to yourself, you will no longer carry other people's stuff in your purse.

Nothing to dump out.
Case closed.
Literally.

You don't want to void the warranty on your new purse. As soon as you allow anyone else and their stuff into your purse, your old purse routine returns with a vengeance. The Care-y Stress purse cycle appears. You open, stuff that purse, dump that purse, have a Tricky Guilt invasion, and then re-open your purse to stuff it with everybody's stuff all over again.

The Care-y Stress Cycle probably won't stop immediately. As you rehearse using your new and different purse, it won't be comfy at first. Owning your Sparkle Power and enjoying VeeVee on your stage more often will feel unusual.

Carrying less stress and owning her Sparkle Power challenged Grandma too. Sparkle, though within her, could be hard to find because of all the familiar Hasty Happy habits Grandma's parts repeated. Her nervous system stage even reset to an edgy baseline because of life's numerous challenges and Energy Kinks. Sometimes having her own purse didn't feel natural. Like Margie's bike ride in the old lot, Grandma's Hasty Happies felt comfortable.

You, like all caring women, feel the routine in your bones. The opening and stuffing of your purse is familiar.

But your new purse and its promise to care for you as you care for others can become the new habit you adore. This allows you to stop the well-meaning but exhausting Care-y Stress Cycle. Your new life purse—clasp closed and full of possibilities that support you—accompanies you everywhere. You take it with you wherever you go and lead the way at work and at home with a warm and engaging élan.

With this purse, you can transform your Energy Kinks and emanate your Sparkle. Your four energies can flow. You have Sparkle Power, the magic you create when you believe in your Sparkle.

In contrast to the Care-y Stress Cycle of open, stuff, dump, and repeat, try instead the Reignite Sparkle Solution.

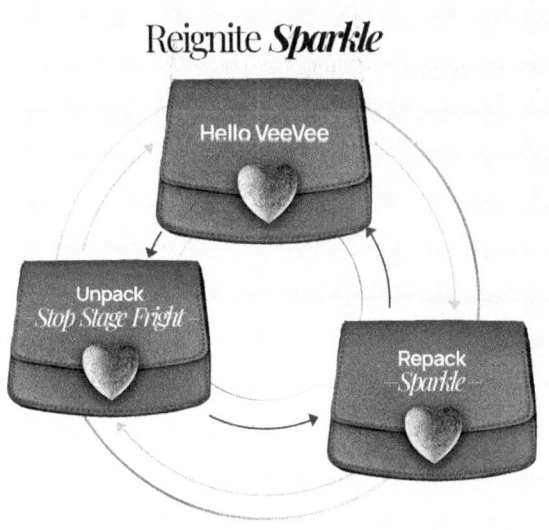

Reignite *Sparkle*

Your one and only life purse, unique as a snowflake, always awaits you. Kindly respect your life purse. Don't grab, shake, or dump it. The cool thing about your own purse is you don't have to care for it in some rigid order. It's just an everyday, regular sort of thing.

Housing your three sisters in your imaginary purse keeps you in charge of your nervous system. VeeVee, the only sister who comes and goes, is the wild card. In some ways, that makes it easier. Just focus primarily on this one sister's whereabouts. Her safety is key. When you say *Hello VeeVee*, Unpack, and Repack anytime and always, your kind wonderment delights her. VeeVee wants to stay and delight you too.

It is different with a new life purse. Your purse will be full of sparkling delight of your own creation—just for you.

Admire the imaginary purse you just made.
Respect it.
Touch it.
Linger over it.

And now, get ready to say *Hello VeeVee*.

CHAPTER 17

Reignite Sparkle: Hello VeeVee

Saying hello is so important. Your VeeVee, scouting for danger and safety all the time, is a hoofer just like the nervous kitty. Assume VeeVee might be offstage, so it's always wonderful to say hello. VeeVee hops off your stage at the smallest sign of Stage Fright. It does not take much: an unexpected phone call, a review of a bank statement, someone's raised eyebrows or sigh—she's off. Given her continual agility, saying *Hello VeeVee* is always your basic go-to.

The warmth of Grandma's tone, gentleness in her eyes, and listening in her ears cast the spell for Kitty, Margie, and her own VeeVee. Saying hello to VeeVee with kind wonderment is your Sparkle Power too. The way you speak to both VeeVee and to all your parts needs to be with kind wonderment. It is clear. It is in the here and now.

The tone and inflection in your voice makes all the difference to VeeVee. She is programmed to know a predator voice, a high pitch, a growl. Loudness scares her. Her neuroception under your face knows the looks that could kill—the flares, the stares—and the looks that neglect. She needs warm eye contact, or she feels alone. She also sees body motions that show openness and welcome. Also, a true hello to someone else happens now, in each moment, not bathed in the Stage Fright of past encounters or trepidation about what will be said.

Stay here. Kindly wonder. VeeVee will purr.

A good hello, genuine and present, inspires VeeVee to stay with or return to your stage and care for those you love with Double Delight. This is something you simply cannot do when you carry people and their stress. As VeeVee stays on your stage, you find kindness within you, delighting your inside energies. This kindness glows to people. You connect with others, VeeVee-to-VeeVee, heart-to-heart.

How to Say Hello

1. Keep your own purse and clasp closed and say:

    I choose to own my Sparkle Power. I will connect, not carry stress.

2. Your Sparkle Lining

    Imagine opening your purse only to yourself. Breathe in your Sparkle lining.

3. Your Compact Mirror

    Flip open your compact mirror and wonder, *Where are ya, VeeVee?* Then ask yourself the following questions:

    a) Am I in a Hasty Happy? Yes or No? If No, then proceed to #4. If Yes, say, *Thank you part of me that is protecting me with this Hasty Happy.* Then ask:

    b) Who is running my stage, SpeeDee or DeeDee? *Thank You SpeeDee. Thank you DeeDee.* Then ask:

    c) Are there any Sticky Notes of how I once had an Energy Kink? If No, it's okay not to know— simply proceed to #4. If Yes, jot down some basic info—current date, time, and a one liner about your Sticky Note, then:

    d) Place the Sticky Note in your Yesterday's News box and say, *Thank you, part of me, for using this Sticky Note to protect me.*

4. Say, *Hello VeeVee.*

Each step of saying Hello VeeVee helps you own your Sparkle Power. Let's see each step in more detail so you get the meaning behind the magic.

Step 1: Your Purse Clasp

Imagine your purse with its clasp closed.

It all begins with *the clasp on your purse closed* before you open it up and look inside. This love moving through your heart needs the clasp on your purse; it helps stop the Care-y Mix-Ups so you can focus on your own VeeVee. With your clasp closed, you can truly connect with others using your Sparkle Power.

Your clasp provides an entryway through your heart intuition. Connecting to others through this path makes your love clearer and shinier and keeps you from smooshing your energy with others.

Only your loved ones can know their VeeVees and their own unique sense of safety. They have different needs and wants, separate from you. All you can do is respect when they say no to something you ask for. Be clear with them about what you agree or not agree to do. Offer support or care as they choose their own answers. The clasp on your purse respects and celebrates the separate purse each of your loved ones own.

It is loving to keep your purse closed. As soon as you let people and their stuff into your purse, a Hasty Happy will ensue. Carrying, though well-intentioned, might make you think you have power over other people's VeeVees. You don't.

The clasp also separates your VeeVee from others' Hasty Happy habits. You choose to love from your heart clasp, not from your Hasty Happy. You choose to love with your whole and separate self, maximizing the delight you offer. You choose not to mix up your lovingness. After all, Grandma Irene knew the rule. Never go into somebody else's purse. And do not let them go into yours.

Keeping your purse clasp firmly in place with others and opening your purse to yourself shows people that you believe they have their own clasp too. You have your own purse, and it is delightful. Imagine the clasp on your purse and say: *I choose to own my Sparkle Power. I will connect, not carry stress.*

I will connect, not carry stress.

When Grandma Irene in that mini-mighty moment kept her purse clasp firmly in place with others and open to herself, she called on her brain to make a heartfelt choice. Her heart and prefrontal cortex brain (PFC) made beautiful music together. Her PFC sorted and integrated the juicy info of her four Energies into a clear flow. Grandma's PFC coordinated her from left to right, from up and down. A skilled conductor, her PFC directed her left analytical and right creative brain parts. It directed her top thought processes with her lower body-based survival into harmony (Anderson 2021, 30–31).

Grandma's PFC helped her choose her Energy Border—who to care for in each moment by noticing her own needs and being kind to herself and noticing others' needs and being kind to them.

She chose:

- What words and actions to impart by listening and kindly respecting her own needs and wants as she said yes or no to their requests and respecting others as they said yes or no to her requests

- How to speak and act in ways that were connecting not over-powering

- The place and time her caring intentions would be expressed clearly

Sparkle Power

Grandma Irene was able to care for Margie and Kitty and care for herself at the same time. It helped her tune in to and make sense of Margie's feelings while making sense of her own self and her Sticky Notes. When Grandma chose to open her own purse to herself, she owned Sparkle Power. Grandma performed magic and didn't even need a wand. It was a trick, but a necessary one. Her VeeVee may even have said goodbye, but owning her Sparkle Power let her mimic a stage set to Sparkle. VeeVee felt safe to return.

Presto! Sparkle Power! Grandma borrowed the Sparkle feeling even when her stage was set to On Guard.

Grandma owned her Sparkle Power. So can you.

Step 2: Your Sparkle Lining

Imagine opening the clasp on your life purse just to yourself.

The moment you open the clasp on your purse just to yourself is the moment you consult your heart, the moment you make for nervous system delight. VeeVee and her Purse Sisters meet at your heart, the place that all the info from your insides percolates. VeeVee gives your heart constant and immediate info about what is safe for you (to what you can say yes) and what is unsafe for you (to what you can say no). In a small but mighty quarter-second moment, this butterfly wink of time makes all the difference.

You can give yourself this quiet time, this undivided attention. Quiet contemplation is a gift to yourself and the people you love. This privacy between you and your heart before meeting the roar of the crowd transforms your stage and your connections with those you love.

Check in with your heart by putting your breathing on manual mode. Inhale slowly and deeply until VeeVee is Safe to Sparkle. Calmly directing your breath in and out will slow your heart rhythm. Your brain and heart love to match rhythms. Your alpha brain waves make it easier for positive thoughts to be created, stick around, and make you happy (Baker 2003, 103).

Imagine your unique sparkle lining.

Even if you are in a Hasty Happy, picturing your Sparkle lining warms your hello to VeeVee.

Put your breathing on manual mode. Imagine breathing slowly and deeply through your heart area. Exhale for longer than you inhale. For example, in for four counts and out for eight. Breathe in gratitude and appreciation for the Sparkle that is always with you, lining your very insides. Breathe out all the Hasty Happies.

We all can create Sparkle Power magic when we *choose* to pause, breathe into our hearts, and rest in the Sparkle within us.

Now, you will emit from your heart clasp the glorious love you have to give.

The Magic Behind the Magic

As Grandma basked in her Sparkle lining, she created that energetic calm needed to make her eventual hello to VeeVee safe and inviting. She recalled her Sparkle lining that infused her, calmed her, energized her. In Sparkle, an appreciative and calm energy enveloped Grandma.

Poof! Stage Fright vanished. Why? Stage Fright and Sparkle cannot coexist.

Grandma was wired to experience one or the other, not both. You can pause like Grandma did, for the short time it takes a butterfly to flick its silky wings or a bee to drink nectar from a bud, basking in your ever-present Sparkle even when it is hard to believe Sparkle is there. Whether VeeVee had gone to the wings of your stage or is on the cusp of doing so, the Sparkle sense of self creates a genuine hello that VeeVee's neuroception senses as safe.

Step 3: Your Compact Mirror

As you bask in your purse's Sparkle lining, relax your jaw and take out your compact mirror. The compact mirror in your physical purse is used for touch-ups. As the day or evening unfolds, life events will mess with your makeup. It's a given. You bite your lip. Your lipstick needs a reapplication. A windy day? Your mascara runs; your hair blows. Your compact mirror lets you know if you need a tissue, a brush, or hairspray. Your ever-ready compact mirror lets you assess and redress.

Before Grandma Irene taught little Margie about the barn kitten, she was curious about a part of herself, who must have had some Stage Fright in that grandparenting moment. She then smiled to herself and, using her compact, imagined asking, *Where are ya, VeeVee?*

That's a great place for us all to start.

Begin by flipping open your compact mirror, breathe through your heart, and wonder: *Where are ya, VeeVee?* Then look for a clue in your face and wonder: *Do my face, thoughts, feelings, or actions give me a clue about what Hasty Happy habit I might be doing?*

Notice your face, your eyes, your mouth:

- Are you kind and inviting?
- Are you glaring and biting?
- Are you pleading and woeful?
- Are you bouncing around so much you do not even see yourself?

- Do you look over people with an *I know what's best tsk, tsk* kind of face?
- Are you icily staring?
- Are you so downtrodden you can't even look in the mirror?
- Are you one big ice cube?

These facial expressions also help you think about the actions and words you might possibly be doing. If your look in your compact mirror reveals a face that is not one of kind wonderment—a face that is not looking warmly with your eyes, smiling gently, and showing signs of genuine listening—you are probably in a Hasty Happy.

Say, *Thank you, part of me that is protecting me with this Hasty Happy.*

One More Helpful Assist

Use the spidey-sense detecting you do so well on behalf of others for yourself. In spy movies, women often pull out their compact mirrors as if to check their lipstick. But the clever femme fatale slightly adjusts her mirror to view what is behind her. Be that daring detective on your own behalf.

Take the compact mirror. Angle it over your shoulder to see your Purse Sisters' stage. Keep breathing through your heart and playfully ask yourself, *who is running my stage? SpeeDee, perhaps DeeDee?*

Focus on having your VeeVee on your stage, ensuring all your Purse Sisters have your back. Breathing through your heart and checking in on your Purse Sisters will adjust your stage and line up all three of your Purse Sisters. With VeeVee present, your eyes, ears, and voice align with caring grace. Then your love can be true and rich and deep, a love of peace with no comparisons or conditions. The love you clearly wish to share.

If you found a Hasty Happy in your facial review, VeeVee must not be there. Given what you just glimpsed, you now have either signs that you are amping your energy amok or slowing your energy to glacial proportions. You now have a clue if its either SpeeDee or DeeDee running your stage.

Say, *Thank You SpeeDee* or *Thank you DeeDee*.

Your Discovery

SpeeDee and DeeDee both adore reading Sticky Notes. They make quite the habit of it. Aha! Sticky Notes must be here. Take a wee moment and close your purse. Turn the clasp. No sense in letting any Sticky Notes get caught by a breeze and blow out willy-nilly, harming others or yourself. Congratulate yourself for being such a fine sleuth.

Imagine peering into your purse. Focus on the beautiful lining, the foundation of your new and different purse. Inhale through your heart this Sparkle lining and exhale your SpeeDee or DeeDee energy. Peer again into your purse. Notice any notes stuck on your Sparkle lining that have come to your attention during this Hasty Happy moment.

Like Grandma, you can then look to see if you have a Sticky Note, old news perhaps, but a reminder of how you once had an Energy Kink. Wonder to yourself, *Are there any Sticky Notes of how I once had an Energy Kink?*

If you don't know of a Sticky Note, that is okay. Simply say, *It's okay not to know*. If in that moment, you already know what part of you might be giving VeeVee Stage Fright, you can quickly jot down on the note some basic info: the current date, time, and a one liner about what was happening in the here and now when you noticed your Hasty Happy. Keep it short; it's just a memo.

Then imagine gently removing the Sticky Note stuck to your Sparkle lining. No need to rip or tear. Acknowledge the part of you that is protecting you with this Sticky Note by saying, *Thank you, part of me, for using this Sticky Note to protect me.* Even if it is Yesterday's News, a part of you wrote it down because you thought it would help once upon a time.

Then gently place the Sticky Note in your imaginary or real Yesterday's News box to look at when you are ready. That's how you begin to unpack the Sticky Notes from your Yesterday's News box. We will let you know how to Unpack your Sticky Notes from your Yesterday's News box in Chapter 18.

Step 4: Say Hello

Sparkle infused, now is the time for you to say Hello VeeVee.

Say Hello VeeVee as warmly as you can, with kindness, love, grace, and an oomph of gusto. Say it to your VeeVee just as you speak to your cherished pet at the end of the workday, the greeting you give your bestie when ya meet up, the twinkling eye-way you engage a child. With your own purse, say *Hello VeeVee* wherever VeeVee happens to be—on or off your stage.

Say hello when VeeVee is off your stage. Even during Margie's Hasty Happies, Grandma appreciated Margie the night before they went to the barn. You, too, can say *Hello VeeVee* with appreciation and wonderment even when she *exits your stage.* VeeVee can then use her neuroception for safety and make a comeback.

Say hello when VeeVee is *on your stage.* Grandma reminded Margie each night about how wonderful she was. You, too, can say hello and appreciate VeeVee when she is doing her job on stage. With such warm reward, VeeVee will stay. From this sparkly place within yourself, you can know love does not have to feel so hard, so urgent. Love loves spaciousness and tenderness. You can make your caring intentions clearly Sparkle.

When VeeVee joined Grandma Irene's stage, she showed Margie how kind wonderment could help Margie create a new friendship with Kitty. Her nerves softened. Grandma, filled with kind wonderment and a clear, soft, and inviting tone, said hello to her own VeeVee.

You can too.

That's it. Say, *Hello VeeVee*.

As you continually welcome your VeeVee with a warm hello, you can encourage her to stay on your stage by reducing the Stage Fright you give yourself. When you say Hello VeeVee, you will probably start to notice the Sticky Notes within.

Next, let's continue to Reignite your Sparkle by unpacking your Sticky Notes.

CHAPTER 18

Reignite Sparkle:
Unpack to Stop Stage Fright

We invite you to take out your compact and unpack your purseonal baggage. As much as other people seem to fill up your life purse, the real purse filler that gives you Stage Fright is intimately yours—your purseonal baggage. Your life purse is filled with joyful connections and inevitable Energy Kinks; you have a stack of memories.

Your parts dutifully carry copious notes. Clusters of information from your Body, Mind, Emotion, and Connection Energies are as concrete as the little pad of notes you keep in your actual purse. Your parts make Sticky Notes with every kink. These Energy Kinks have power. Tenacious and stubborn, they hold to your past. Invisible to the eye yet mighty in strength, the kinks in your energies disrupt your smooth energy flow. The body responses you used to protect yourself from harm lock into your tissues, ensnaring old Stage Fright and ditching your present delight. Yesterday's News.

The Sticky Notes scare your VeeVee. What you remember as scary before seems like it's happening now, so she says goodbye. Old Sticky Notes appeal to SpeeDee and DeeDee. With social niceties out of the way, your parts can use Energy Kink memories jotted down on Sticky Notes. Quick and easy, lemon squeezy. All this repetition, boring to some, gives SpeeDee and DeeDee comfort.

Another Sticky Note Bonus

Sticky Notes are as convenient as a TV dinner.

Connection Energy Kinks are auto-tragic. Your Sticky Note barcodes alert you without your knowledge or consent. Remembering computer passwords or your notes at school takes a lot of repetition and study. Unlike this slow-burn memory, you download the scary pains in one single lesson.

Touch a hot stove? Seared in your memory forever.

You have another pain that your survival brain hates: the Alone Zone. Your amygdala acts instantly to warn you about anything that reminds you of these fear-flavoured *owies*. Confusing.

You don't know how and when you first scribbled them down.
Are they still true today?
Are they Yesterday's News and clogging up your purse?

You don't know, so with SpeeDee's or DeeDee's directions, you recite and believe them over and over again.

SpeeDee and DeeDee revert to their love for routine and reenactment. Sticky Notes are perfect for that. They can read off these notes and direct your moves in an instant. The notes replay over and over, ensuring you remember the original safety plan you wrote on your Sticky Note. You can use that plan even if it doesn't fit now.

One thing is for sure. Your pursesonal baggage makes your life purse a bottomless pit. Old wrinkled up notes and crisp recent notes vie for space, coating your Sparkle lining. Your purseonal baggage—the loves, unexpected events, the heartbreaks—bring your purse to the bulging point. Your life purse grows full with Sticky Notes about your life and with other people's stuff. It's a full and mixed-up place. Years of memories of what you did to help yourself fill your purse with Stage Fright—something you never intended.

To Sparkle, you want VeeVee to stay on your stage as often as she can. Luckily, you have the power to transform the Stage Fright your Sticky Notes create. With kind wonderment, you can explore these Sticky Notes and notice if they are still helpful or not. You dispel the spell they may have had on you, improving VeeVee's odds for staying on stage. Unpacking your purse clears the old things taking up valuable space and preventing you from noticing the beauty of your Sparkle. Unpacking Sticky Notes clears out past Energy Kinks. Life goes on.

Daily Packing

You add to your purseonal baggage almost daily.

You can unpack all you want, but you face Energy Kinks all the time. You must unpack the playlist that VeeVee keeps hearing as your old Sticky Notes stay stuck on repeat—ones you know and ones you don't know. Unpacking Sticky notes clears out Energy Kinks that make it hard to see your Sparkle.

Here are the steps to use your compact to unpack and release your Sticky Notes.

Unpack a Sticky Note

Now that you have a specific Sticky Note in your Yesterday's News box, you can Unpack and release the Sticky Note itself. Start with the steps outlined in Chapter 17 for *Hello VeeVee* and continue to breathe in and out of your heart.

Take a Sticky Note and say, *I choose to look at the Sticky Note a part of me made.*

1. Read the Sticky Note and say, *Even though a part of me had a Hasty Happy habit, I deeply and completely accept I am APNP* (always practicing never perfect).

2. Notice what unhelpful thoughts or feelings (Stage Fright) come up for you about the Sticky Note as you breathe into the Stage Fright in your body. Notice its location if you can.

3. Appreciate something in the here and now as you continue to breathe in and out through your heart. This alone lightens your load.

4. Sticky Note Bar Code Match: Think about how your part's Hasty Happy might have tried to help you in a past time. If there is no match, just keep breathing.

5. Jot down what you really needed or hoped for instead of what happened on the Sticky Note.

6. Thank your part for holding the Sticky Note and trying to protect you.

7. Remind yourself of how you are different now from when your part created your Sticky Note.

8. Breathe beautiful air into the front of your head while touching your forehead.

9. Make a Sparkle Note of a new thought, feeling, and action. Pop it in your purse.

Well done. Take a bow. So many people do not Unpack their Sticky Notes. You have the Sparkle Power to transform the Stage Fright your Sticky Notes created. It's as therapists are often known to say, *a process*.

If you discover there is more to Unpack and release about your Sticky Note, it would be marvellous to Unpack it with a safe person or group. Being safe in the here and now with another person or group may prevent you from going to the Alone Zone when you reread the Sticky Note.

Unpacking Yesterday's News from your Sticky Notes creates a more spacious purse. You have more room to repack using your cell phone to encourage VeeVee to stay on your Stage.

CHAPTER 19

Reignite Sparkle: Repack Sparkle

Repacking your new purse with Sparkle keeps your Sparkle essence vibrant. Your Body, Mind, Emotion, and Connection Energies within you and around you flow.

To Sparkle, you need VeeVee to stay as often as possible. As you cherish VeeVee, she wants to stay with you. VeeVee's presence on your stage depends upon how you treat yourself and your energies, how you connect to yourself in your talk, thoughts, and actions.

Sparkle Notes

You write notes to remember things. You jot down Sticky Notes to recall the times VeeVee left your stage and you were On Guard. **Sparkle Notes** record the opposite. Sparkle Notes recall the delightful moments VeeVee stayed on your stage and you were set to Sparkle.

Sticky Notes imbue you with Stage Fright. Sparkle Notes fill you with delight.

- Sparkle Notes can stop the Stage Fright that makes your VeeVee leave. Sparkle Notes can help you Unpack and release Sticky Notes so that VeeVee does not get Stage Fright.

- Sparkle Notes help VeeVee stay. Use these notes to Repack actions that encourage your four energies to flow and help you engage in Sparkle connection with yourself and others.

Grandma Irene Made Sparkle Notes

Grandma Irene had a notebook and a pencil. She purposely jotted down some ways she could help her own VeeVee either come back or stay on her stage. First, she wrote down a way to help VeeVee with Stage Fright when she leaves. Then she jotted down some ways she could help VeeVee stay more often. To this end, Grandma often took a tally of how her energies were doing. It was grand if all energies aligned in a sunny blue-sky kind of way, but her energies ebbed and flowed all the time. Grandma's VeeVee felt safe if her Energy Sparkle flowed, but as soon as an Energy Kink occurred, VeeVee got Stage Fright and easily said goodbye.

Checking in on her Body Energy joys and uh-ohs—her Mind Energy thoughts, her Emotion Energy waves, and her Connection Energy hits and misses—helped Grandma know where she might have an Energy Kink. After she figured out where she might have a kink, she used her Sparkle Note reminders about what she could do for her different energies.

Your Sparkle Notes are delightfully deliberate.

Grandma Irene, with her purposeful record keeping, was in good company.

The Obama Download

On the second inauguration of President Barack Obama, news reports focused on his behaviour just after the swearing-in ceremony. A million people had gathered to witness this historic event, even more notable for occurring on the fiftieth anniversary of Martin Luther King Day. Celebration was alive in voice, sound, colour, and feeling. After he was sworn in, the President and his family began to walk offstage, no doubt to be whisked to the next event.

Then it happened. The President turned around and stopped. His wife and children were heading offstage as planned.

He stopped.

The President turned around and looked out at the sea of people. His eyes seemed to photograph this present blink of time. The camera and microphones weren't primed for this spontaneous turn of events. On television that night, subtitles told us what he said, "Let me have a moment to take this all in. I won't be seeing this again." He stopped, he looked, and he let the experience seep throughout him. On future rainy days or hard days or even gentle days talking to his grandkids, he could recall from his being this extraordinary moment, a millisecond in time as we measure it, yet timeless in its truth.

You, too, can drink in and bathe in the goodness life has to offer. Negative, unhappy, and scary events automatically download. Sticky Notes adhere to you even though you did not plan for them to land inside. Sparkle Notes as you have seen in movies, read about in books, or diligently have written yourself, are crafted, designed, and chosen.

Noted psychologist Rick Hanson recommends you pick and choose what to download into your intricate lovely self. Look, hear, smell, taste, or touch Sparkle like the President did that day and soak the experience in by holding the sensation for about thirty seconds. Make a note about the Sparkle as Grandma Irene did and read your note, as Dr. Hanson encourages, for about half a minute. Hey, you can even set an alarm on your actual phone to time it.

Repacking your purse mindfully with Sparkle Notes cheers VeeVee on—encouraging, inspiring, and celebrating her. VeeVee needs Sparkle Notes that boost her. If she is not appreciated and supported, she could burn out. That would just be so sad.

Sparkle Notes tell VeeVee you are so glad she is there. Cherishing VeeVee cherishes you. Choosing to repack Sparkle Notes to rehearse Sparkle simply takes a little planning. In Repacking, choose Sparkle Notes for each energy. The Sparkle Note you choose has an action that inspires VeeVee to stay.

Sparkle Notes tell VeeVee you are so glad she is there.

You can prerecord or jot down Sparkle Notes and put them in your purse to help your VeeVee stay. You have the perfect piece of equipment.

Your Cell Phone

Like a fab BB face cream that moisturizes, sun protects, anti-ages, all with a hint of colour, your cell phone—a pocket-sized powerhouse—multitasks. Your cell phone holds and offers important info that makes you feel safe. It houses everything all in one place, providing: a place to surf the net, notes to remember to do things, a camera, your schedule, drawings, scanned documents, and checklists. You trust it to find things that give you delight—photos, meditations, poems, and quips. Heck, you can even make a phone call on it. You can choose how and when to use your phone to communicate with people. You can connect with people in a way you choose by text, email, or an actual call. Your contacts list has all the ways you can reach out and not be alone.

Your phone keeps you connected to yourself and all your energies. Your apps make it easy to hold your passwords and points for shopping. You can look up info on the internet. You can keep favourite pics that you can look at to feel immediate calm. You can call, text, and send emojis filled with oodles of love and caring. You can give and receive love. Your phone can do things that soothe you. You feel safer.

Get out your imaginary cell phone and go to the notes or reminders app.

Imagine you have a list.

My Sparkle Notes

You can imagine, of course, but we find doing the Repack on our actual cell phones is so helpful.

First set up the main categories of each energy:

- Body Energy Sparkle Notes
- Mind Energy Sparkle Notes
- Emotion Energy Sparkle Notes
- Connection Energy Sparkle Notes

Use Sparkle Notes when you sense an Energy Kink.

> Feel too wired or too tired? Go to a Body Energy Sparkle Note.

> Super worrying or your thinking is non-existent? You can go to a Mind Energy Sparkle Note.

Stuck in one emotion or totally devoid of feeling? Go to an Emotion Energy Sparkle Note.

Longing for a connection to someone or something? Go to your Connection Energy Sparkle Notes.

In each of these four categories, you will be keeping two types of Sparkle Notes.

Note to Self: Something to Remember

These notes reflect the times you have experienced Sparkle and are good to refer to when your VeeVee is off or could be leaving your stage. For example, if you are getting a filling at the dentist, you could remember yourself playing or running on a beach to help you feel Sparkle.

Remember that Stage Fright and Sparkle literally cannot coexist within you at the same time. You want to fill yourself with Sparkle. Be deliciously deliberate. You can read these notes or look at a picture of a Sparkle time. Leslie keeps a picture of catching her first fish. Lynda has a pic of her grandchildren.

Bask in this Sparkle reminder for thirty seconds.

Note to Self: Something to Do

These Sparkle Notes are directions and encouragements to bring VeeVee back or to prevent her from leaving. These notes inspire you to take actions that can help reignite Sparkle. They can simply say things like, *I can do this*.

To get the ball rolling, we are going to give you some examples of Sparkle Notes in each category.

Body Energy Sparkle Notes

Body Energy Sparkle Notes take care of your body. They remind you to allow your body to move or to enjoy stillness with flow, not Stage Fright.

Note to Self: Something to Remember

Recall times you felt relaxed energy in your body. Using one hand, touch your thumb to each finger, one at a time. When you touch each finger, stop and recall.

Breathe.

Touch your thumb to your index finger. As you do so, remember a time your body felt healthy fatigue, when you had just engaged in an exhilarating physical activity. You might imagine that you have just played tennis, jogged, swam, or been to an aerobics or yoga class.

Now breathe.

Touch your thumb to your middle finger. As you do so, go back to a time when you experienced a pleasant scent or aroma. Breathe in this pleasant scent or aroma and the feeling you had as you remember this special time.

Now breathe.

Touch your thumb to your ring finger, and as you do so, remember the loveliest place you have ever been and dwell there for a while. This place may be a place you visited or a wonderful place you have created in your mind. Notice if there is a breeze, if it's cool or warm, and what you hear as well as what you see in your lovely place.

Now breathe.

Touch your thumb to your little finger and remind yourself that these memories you have just recalled are part of your unique and separate self. Imagine a colour surrounding your unique and separate self.

Note to Self: Something to Do

Breathe: VeeVee loves to stay when your breath is focused. Inhale with four breaths in through your heart; exhale with eight breaths.

Exercise: Set your timer and walk for twenty minutes to your favourite music.

Relax: Read a mystery book with a cup of tea.

Mind Energy Sparkle Notes

Sparkle Notes on your cell phone are great for getting to know yourself and your different parts. Mind Sparkle Notes are great to help you Unpack a Sticky Note. Your Mind Energy tries to make sense of your world and how to survive in it. The mind helps you by sorting itself into parts. Each part deals with any tough stuff you go through.

These notes build up your here-and-now ability. Your mind, thoughts, and decision-making are grounded and present. You will not need to rely on Sticky Notes to make choices and interpret data in either the past or future time frame.

Note to Self: Something to Remember

Recall when your mind was working well—jived about something you learned.

Remember a compliment you received about a good idea you offered.

Note to Self: Something to Do

Unpack a Sticky Note.

Do a fifteen meditation on your phone app.

Do a crossword puzzle.

Listen and talk kindly to your parts.

Pick up a pen. Start journaling. Don't worry where the pen will take you.

Emotion Energy Sparkle Notes

Each emotion is simply information. For example, your body temperature ranges, and you experience this sensation as hot or cold. You are not bad or good because you are hot or cold. Perhaps your body has a tummy ache when you meet a new person. You might say, *I feel anxious*, then you might judge that feeling as silly. Your VeeVee just picked up a clue for you to consider. Just information. Emotions are the info that lets you know how your insides and outsides are doing.

Sparkle Notes in your emotion collection help VeeVee find the information your emotions are trying to convey. With that info, VeeVee can accurately sense if she should stay or vamoose. You can create Emotion Sparkle Notes that help you know what you are feeling and remind you of ways to release emotions without clamming up or fanning the flames.

You can give VeeVee a Sparkle Note full of genuine emotion.

Note to Self: Something to Remember

Recall a movie or series you enjoyed that brings up many emotions for you. Your overall experience is one of interest and engagement, even with all its ups and downs. After all, you kept watching that show.

Remember a time when you felt sad, happy, scared, and mad all at once, perhaps a milestone celebration like a good-bye party. You felt many feelings, and somehow it was okay to do so.

Note to Self: Something to Do

Say, *Thanks for this wave of Emotion Energy info.*

Try the "Emptying the Jug" exercise.

This exercise was taught to us by Lori Gordon in our training to become approved teachers of PAIRS (Practical Application of Intimate Relationship Skills). We have slightly adapted it.

Take a moment in the day. Breathe like you do with *Hello Vee Vee*—hand on heart, breathing in for four counts and out for eight through your heart area. Be a detective on your own behalf. You are simply gathering clues with no judgment. Just the facts, Ma'am.

Ask yourself:

> *What am I mad about?* Jot down whatever comes up without judgment.
>
> Say to yourself, *Thank you for this information.*
>
> *What am I sad about?* Jot down whatever comes up without judgment.
>
> Say to yourself, *Thank you for this information.*

What am I scared about? Jot down whatever comes up without judgment.

Say to yourself, *Thank you for this information.*

What am I glad about? Jot down whatever comes up without judgment.

Say to yourself, *Thank you for this information.*

Connection Energy Sparkle Notes

These Sparkle Notes promote enjoyable, enriching relationships with people, all living things, and Love beyond time and space. You need connections. Solitude is great at times to restore your reserves, but the Alone Zone is scary and harmful. People need people.

There is a special bonus as you rehearse your Body, Mind, and Emotion Sparkle Notes. As you attend with deliberate attention and curiosity to these three energies, you transform your relationship with yourself.

As you notice your body, mind, and emotions with this tender curiosity, your Purse Sisters unite to set your stage. As they dance together, you notice what your body needs, you talk more patiently to yourself, and you consider your emotions as information that can help you. You start a new habit.

You **Sparkle Talk** to yourself.

This parlays easily into the Sparkle Talk you give to others.

Note to Self: Something to Remember

Recall warm, engaging times you were in connection. You could look at pictures of friends, family, pets, or favourite places you have visited. You might remember a prayer or a song.

263

Note to Self: Something to Do

Call or text a buddy once a week.

Enjoy the sunshine and look for bees and butterflies in the garden.

Read inspirational passages.

Engage in Sparkle Talk with others. Let's look at this a bit more closely.

With Sparkle Talk, You Face-Heart It

Sparkle Talk: The way you listen and talk to yourself and others that is respectful of your needs and theirs.

Imagine—

- Your eyes look with kind wonderment.
- Your jaw is relaxed.
- Your ears listen without interruption.
- Your mouth curves up.
- You speak clearly in a calmly energetic and kind tone.
- You let others finish sentences.
- You let yourself finish your sentences.
- You speak facts.
- You enjoy talking.

Sparkle Talk: Focus on your VeeVee to inspire.

- Listen with compassion. Normalize the stress. Focus on facts.
- Gently approach others' VeeVees—you have no idea how skittish they are.

- Try not to take it personally as their VeeVee has Stage Fright, not them.

- Suggest a time-out and meet later if they cannot chillax or rev up immediately.

- Use compassion for their frustration *without* taking the blame or accepting the invite to ignore your own needs and thoughts.

- Acknowledge their concerns without necessarily agreeing with what they are saying.

- Listen deeply to your others' concerns and respond with what you heard them say.

- When you respond, focus on facts and what you want to share about what you're selling rather than your perceptions or beliefs about the person.

Your Sparkle Power is your presence. It's magic.

All These Sparkle Notes

Adding Sparkle encourages VeeVee to stay. Your stage is set at Safe to Sparkle. With Sparkle, you simply cannot carry people and their stress. Your Hasty Happy habit halted, you choose when and how to place or receive calls. As VeeVee tap dances in synch with SpeeDee and DeeDee, you appear inviting and friendly, safe to people—delightful for you both. You choose to *make a call* when your stage is set at Safe to Sparkle. You connect, not carry.

Rehearsing the Reignite Sparkle Solution: Hello VeeVee, Unpack, and Repack transform the harshness and judgment of yourself and others into a tender curiosity.

When you recognize other people are in a Hasty Happy, use Sparkle Talk:

Sparkle Talk

Their SpeeDee Hasty Happy	Their Energy Is	Their Hope	You Do *Not* Do or Say This	Instead, You Can Try Sparkle Talk
Too Bossy	Too Revved Up	They hope saying "Do What I Say" will *make* you stay. Or They blame you, hoping your guilt will make you stay.	Fight back. Or Be sorry for everything. Or Be too helpful.	"I hear your concerns and would like to talk this through with you." Or "Let me think about what you said and get back to you."
Too Pleasing	Too Revved Up	They hope by trying to make you happy, you will stay.	Lose sight of your needs and cajole or get overwhelmed. Or Say, "Stop it. Enough already."	"Sounds like a lot happening for you. Let's keep talking about what could work better for us."
Too Escaping	Too Revved Up	They make light of anything serious or entice you to have fun in hopes you will stay.	Yell at them to stay put. Or Get swept up in their speed.	"I'll give you a call next week." Keep your eyes focused and look at them, even if they divert.
Too Helpful	Too Revved Up	They hope if they show you how much you need them, you will stay with them.	Keep letting them do it all. Or Yell, "Stop!"	"Thank you. Let's do it together."
Too Frosty	Too Revved Up and Too Chilled	They hope if they don't express their feelings, you will stay.	Blame and yell Or Shame Or Frost back Or Say "sorry" even if you did nothing wrong.	"Thanks for letting me know what you are thinking. Tell me more."

Their DeeDee Hasty Happy	Their Energy is	Their Hope	You Do *Not* Do or Say This	Instead, You Can Try Sparkle Talk
Too Helpless	Too Chilled	They hope you will stay if they show you how much they need you.	Ignore all your own needs and jump in to help. Or Shout, "Snap out of it!"	"It all seems like a lot. Let's take it one step at a time."
Too Iced Over	Too Chilled	They have stopped hoping for people to stay with them.	Ignore and leave them alone. Or Shout, "What's wrong with you? Speak up! Cat got your tongue?"	Can't really have a conversation. "Perhaps you would like to think about it and get back to me. I'm happy to follow up a little later if I don't hear from you."

CHAPTER 20

The Purse Rehearsals

The constant mystery of VeeVee's travels keeps us asking: *Will she stay, or will she go?* Purse rehearsals are all about answering this question because when VeeVee is on stage, your vagus nerve is working at its best.

Like any great stage production, rehearsals make all the difference. As Grandma Irene often said, "How do you get to Carnegie Hall? Practice. Practice. Practice."

New paths in Grandma's brain helped her rehearse her own new purse. After Grandma helped Margie design her purse, Grandma showed Margie how to rehearse with her purse too. Grandma knew rehearsals were essential for Margie. Stage Fright was auto-tragic. By stopping Stage Fright and adding Sparkle, Grandma created auto-magic.

Stage Fright automatically downloaded inside her beloved granddaughter. The luscious, good memories of the summer of love were not superglued by her brain and could easily inch out of Margie's memory. Purse rehearsals back in the city could have helped Margie say hello to her own VeeVee and Unpack and Repack her purse often and well. With rehearsal, these actions could have grown to be auto-magic.

Rehearsing ways to keep your VeeVee on stage can eventually make them auto-magic for you too. Your purse lining is hard to see when it is stuffed with other people's stuff. It is difficult to see when it's layered with Sticky Notes too. The Stage Fright dims or covers over the Sparkle delight in your life purse.

Rehearsals make cherishing VeeVee auto-magic. The three types of rehearsals in the Reignite Sparkle solution set your life stage for a sparkly show. Purse rehearsals encourage VeeVee to stay. Your nervous system resets to safe more often. Also, with rehearsals, resets are quicker.

You don't want to stay in the Alone Zone for long. VeeVee stays if she experiences safety within, and your Sparkle shines around you. Does it sound like a piece of cake? Yes, but it is no cake walk.

Purse Rehearsals to Reignite Sparkle

Like Care-y Stress, purse rehearsals are labours of love. They require a commitment. But the rewards of purse care are fabulous.

Hello VeeVee Rehearsals

Given VeeVee's penchant for saying goodbye, a continuous sweet greet to her helps her feel safe to stay on your stage as often as she can. We encourage you to set aside time to just rehearse *Hello VeeVee* to get the hang of it. If you don't know if your VeeVee is on your stage or off your stage, don't fret, Bette. Just say Hello VeeVee. Say this warm hello as often as you can.

You can use the steps outlined in Chapter 17 to say *Hello VeeVee*. You might notice it's not as easy as you think. That's okay. Your VeeVee might have vetted an Energy Kink you haven't explored or released yet. Use your compact to rehearse unpacking practices, to stop fright, and to rehearse repacking practices using your cell phone to add Energy Sparkle.

Unpack Rehearsals

Compact rehearsals allow you to Unpack your purse with calm energy. With rehearsal, purse dumps begin to seem drearily dramatic. Unpacking your purse reduces the Sticky Note scripts for SpeeDee and DeeDee. You reduce the Stage Fright you give to yourself. Your compact mirror—your self-reflection—helps you respect your Sticky Notes and release Yesterday's News that gives you Stage Fright. You can use the steps outlined in Chapter 18.

Less Stage Fright leaves room for more Sparkle. As alert to danger and quick to say goodbye as VeeVee is, she prefers to stay with her sisters. Your private, wonderous purse holds all you need to delight your VeeVee. Your delight can Sparkle forth from your own purse, much to the delight of those you love.

Repack Rehearsals

Repack rehearsals help add Sparkle. Your cell phone is your wondrous ability to delight VeeVee directly with actions to prevent or smooth out an Energy Kink or show your Sparkle.

Your cell phone stores Sparkle Notes, so you know where to find them. Ahh. VeeVee feels cherished as you read her these Sparkle Notes. By unpacking your Sticky Notes, you have more space for Sparkle Notes.

Just Imagine

As you rehearse, you can imagine how all these wondrous aspects are precious elements of you. You are totally lined with Sparkle. Your heart is the gorgeous clasp that you tend to privately and separately from others. As you take care of your heart, you magnify its power to share with others. You shield it from others' Hasty Happies, so you don't add your Hasty Happy to the fray.

That is so loving.

Purse rehearsals create a healthy baseline in your body. Your amygdala rests more with fewer of your parts in Hasty Happy from your Sticky Notes. Your heart, with VeeVee moderating SpeeDee and DeeDee, can be at the normal rhythm. As you leave the Hasty Happy habits, you recalibrate to Sparkle. You are kind to yourself, making you more kind to people. Even when people are unkind to you. Rehearsals harmonize your energies, adding glow to your health.

Remember you need safe people too. We are team players by nature. Your safe nervous system is designed for safe connection with safe people. Double Delight is essential. Kindness to yourself and kindness to people are both needed to keep VeeVee on your stage. You connect, not carry. You are kind to people even in their Hasty Happy. You don't take it personally. You just know this person has a nervous system without a VeeVee on their stage.

You experience Double Delight.

Attending the Purse Rehearsal studio keeps VeeVee on your stage more often. Your VeeVee is a teacher too. On your stage, VeeVee shows people how they might use their VeeVees. You never know. They might want their VeeVees to meet up with your precious VeeVee and go to their own Purse Rehearsal studios.

Do you want to do Purse Rehearsals?

Would change be good for you?

Night Out

As a treat and reward, you planned a night out with your best friend for weeks. Dinner and a show. You have had it on the calendar, a loving joy to put your sights on when times have been tough. Earlier in the week, you made sure you had a clean dress and laid out a little purse that simply holds lipstick and cash.

The night was planned to be about you, starring you *by your name* and not: Honey, Daughter, Mom, Grandma, Aunt, Boss, Assistant. When you and your buddy get together, it will be about you by your own names with no expectations—no one tugging or rolling their eyes at you, wanting your advice desperately then, in the next second, ignoring you. With your best friend, you will reminisce and wag on, remembering former times of angst compared to now, delightful life distractions. Somehow you both survived school, your first jobs together, your first heartbreaks, and as life unfurled, the aches and joys of Care-y Stress.

The day arrives. As it unravels, the bone tiredness of the last few weeks leaks into your pores. You long to put on your sweats and veg out. It has nothing, absolutely nothing to do with seeing your friend. You are just too tired to change into something else.

Fatigue

We get so tired from the inevitable Hasty Happy of our habitual routines that even when something is gloriously good for us, we balk. Daily routine is tried, familiar, and easier—even if it won't get us anywhere new.

We balk.

It's more than the neural rut pathway to the old library that Margie experienced. As Margie became adult Margie, her experiences in life layered into her sinew and bone. Unlike the trip to the library—a divine solo journey for her—the more she lived and loved, the more other people's stories entwined with hers. She learned about worry and making time and doing more stuff for herself and for them.

Tense.

She might have played on a team and worried about the team. She might have fallen in love and worried about her loved one's heart. She may have a child or children, and with each piece of love for each important person, she always found responsibility. Often there were crisis points for herself or someone she loved; she rallied then and rallied well.

She fed and drove and soothed and continued working at her job. She analyzed and met with specialists in health, aging, or education. She googled. A lot. She knew she should include herself in the puzzle of life, and the knowingness of this and her inability to do it made her feel the guilt that always nipped at her heels.

The fact that we do not always kindly treat ourselves right stems from habits and guilt.

So, when we have a night of fun planned just for us, we are simply too tired to change.

So pooped, you pop.

The weight of your purse is heavy. You are tired. Too pooped to rehearse your own new purse. Like your real purse, you don't take stuff out of your life purse until the bulge is so big the clasp won't close.

Until its ready to—ack! Too late. Pop!

Your purse spills over in the Hasty Happy purse dump. If you are not careful, you will fall back into the Care-y Stress Cycle. You will dump, then feel that Tricky Guilt. Then you take on more responsibility, so you open your purse again, only to create more Energy Kinks and, yes, more Sticky Notes. These wondrous Sticky Notes and their good intentions stick so well that you cannot see your Sparkle.

Your current purse must lead to a purse dump. You end up carrying other people's stress and forget to put in any rehearsal time just for you. You went to Carnegie Hall, but you practiced that same old tune: *Carrying your purseonal baggage, carrying their stress.*

Lynda and Leslie had this happen to not only their lovely clients, but to themselves. The trouble is this statistically tends to be the reality for all of us: 80 percent for them, 20 percent for me or sometimes 95 percent for them, 5 percent for me.

Oops! We forgot too. Lynda and Leslie have also been thigh deep in our different years of new purses. We know about this because we do it. No judgment here.

APNP. Always Practicing. Never Perfect.

We both had significant losses and caring dilemmas with family and friends that propelled each of us into action. And probably because our systems had assessed the situations as dangerous but not life threatening to us, our SpeeDees ignited us so we could multitask, drive, cook, and see clients during these difficult times.

APNP. Always Practicing. Never Perfect.

Sometimes, our DeeDees ran our shows with Yesterday's News Sticky Notes, and we just pooped out. No one prepared us for the aftermath our Energy Kinks felt after various crises. In the calm after the storms we weathered, we felt the impact. And it tired each of us. We never seem to talk about the letdown after the crisis.

Our televisions honour crisis by doing play-by-play coverage of the devastation of tornados, hurricanes, crashes, and murders. But how much coverage is allotted to the aftermath? It's not breaking news to see the mother trying to find clothes at the shelter and sweeping mud out of her basement three weeks after the tornado hit. It is especially not news-breaking to visit the same woman a year and a half later when the house is semi-fixed, the kids are back to school, and she and her partner are working full time. She blames herself for finding it hard to get off the couch. After all, the tornado isn't there anymore.

No one told you. No one told us. It is one of the worst kept secrets we continue to hold.

Tired to the bone is the killer.

Even in this book, we are asking you to put on a fresh face.

Not bloody likely, you should say. *I am too tired, and I have earned a rest.*

Darn straight. You can rest before you do anything else. Feel free to put the book down and have a nap. Put the book down for a few days or months, whatever you need. When you are ready, you can look at our ideas for rehearsing your new purse. You will know when you are ready to put your little blue bike on a path to your own Purse Rehearsals. You will know when the time is right.

Until then:

Let your eyes be less tired.
Let your shoulders come down from their perch.
Let the sun touch the places you froze for safekeeping.
The world absorbs you.
The world absolves you.

Butterflies by day, fireflies at night,
Soar softly.
Like the gentle strength from your heartfelt wings.
Open your weary eyes, unfold your working arms, drink in
sundrops.
You are safe here. We will be waiting.

Contact the Authors

Lynda Rees and Leslie Gillespie

Thank you for reading our book.
Please collect your gift from us to you:
www.reegill.ca/bookgift

Mailing Address:
Box 22
Waterdown, Ontario
Canada, L0R2HO

Email:
hello@reegill.ca

Website:
www.reegill.ca

Social:
LinkedIn:
www.linkedin.com/in/lynda-rees-a42373173
www.linkedin.com/in/leslie-gillespie-b461a4145

Appreciations

To Denis and Robert—thank you for your love and patience. You challenge us to be our sparkly selves and cheer us on every step of the way.

To our children, grandchildren, siblings, niblings, and godchildren—we hope this inspires you to own your Sparkle Power wherever you go.

To our friends and clients—you have taught us so much about who we are as people and what it means to love and care for ourselves, amid our caring for others.

To the Relationship Collaborative where some of our ideas have been birthed—you have been our place to connect, experiment, explore, and release our *purseonal baggage.*

To Dr. Jim Brown and Jean Brown—you have cheered us on with loving support through the ups and downs of writing this book. We are grateful to have you in our lives.

To Rosemary Slivinskas—your foresight in creating stress workshops for teachers allowed us to practice our emerging ideas.

To Cathy Lane, our illustrator—your brilliant vision and creative artistry made VeeVee, SpeeDee, and DeeDee come alive. You really got our take on the nervous system.

To Laura Newton, our gifted photographer par excellence.

To the Capucia Publishing team—you are all amazing.

Christine Kloser—you created a publishing home of encouragement, vast resources, and warm support.

Carrie Jareed—your organizational acumen is only surpassed by your kind nature.

Jean Merrill and your team—your eye for designing and marketing wizardry produced our colourful book.

Penny Legg—your verve, marketing expertise, and wise counsel guided us as we traversed from writers to authors.

Karen Burton, our editor—our quirky take on neuroscience research in our first draft could have made any editor run for the hills. Your gifts as a published poet and writer, your patience, and your razor-sharp ability to cut to what matters transformed our hopeful intentions into this book. We are deeply grateful.

Karen Everitt, our book midwife. You have delivered our book into the world with tender loving care.

Appendix

Little Doodle's Energies Further Explained

Energy is movement and action and power. We are all a mass of energy. We resonate with the energy around us and within us all the time. Often, you experience energy when you see or hear things in life. Yet when a breeze caresses your face or the sun's rays hug you, know these moments are energy too. Although we can't always see them or hear it, we are all packets of energy.

Little Doodle comes to life's party with wondrous energy gifts. These energies help Little Doodle connect with herself and with people. Experiences and the people she meets will affect how she learns about these energies and how she will use them.

We sorted them into four areas.

Body Energy

Her body always seeks to heal itself (Rankin 2020, 81–85; Mate 2003, 7–12). To do this, there are different energetic body parts within Little Doodle.

Her vagus nerve connects to almost all her insides, allowing communication between her organs to nourish and maximize her vitality (Rosenberg 2017, 7–8).

Her nervous system seeks safe people for connection who will help her and simultaneously alert her to the danger of unsafe people and unsafe events (Porges 2021, 259).

She has an automatic knowingness, a sensing, of what feels safe or unsafe called neuroception (Dana 2018, 36). Her chemical messengers (hormones, neuropeptides, neurotransmitters, pheromones) help her neuroperceive safety or danger (Dispenza 2012, 53–56).

Amazing organs of energy, her heart (Rozman 2022, chap. 3), her gut (Gershon 1999, 3), and her skin (Denda 2015; Linden 2015, 7–32) are all resplendent with their own brains and emotional memories. These organs also help her decipher who and what may be safe or unsafe.

Her heart *receives* information from inside and outside her body. Her heart *sends* information to the rest of her body through her nervous system, hormones, pulse waves, and electromagnetic field. This hero heart *responds* to her ever-changing emotions (Rozman 2017, chap. 3).

Her skin and its sense of touch, the earliest sensory organ to develop in the womb before her ears or eyes, is like a "nervous system" responding to skin-to-skin contact since before she was born (Montagu 1986, 4–6).

Her brilliant brain thrives on routine, repetition, and reenacting what has happened before (De Beauport 1996, 228). To take special care of Little Doodle, her brain errs on the side of safety and stores emotional memories with a bias to take in more negative memories than positive (Graham 2013, 23–24, 39; Hanson 2009, 41).

Her brain is social. It loves and learns in connection with others, so much so it has a "default" setting to seek connection with people (Lieberman 2013, 19–23). It can signal danger, register pain or pleasure, and use mirror neurons to learn from other people's actions (Banks 2015, 40–63).

The waves of her brain will share information about her body's level of awareness. Of these magical wavelengths, the delta and theta brain waves are predominant in her early years. In those years, Little Doodle will automatically download information to learn from others without analysis (Dispenza 2012, 184–190).

Her brain will adapt and change as she experiences life thanks to its flexible "neuroplasticity" (Doidge 2016, xv). This brain develops over time to help her mind analyze and reflect, and eventually choose. As she grows, she will have the ability to choose her thoughts, actions, and words. She will have empathy and imagination and be creative, crafting meaning and purpose (Graham 2013, 20).

As she faces challenges, she has an immune system to cushion, nurture, and defend her. This immune system grows even stronger when she connects with safe people. Little telomeres on her chromosomes protect her luscious DNA. These telomeres stay preserved and intact when she kindly connects with herself and other kind doodles (Hamilton 2017, 94–101). Her DNA stores memories in her cells from her ancestors (Dispenza 2012, 76–79; Pearsall 1999, 66).

Mind Energy

Mind energy regulates and tries to make sense of the flow of information she receives from all her energies and is shaped by her life and relationship experiences (Siegel 2012, 1–4).

This mind energy can create parts within her that each have a caring intention to keep her safe (Schwartz and Sweezy 2020, 31).

Mind parts relate like a family, each one with their own emotions, actions, thoughts, interests, natural abilities, and ways of making meaning and purpose (Schwartz and Sweezy 2020, 24–35).

Mind parts use the whole body to give them information. These parts can trigger her body and emotions, and in turn, her body and emotions can affect her parts (Anderson 2021, 147–148).

Emotion Energy

Emotional energy flows within and around her as waves of body sensations (McLaren 2010, 25–37; Graham 2013, 251).

Information from her body goes to her emotional brain a quarter second before her thinking brain registers a thought (Baker 2003, 135).

Peptide receptors throughout her body accept emotion, especially where her five senses of sight, sound, taste, smell, and touch connect with her nervous system, emotional brain, and gut (Pert 1997, 133–142; Gershon 1999, 3).

These emotions are information she can use to help her mind and body work together, and she has the ability to learn how to use this information (Pert 1997, 192; Graham 2013, 252).

Connection Energy

Sparkle self can connect and bring healing to all her parts. This Sparkle will never be damaged or cease to exist because of negative life events and people (Schwartz and Sweezy 2020, 276–277).

This Sparkle self can connect to people, all living things, and the Love beyond time and space (Dispenza 2017, 61–83; Pearsall 1999, 38–61, Schwartz and Sweezy 2020, 45).

Glossary

Created for you to make the science more fun to understand

Alone Zone

No one is with you, or you don't recognize someone as safe. It is chill, stark, and gripping in your biological core. There could be a kazillion people around, and you will still feel alone. Your Purse Sisters are On Guard, set at solo, not sisterly love. Often your adult self does not clearly remember the Energy Kinks from your younger years, but your unawares remember.

Body, Mind, Emotion, and Connection Energies

Body, Emotion, Mind, and Connection Energies are flowing within you and around you. Your four energies are interconnected and inseparable. When one energy is kinked, all your energies are affected in some way.

Care-y Mix-Ups

You try to change someone else by getting their VeeVees back on their nervous system stage. You hope they will stop their Hasty Happy habits and get back to being at Safe to Sparkle.

Care-y Stress

The tug in your mind, heart, and gut created from the act of caring for people intently. People's life stress and your life stress mix up together. It feels like a push-pull within you. You cannot figure out whose stress is whose. You try to take care of relieving their stress and then forget about yourself. Not taking care of yourself upsets you. You act out on the people you love. Then you feel guilty and upset with yourself.

Care-y Stress Cycle

You open your life purse and carry everybody's stress, including your own. When you are tired of all the stress, you do a Hasty Happy purse dump, only to feel Tricky Guilt and start this cycle all over again.

Double Delight

Caring for yourself and your loved ones at the same time. Amid caring for those you adore, there is place and space for you. There is place and space for those you love. These spaces are not mutually exclusive.

Energy Border

Your energetic border is inside you and around you. Body, Mind, Emotion, and Connection Energy Borders are separate from others and yet connected. You can reach out to others and be grounded in your own energies, knowing where you leave off and others begin. Your energy is not mixed up with others, and you can choose actions of compassion for your parts and toward others.

Energy Kink

When the Body, Mind, Emotion, and Connection Energies within you and around you are not flowing.

Hasty Happy

A quick fix for momentary gain, the reactive salve for a relationship wound. When VeeVee neurocepts unsafe, she lifts her foot off the brake and SpeeDee, then DeeDee, take over. You reclaim your life purse. A caring-intentioned attempt at carrying less. You may even feel some satisfaction that you are free of others' Hasty Happy.

Hasty Happy Habits

SpeeDee and DeeDee fuels seven habits that your parts use to protect you. SpeeDee fuels Hasty Happy Habits that makes you move with Stage Fright. These are Too Bossy, Too Pleasing, Too Escaping, Too Helpful, Too Frosty. DeeDee fuels Hasty Happy habits that makes you stay still with Stage Fright. These are Too Helpless and Too Iced Over.

Hello VeeVee

Given VeeVee's penchant for saying goodbye, a continuous sweet greet to her helps her feel safe to stay on your stage as often as she can.

NeuroGoof

When VeeVee finds a Sticky Note, she doesn't know if it's happening now or not. She acts on information that is Yesterday's News. She makes a mistake and signals something or somebody *is safe* when they *are not safe,* or something or somebody is *not safe* when they are *safe.*

On Guard

When VeeVee neurocepts unsafe, she lifts her foot off the brake and hoofs it to the wings. SpeeDee, then DeeDee, take over to keep you safe. With caring intention, parts of you will protect you with their Hasty Happy Habits.

Purse Rehearsals

Choose to rehearse the Reignite Sparkle Solution. Say *Hello VeeVee,* Unpack to stop Stage Fright, and Repack to add Sparkle.

Purse Sisters (VeeVee, SpeeDee, and DeeDee)

Your automatic nervous system that backs you up on your life stage. VeeVee the parasympathetic baby sister, loves to connect and keep her peeps safe. When VeeVee senses safety, she stays on your life stage with her sympathetic nervous system middle sister, SpeeDee, and her parasympathetic oldest sister, DeeDee. If there are no safe people and/or safe situations, VeeVee develops Stage Fright and takes her foot off her brake. SpeeDee takes over and when SpeeDee has done all she can, DeeDee takes over.

Reignite Sparkle Solution

Say Hello VeeVee, Unpack, and Repack your Purse on an everyday basis with fresh thought and kind intention to repair the Energy Kinks that happen as life unfurls and to encourage Energy Sparkle. You transform your relationship with yourself and those you love. You connect, not carry.

Safe to Sparkle

When all three Purse Sisters work as a team, or VeeVee teams up with either SpeeDee or DeeDee, you have everything you need to Sparkle. Your parts feel safe enough to let your Sparkle show.

Sparkle

Your birthright essence of wise compassion that is always with you throughout your life. Life experiences can diminish or obscure your Sparkle, but it is waiting patiently to be known.

Sparkle Notes

Repack *Notes to self: Something to remember* and *Notes to self: Something I can do.* These two types of notes encourage VeeVee to stay on your stage and your Sparkle to shine through.

Sparkle Power

The magic you create when you pause, breathe into your heart, believe in, and embrace your Sparkle.

Sparkle Talk

The way you listen and talk to others that is respectful of your needs and theirs.

Stage Fright

Like the classic jitters you can feel on stage. When VeeVee has Stage Fright, she says goodbye. These dreads make VeeVee adept at revealing impending doom but can also be inaccurate and, well, not real.

Sticky Note

You put together Body, Mind, Emotion, and Connection Energies and mix them together as an information cluster at the time you experienced an Energy Kink. You sum up the note with your opinion about what helped or could have helped you survive the Energy Kink. It sticks inside you so you can recall it should a similar Energy Kink recur.

Tricky Guilt

Your tricky call to be responsible for others even when you are not. Your Sticky Notes twist and twizzle within you as your needs and others' needs collide. These two opposites are physically uncomfortable. You label it as guilt, even when their needs or desires are not yours to take on. You haven't done anything to feel guilty for. It is tricky to decipher whose responsibility it is: yours or theirs.

Yesterday's News

Real past events you might have made Sticky Notes about.

References

Amen, Daniel G. 2007. *The Brain in Love: 12 Lessons to Enhance Your Love Life.* New York: Three Rivers Press, division of Random House, Inc.

Anderson, Frank, G. 2021. *Transcending Trauma: Healing Complex PTSD with Internal Family Systems Therapy.* Eau Claire, WI: Pesi Publishing.

Baker, Dan and Cameron Stauth. 2003. *What Happy People Know: How the New Science of Happiness Can Change Your Life for the Better.* New York: St Martin's Press.

Banks, Amy with Leigh Ann Hirschman. 2015. *Wired to Connect: The Surprising Link Between Brain Science and Strong, Healthy Relationships.* New York: Jeremy P. Tarcher/Penguin.

Bepko, Claudia and Jo-Ann Krestan. 1990. *Too Good for Her Own Good: Searching for Self and Intimacy in Important Relationships.* New York: Harper and Row.

Blackburn, Elizabeth and Elissa Epel. 2017. *The Telomere Effect: A Revolutionary Approach to Living Younger, Healthier, Longer.* New York: Grand Central Publishing.

Blakemore, Sarah-Jayne. 2018. *Inventing Ourselves: The Secret Life of the Teenage Brain.* New York: Hachette Book Group, Inc.

Brach, Tara. 2021. *Trusting the Gold: Uncovering Your Natural Goodness.* Boulder, CO: Sounds True, Inc.

Buczynski, Ruth and Emiliana Simon-Thomas. 2019. "Clinical Applications of Compassion, Module 1: The Neurobiology of Compassion." *The National Institute for the Clinical Application of Behavioral Medicine.* www.nicabm.com/program/compassion/

Buczynski, Ruth and Ashley Vigil-Otero. 2019. "Clinical Applications of Compassion, Module 1: The Neurobiology of Compassion." *The National Institute for the Clinical Application of Behavioral Medicine.* www.nicabm.com/program/compassion/

Childre, Doc and Howard Martin. 1999. *The Heartmath Solution: The Institute of HeartMath's Revolutionary Program for Engaging the Power of the Heart's Intelligence.* San Francisco: HarperCollins.

Chutkan, Robynne. 2013. *Gut Bliss: Feel Light, Tight, and Bright—the Healthy Way.* New York: Penguin Books.

Cómitre-Mariano, Blanca, et al. 2021. "Feto-maternal microchimerism: Memories from pregnancy." *iScience.* 21 Jan. pubmed.ncbi.nlm.nih.gov/35072002/

Dana, Deb. 2018. *The Polyvagal Theory in Therapy: Engaging the Rhythm of Regulation.* New York, London: W.W. Norton & Company, Inc.

De Beauport, Elaine with Aura Sofia Diaz. 1996. *The Three Faces of Mind: Developing Your Mental, Emotional, and Behavioral Intelligences.* Wheaton, IL: Theosophical Publishing House.

Denda, Mitsuhiro. 2015. "Epidermis as a Third Brain?" *Dematologica Sinica.* June. www.sciencedirect.com/science/article/pii/S102781171500049X

Dessanti, Claudia. 2020. *The She-Covery Project: Confronting the Gendered Economic Impact of COVID-19 in Ontario. Ontario Chamber of Commerce.* occ.ca/wp-content/uploads/OCC-shecovery-final.pdf

Devi, Gayatri. 2012. *A Calm Brain: Unlocking Your Natural Relaxation System.* New York: Dutton/Penguin Books.

Dispenza, Joe. 2012. *Breaking the Habit of Being Yourself: How to Lose Your Mind and Create a New One.* Carlsbad, CA: Hay House, Inc.

Dispenza, Joe. 2017. *Becoming Supernatural: How Common People are Doing the Uncommon.* Carlsbad, CA: Hay House, Inc.

Doidge, Norman. 2015. *The Brain's Way of Healing: Remarkable Discoveries and Recoveries from the Frontiers of Neuroplasticity*. New York: Penguin Books.

Friedan, Betty. 2013. *The Feminine Mystique*, 50th anniversary ed. New York: W.W. Norton.

Gershon, Michael D. 1999. *The Second Brain: A Groundbreaking New Understanding of Nervous Disorders of the Stomach and Intestine*. New York: Harper Perennial.

Gilligan, Carol and Naomi Snider. 2018. *Why Does Patriarchy Persist?* Medford, MA: Polity Press.

Gordon, Lori, H. with John Frandsen. 1993. *Passage to Intimacy: Uniquely Effective Concepts and Skills from the dynamic Internationally acclaimed PAIRS Program*, revised ed. Weston, FL: The PAIRS Foundation, Inc.

Graham, Linda. 2013. *Bouncing Back: Rewiring Your Brain for Maximum Resilience and Well-Being*. Novado, CA: New World Library.

Habib, Navaz. 2021. "Symptoms and Root Causes of Vagus Nerve Dysfunction." Dr. Eva Detko, interviewer. *Mind-Body & the Vagus Connection: Health Means*. Ergos Institute of Somanatic Education. August.

Hamilton, David. 2015. *I Heart Me: The Science of Self-Love*. London: Hay House, Inc.

Hamilton, David. 2017. *The Five Side Effects of Kindness*. London: Hay House, Inc.

Hanson, Rick with Mendius, Richard. 2009. *Buddha's Brain: The Practical Neuroscience of Happiness, Love & Wisdom*. Oakland, CA: New Harbinger Publications, Inc.

Leal, Kristin. 2021. *Meta Anatomy: A Modern Yogi's Practical Guide to the Physical and Energetic Anatomy of Your Amazing Body*. Louisville, CO: Sounds True, Inc.

Lembke, Anna. 2021. *Dopamine Nation: Finding Balance in the Age of Indulgence*. New York: Dutton, Penguin Random House.

Levine, Peter A. with Ann Frederick. 1997. *Waking the Tiger: Healing Trauma. The Innate Capacity to Transform Overwhelming Experiences*. Berkley, CA: North Atlantic Books.

Levine, Peter. 2018. "Polyvagal Theory and Trauma." In *Clinical Applications of Polyvagal Theory: The Emergence of Polyvagal Informed Therapies*, edited by Stephen W. Porges and Deb Dana, 3–26. New York: W. W. Norton & Company.

Lieberman, Matthew D. 2013. *Social: Why our Brains are Wired to Connect*. New York: Broadway Books, Random House.

Lindaman Sandra and Jukka Makela. 2018. "The Polyvagal Foundation of Theraplay Treatment: Combining Social Engagement, Play, and Nurture to Create Safety, Regulation, and Resilience." In *Clinical Applications of Polyvagal Theory: The Emergence of Polyvagal Informed Therapies*, edited by Stephen W. Porges and Deb Dana, 227–247. New York: W. W. Norton & Company.

Linden, David J. 2015. *Touch: The Science of Hand, Heart, and Mind*. New York: Penguin Books.

Maté, Gabor. 2003. *When the Body Says No: Understanding the Stress-Disease Connection*. Canada: Alfred A. Knopf.

McCraty, Rollin. 2022. "The Intuitive Heart." In Doc Childre, et al. *Heart Intelligence: Connecting with the Heart's Intuitive Guidance for Effective Choices and Solutions*, 2nd ed. Cardiff, CA: Waterside Productions.

McCraty, Rollin. 2015. *Science of the Heart, Volume 2: Exploring the Role of the Heart in Human Performance*. Heart Math Institute.

McLaren, Karla. 2010. *The Language of Emotion: What Your Feelings Are Trying to Tell You*. Boulder, CO: Sounds True, Inc.

Miller, Jean Baker and Stiver, Irene. 1998. *The Healing Connection: How Women Form Relationships in Therapy and in Life*. Boston, MA: Beacon Press.

Montagu, Ashley. 1986. *Touching: The Human Significance of Skin*. New York: HarperCollins.

Moore, Fiona. 2018. "Harness the Intelligence of Consciousness." Video. *Beyond Anxiety*. beyond-anxiety-2018.s3.us-west-2.amazonaws.com/BeyondAnxiety-Masterclass.mp4

Mulkey, Sarah B. and Adre J. du Plessis. 2019. "Autonomic nervous system development and its impact on neuropsychiatric outcome." *Pediatric Research*. Jan. doi. org/10.1038/s41390-018-0155-0

Nagoski, Emily and Amelia Nagoski. 2019. *Burnout: The Secret to Unlocking the Stress Cycle*. New York: Ballantine Books.

Ogden, Pat. 2018. "Polyvagal Theory and Sensorimotor Psychotherapy." In *Clinical Applications of Polyvagal Theory: The Emergence of Polyvagal Informed Therapies*, edited by Stephen W. Porges and Deb Dana, 34–49. New York: W.W. Norton & Company.

Pearsall, Paul. 1999. *The Heart's Code: Tapping the Wisdom and Power of our Heart Energy*. New York: Broadway Books.

Pert, Candace B. 1997. *Molecules of Emotion: Why You Feel the Way You Feel*. New York: Scribner.

Porges, Stephen W. 2018. "Polyvagal Theory: A Primer." In *Clinical Applications of Polyvagal Theory: The Emergence of Polyvagal Informed Therapies*, edited by Stephen W. Porges and Deb Dana, 50–71. New York: W.W. Norton & Company.

Porges, Stephen W. 2017. *The Pocket Guide to The Polyvagal Theory: The Transformative Power of Feeling Safe*. New York: W.W. Norton & Company.

Porges, Stephen W. 2021. *Polyvagal Safety: Attachment, Communication, Self-Regulation*. New York: W.W. Norton & Company.

Rankin, Lissa. 2020. *Mind Over Medicine: Scientific Proof That You Can Heal Yourself*, revised. Carlsbad, CA: Hay House.

Rohr, Richard. 2013. *Immortal Diamond: The Search for Our True Self*. San Francisco: Jossey-Bass, A Wiley Imprint.

Rosenberg, Stanley. 2017. *Accessing the Healing Power of the Vagus Nerve: Self-Help Exercises for Anxiety, Depression, Trauma, and Autism*. Berkeley, CA: North Atlantic Books.

Rothschild, Babette. 2017. *The Body Remembers, Volume 2: Revolutionizing Trauma Treatment*. New York: W.W. Norton & Company.

Rozman, Deborah. 2022. "Attributes of Heart Intelligence." In Doc Childre, et al. *Heart Intelligence: Connecting with the Heart's Intuitive Guidance for Effective Choices and Solutions*, 2nd ed. Cardiff, CA: Waterside Production.

Satir, Virginia. 1972. *Peoplemaking*. Palo Alto, CA: Science and Behavior Books, Inc.

Scaer, Robert. 2007. *The Body Bears the Burden: Trauma, Dissociation, and Disease*, 2nd ed. New York: Routledge, Taylor & Francis Group.

Schwartz, Richard C. and Martha Sweezy. 2020. *Internal Family Systems Therapy,* 2nd ed. New York: The Guilford Press.

Schwartz, Richard. 2021. *No Bad Parts: Healing Trauma and Restoring Wholeness with the Internal Family Systems Model*. Boulder, CO: Sounds True, Inc.

Seppälä, Emma. 2016. *The Happiness Track: How to Apply the Science of Happiness to Accelerate Your Success*. New York: Harper One.

Siegel, Daniel J. 2012. *Pocket Guide to Interpersonal Neurobiology: An Integrative Handbook of the Mind*. New York: W.W. Norton & Company.

Tavris, Carol and Elliott Aronson. 2007. *Mistakes Were Made (but not by me): Why We Justify Foolish Beliefs, Bad Decisions, and Hurtful Acts*. Orlando, FL: Harcourt Books.

Taylor, Shelley E. 2002. *The Tending Instinct: How Nurturing is Essential to Who We Are and How We Live*. New York: Times Books, Henry Holt and Company.

Tucci, Joe, Angela Weller, and Janise Mitchell. 2018. "Realizing 'Deep' Safety for Children Who Have Experienced Abuse: Application of Polyvagal Theory in Therapeutic Work with Traumatized Children and Young People." In *Clinical Applications of The Polyvagal Theory: The Emergence of Polyvagal Informed Therapies*, edited by Stephen W. Porges and Deb Dana, 89–105. New York: W.W. Norton & Company.

Van Der Kolk, Bessel. 2014. *The Body Keeps the Score: Brain, Mind, and Body in the Healing of Trauma*. New York: Viking, Penguin Group.

Walker, Pete. 2013. *Complex PTSD: From Surviving to Thriving*. Lafayette, CA: Azure Coyote Books.

Watt, Jaime. 2020. "The 'she-cession' may be new but its underlying causes are not." *Toronto Star*. 24 May. *Toronto Star*. www.thestar.com/opinion/contributors/2020/05/24/the-she-cession-may-be-new-but-its-underlying-causes-are-not.html

About the Authors

About Leslie and Lynda

Leslie Gillespie and Lynda Rees are innovative leaders in transforming relationships in couple, family, and organizational systems. They are passionate about educating and supporting people to create compassionate relationships with themselves and others. Lynda and Leslie have a unique team approach to help women leaders perform under pressure by optimizing their nervous system. In addition, they have created a program for helping workplace teams perform with more joy and productivity.

About Lynda

As an RN, Lynda Rees first specialized in mental health inpatient treatment in Toronto. She then received her Master of Science degree in Marriage and Family Therapy from the University of Guelph. She is an AAMFT Clinical Fellow, Registered Marriage and Family Therapist, and Lifestyle Prescriptions Root Cause Health Coach.

In her private practice in Ontario, Canada, Lynda uses an integrative approach, combining Family Systems, Internal Family Systems, Psychodramatic Bodywork, and Energy Psychology. She mentors and supervises therapists in her approach. Lynda has designed curriculum and led courses and workshops for nonprofit and for-profit organizations about relationships, self-leadership, leadership, team building, and natural abilities.

Lynda was the former director of Behavioural Health with a health organization in Toronto. She is chair of Ledge Leadership, a charity providing leadership training and whole person well-being support to emerging adults ages eighteen to thirty.

Lynda has been married to Denis for over fifty years. They have three children and seven grandchildren. She loves being by the water, watching movies, reading, experimenting with cooking interesting recipes, and connecting with family and good friends.

About Leslie

An American Association for Marriage and Family Therapy Clinical Fellow, Leslie uses collaborative and unique methods to help people enjoy their relationships. Obtaining a degree in Family Studies at the University of Guelph, Leslie began her career as a youth counsellor. She then attended Osgoode Hall Law School and subsequently practiced family law. Seeing the possibilities for reconciliation, Leslie returned to the University of Guelph and received her master's degree in Marriage and Family Therapy.

Conducting a private therapy practice in Mississauga, Leslie co-created a successful Custody and Access clinical team. At a multidisciplinary healthcare facility in Toronto, she helped develop and implement programs regarding sleep challenges, the mind/body connection, and women's health.

She was a board member of the Social Planning Council of Peel and the Ontario Association for Family Mediation. Leslie has created curricula and trained leaders in the fields of law, the judiciary, and education. As a consultant for the Peel Board of Education, Leslie provided counselling and workshops to teachers and support staff regarding stress, relationships, and grief.

Leslie met her husband Robert at Osgoode Hall Law School. She loves to write, swim, garden, binge British thriller movies, and travel. She and Robert delight in creating festive themed events for their friends.